Boston 1945-2015

Also by Russ Lopez

Boston's South End: The Clash of Ideas in a Historic Neighborhood, 2015

Building American Public Health: Architecture, Urban Planning, and the Quest for Better Health in the United States, 2012

The Built Environment and Public Health, 2011

Urban Health: Readings in the Social, Built and Physical Environment of U.S. Cities, 2011 (with H. Patricia Hynes)

Boston 1945-2015

The Decline and Rebirth of a Great World City

Russ Lopez

Shawmut Peninsula Press
Boston, Massachusetts

Copyright © 2017 Russ Lopez.

ISBN: 978-0-692-82935-6

To Andrew Sherman

Table of Contents

Photo Credits

Pages x, 231, 248. Russ Lopez

Page 12. Courtesy of the Boston Public Library, Leslie Jones Collection (and thank you to the Jones family)

Pages 18, 82, 117, 130, 147. Boston Landmarks Commission Image Collection

Pages 27, 95, 160, 192, 201. City of Boston Archives

Pages 42, 45, and Cover. Urban Redevelopment Division – Boston Housing Authority

Pages 80, 114. Boston Planning and Development Agency

Page 174. Historic American Engineering Record – Library of Congress

Preface

I REMEMBER A Boston where every Friday morning, we would walk the blocks around Dudley Street to see which houses had burned the night before. I visited apartments where the plaster was falling off the walls and whose heat was sporadic at best. Parks lacked grass, streets were littered with abandoned cars, and racial violence was a constant threat. It seemed that no one was happy with the state of the city.

But Boston was also a place where families would boast of one son who was in the service, another was a priest, and the daughters who were teachers or working in one of the new highrises downtown. There were friendly arguments regarding whether Puerto Ricans or Cubans made better platanos and heated discussions regarding the talents of various Dominican merengue bands. And the architecture was beautiful. Everyone knew the city had potential.

Today, Boston has million dollar condos, slick restaurants, an economy that is the envy of the world, and it could easily grow to twice its size if it could build enough housing. The views from the rooftops, boats on the harbor, or an airplane are spectacular. Its people make a resident proud. No one wants to leave.

This book chronicles the great changes in Boston, its high points and its lows. It is the story of how we became what we are today.

Acknowledgements

SELLING A BOOK is like an election campaign for a local office: some nights you find yourself pumped up by the energy of a hundred people hanging on every word you say, other times you find yourself speaking to a room with barely ten people in it. But in both cases the encouragement of people for your last book helps you through the slow times of writing the next. My most heartfelt thanks go to everyone who has read my books and told me they wanted to read more.

Boston is blessed by a rich array of archives, libraries, and resources for researching its history. Writing this history involved visits to the Boston Public Library at Copley Square, the South End Branch Library, the Boston Athenaeum, several libraries at Harvard, the Healey Library at the University of Massachusetts Boston, the Yale Library, and the archives at the Snell Library of Northeastern University. A special thanks must be given to the people at the History Project, the South End Historical Society, and the countless unnamed people who have digitized the many sources for this book. The family of Leslie Jones were very courteous in allowing me to use his picture of Mayor Curley.

Among the people who I must thank are Ann Hershfang, Alison Barnet, Judy Watkins, Michelle Romero, and Andrew Elder. There should be a national "hug an archivist" day. Susan Paton was a great editor and helped make this book readable.

My writing must be a burden to my friends and family who are forced to listen to my rapturous excitement at finding a new source and bitter disappointment when a lead on a cataloged item goes nowhere. I thank them all, especially Andrew Sherman and Steven Lopez.

Boston and its neighborhoods

INTRODUCTION

THE EXUBERANT PROSPERITY of modern Boston is a mytery. The city awakened itself from decades of gloomy decline and merciless decay. Once it was the poorest major city in the United States and a backwater noted for its provincialism; now it is one of the most important cities in the world, a powerhouse in medical research, technology, and financial services. How did this happen?

The rebirth of Boston was not inevitable; it could have spiraled ever downward into the twenty-first century urban nightmares of St. Louis, Detroit, and many other once prosperous places. Even as late as 1978, these cities were ranked higher than Boston in quality of life, and there was no reason to think Boston wouldn't rot and hollow out as so many other great cities had.[1] Yet it rebounded and thrived. Why?

The reasons for Boston's (and other select cities') great U-turn are debated. Some urbanologists have proposed that it is a concentration of a creative class—architects, scientists, and so forth—that enable cities to grow.[2] Yet from New Haven to Cleveland, there are many examples of clusters of universities and research institutions that have failed to revitalize their surroundings. Others contend that it was the arrival of millennials who wanted to dwell in walkable neighborhoods that reinvigorated Boston and other cities.[3] But Boston's revival began in the 1970s when preference for suburban living, among the then dominant baby boomers, was at its peak. Another oft-cited reason for its success, urban renewal, also did not save the city.[4] On the contrary, it nearly destroyed Boston as it too often created blocks of drab development that had to be replaced within a few decades. Nor was it Mayor Kevin White's management style or Mayor John Collins's vision for a New Boston that revived the neighborhoods. It was the people of Boston who deserve credit for making the city what it is today.

The theory that drives this book is that Boston rebounded because at its heart it is a beautiful and comfortable city to live in, one that its people fought hard to protect and preserve. From Brighton to South Dorchester, from East Boston to Hyde Park, it is a city of compact neighborhoods that residents did everything they could to stop outsiders from destroying. For many years, these neighborhoods were unappreciated; calculating politicians, ruthless businessmen, and greedy downtown bureaucrats wanted to bulldoze the hundreds of thousands of buildings they thought obsolete and ugly. At the same time, they tried to force out of the city those residents they despised as too poor, too non-white, and too uneducated to bother with. If these developers of doom had had their way, Boston would have been transformed into something uninhabitable. It would have decayed beyond recovery.

The people and events that drove the city's revival are the focus of this book. Despite the powerful forces arrayed against them, Boston's residents refused to be displaced. They fought bulldozers to protect their families, homes, and way of life, and they organized themselves to create alternatives to destruction. Along the way they built and renovated housing, opened new businesses, cared for those who were fragile, and created a vibrant city. Oftentimes residents failed, and the people who now live in the South End, North End, Mission Hill, and elsewhere are very different from those who lived in these neighborhoods in 1945. But even these people, long gone but never forgotten, have left a giant legacy because they protected their communities long enough so that their neighborhoods survived until a time that they were cherished and deemed worthy of living in.

One warning: the decades covered by this book are not times of steady, inspiring improvement. On the contrary, there are parts of Boston's history that are sad and uncomfortable. The city has been rocked by violence and racism, and reading about terrible housing conditions, riots, and displacement is not easy. But to a great extent, the battles of the past seventy years reflect a shared love of Boston that made it worth fighting over. Even the turmoil over busing to integrate the schools, which forty years later still divides the city, has at its core values common to both sides. White ethnics could have left for the suburbs, as their counterparts did in many other cities, and black parents could have moved to other cities, like many of their brothers and sisters, but both groups made their stand here because this was a place they believed in and wanted to be a part of. There were battles in Boston because it was a city worth fighting over.

To explain this history of celebration and heartbreak, victors and the displaced, this book is organized chronologically with chapters that generally correspond to mayoral administrations, though because Kevin White and Thomas Menino served for so many years, their terms are split into two chapters each. When possible, a particular event is covered in one section, but some issues spanned many decades and are incorporated into multiple chapters. Thus the marathon bombing is in one chapter while busing, urban renewal, and highway construction appear repeatedly across this book.

Boston still has problems, but many of them are the products of its success: expensive housing, overburdened public transit, and crowded neighborhoods. It has yet to figure out how to connect low-income neighborhoods to its core prosperity, and its business and cultural elites have been slow to open their doors to the multicultural community that surrounds them.

Yet no one who lives in Boston today is forced to do so against their will; people live in the city because they want to. Boston held on to its Irish, Italians, Jews, and Yankees even though many left other communities. Black Americans are fleeing other cities, but not Boston, and the immigrants who choose Boston are an affirmation of the quality of life and opportunities here. The city has been enriched by students coming to study and the many who stay after graduation while it attracts retirees and older residents from the suburbs. Some families have been here for generations, others have moved in just recently, and both groups contribute to the city's vitality. Today, people are more likely to leave because Boston's success has made it too expensive, and they move out because of high housing costs, not because neighborhoods are bad.

Boston's people can trace their roots to Ireland, Italy, the Mayflower, China, India, Puerto Rico, Cuba, Haiti, Cape Verde, East Boston, South Boston, and all fifty states and six inhabited continents. As a result, Boston is a city of a hundred accents: proudly misplaced 'R's, melodic Caribbean lilts, and impatient entrepreneurial tech speak. In each you can hear the overtones of a person determined to make Boston their own and the sound of individuals who proudly call the city home. Accents vary, but all are bound together by place. This book is the story of how a group of people, often divided into warring tribes, somehow made and preserved a great city.

1. Bradbury KL, Downs A and Small KA. *Urban Decline and the Future of American Cities*. Washington, DC: The Brookings Institution, 1982.
2. Florida R. *Cities and the Creative Class* New York City: Routledge, 2005.
3. Speck J. *Walkable City: How Downtown Can Save America, One Step at a Time*. New York: North Point Press, 2012.
4. Kennedy L. *Planning the City Upon a Hill: Boston Since 1630*. Boston: University of Massachusetts Press, 1994.

Chapter 1

Twilight of the Master: 1945 - 1949

WHEN PRESIDENT HARRY Truman took to the radio to announce that Japan had surrendered and World War II was finally over, famously reserved Boston erupted in jubilation and declared the next day a holiday. From Scollay Square to Chinatown, 750,000 deliriously happy people danced all night in streets ankle deep in confetti, oblivious to the approaching dawn.[1] Across the city, wild celebrations made "every service uniform a ticket for some pretty girl's kiss and every stranger a comrade who shared the joy."[2] So some wept, others prayed, and many joined impromptu parades. Rambunctious Bostonians lit bonfires in the Public Garden, while, in Park Square, three sailors straddled kegs to pass out free mugs of beer. The headline in the *Boston Daily Record* simply stated, "All Boston Goes Mad."

Beyond the joyous relief felt by the war weary, however, there was a tremendous sense of gloom in the city because Boston was dying. Over a third of its housing stock needed to be repaired or replaced, its economy was in a tailspin, and its politics were badly divided between two groups who, like punch drunk rivals, fought over wounds and causes that began generations prior. The end of the war meant that the city now had to address its previous thirty years of decline and its reputation as the country's most distressed big city.

At the center of these problems was Boston's moribund economy. At the end of the nineteenth century, the region's prosperity had been based on multiple foundations: shoes and textiles, other assorted manufacturing, financial services, and the port. Each was decaying for its own reasons. The shoe and textile factories had moved to the South to take advantage of low-wage workers, and while there had been 124,000 textile jobs in the state in 1919, by 1940 there were only 30,000 left. Other industrial activities suffered as well. Boston, sitting at the northeast edge of the United States, was in a weak position to sell chemicals, automobiles, and other mass-produced items compared to those cities in the Midwest or mid-Atlantic regions that were closer to markets. The port had aging facilities, a limited hinterland to draw on for exports and imports, and poor railroad connections to the rest of the continent. It was easier to ship goods in and out of New York or Montreal.

In some respects, Boston continued to be a banking powerhouse, and in 1950 the gross annual value of financial services in the city was $1.3 billion. But that alone was not enough to save the local economy as money management in the city was in decline. In 1900 Boston had been the country's fourth largest banking center; by 1965 it will have slid to tenth.[3] Early Massachusetts laws had established the legal framework for fiduciary liability that led to a network of trust funds for educational institutions, charities, endowments, and family fortunes. A gift from John Harvard in 1638 to a struggling school in Cambridge, for example, established the oldest endowment in what would later become the United States.

By 1945, Boston had ceased to be a place of financial innovation. The conservatism of its mid-century money managers meant that trusts and endowments controlled by wealthy families and institutions were only invested in bank stocks, government bonds, and low yield paper. Middle-class households put their money into savings accounts while the poor had no savings at all. As a result, the total employment needed to manage trusts and endowments was limited.[4]

The economic malaise was a symptom of a greater problem in the region: its lack of imagination and entrepreneurial risk taking. As the war ended, the Yankee (Protestant descendants of pre-revolution British settlers) business class that had once sailed clipper ships to China, created global powerhouses such as General Electric and American Telephone and Telegraph, and financed transcontinental railroads had slouched into a timid group of trust fund families that depended on income from municipal bonds and real estate returns. Boston's increasingly shabby financial district reflected the group's taste and ambitions: even remodeling a State Street office building was seen as a dangerous extravagance, and for almost thirty years, the city went without the construction of a significant new office building.

As a result of this economic stagnation, total personal income in the city declined by 25 percent between 1929 and 1950 and per capita income by 20 percent.[5] This contributed to a reduction in the total assessed value of property in the city from $2 billion in 1930 to $1.4 billion in 1945.[6] Downtown property values, the foundation of the city's revenues, were down by 40 percent and as a result, the city lacked the money to finance its operations as there was neither sales tax nor income tax at this time. Therefore the property tax levy soared from $28.50 per thousand in 1928 to $42.50 in 1945 on its way to $101.20 by 1959.[7] To make ends meet, the city's Irish (by the 1850s the Irish, either foreign born or native, were the city's largest ethnic group) mayors were repeatedly forced to beg the Yankee-dominated state legislature for fiscal assistance, and the conditions it imposed were humiliating. Borrowing money was just as problematic because the banks were controlled by the same hostile Protestant establishment, and the past thirty years of deficits had exhausted the city's ability to float bonds. Almost every year, the city faced bankruptcy as it lurched from crisis to crisis.

The long-term economic decline pressured city residents. As a group they had missed out on the great prosperity of the 1920s, and when the Depression hit, it was long and ugly in Boston. Many were poor with little hope for a better life while many of those with resources moved away. After modest growth in the 1920s, the city's population declined in the 1930s, a decade when other cities in the country continued to grow. While between 1920 and 1950 the city will have grown by a little over 10 percent, only Providence had a smaller increase among major United States cities. The slow growth was regional, not just in Boston, and the metropolitan area had the second smallest percentage increase in population among the 32 largest metropolitan areas in the country between 1920 and 1950 (28.5 percent). In contrast, Detroit's metropolitan area population doubled during this time.[6]

A very influential factor on the state of Boston in 1945 had been the closing down of immigration several decades earlier. The years following World War I, with the Immigration Act of 1921, slammed the door on many people from other countries coming to the United States. In the decades around 1900, almost a third of Boston's population was foreign born. But by 1945, the percentage was only about 25 percent, and it would bottom out at 13 percent before a new wave of immigrants moved to the city in the 1970s.[8]

It wasn't just economic problems that pushed people out; there was the pull of the suburbs that had been beckoning Boston residents since the middle of the nineteenth century. By leaving the crowded tenements and triple deckers of the city, families could now have grass, yards, and privacy. Rather than taking crowded streetcars or the rundown subway, people could drive a new automobile, financed by easy credit, on roads funded by public expenditures. As soon as they could leave, many of the descendants of Irish immigrants who had once packed the city's inner wards moved out to middle-class housing on the city fringe in Dorchester and West Roxbury or further out to the suburbs. At the same time, many Italian residents were moving north of the city, and Boston's Jewish population was departing for suburban towns to the west. These groups were following the Yankees who had abandoned Boston a century before. But now there were no newcomers to replace them.

There was one very significant difference between the mid-century loss of population in Boston and the extreme depopulation of other cities in the 1960s and 1970s that would eventually destroy places such as Detroit and St. Louis. In Boston, though the population fell, the number of households remained stable as much of the population loss was caused by households becoming smaller. Grown up children left the city, leaving their parents behind. There is a famously apocryphal tale told about Massachusetts Senate President William Bulger. A crafty *Boston Globe* reporter was trying to trap him into admitting that he was committing voter fraud to win reelection. As the reporter and Senate President were walking along L Street, the reporter pointed to a triple decker house and asked Bulger to explain how he had received twenty votes from that house in the last election, implying that there was no way so many votes could come from the modest three-apartment building. Bulger shrugged apologetically and explained, "The second floor is vacant."

Thus was the reputation for very large families in many parts of the city. Immigrants may have traditionally had large families, but by the third-generation, fertility rates were approaching the national norm as the average household size decreased from 3.90 to 3.56 during the 1940s.[6] So as other parts of the country saw large growth of people under eighteen, in Boston the number of children decreased while the number of elderly grew rapidly. This change was reflected in the public schools; declining numbers of school children in the 1940s and 1950s were nearly as high as their rate of decline in the 1970s during the busing crisis. There would be no baby boom in Boston.

One result of its economic and demographic troubles was that the city became increasingly rundown. This could be seen in the quality of the city's housing stock as landlords lacked the resources to maintain the apartments so in need of substantial renovation. This relentless deterioration lowered property values and put further pressure on a city budget that was already stretched thin. Most of Boston had been built for working people, not the wealthy, and construction standards had been modest. Now that even the newer of these units were approaching forty years old, they were in need of substantial repairs. Plumbing was not up to current standards and electrical systems were wanting; a full 25 percent of the city's units still lacked central heat in 1950 as many were heated by a coal or oil burning heater attached to the kitchen stove. South End resident Charles Caizzi, for example, wrote about the burden of carrying a five-gallon container of kitchen oil, refilled from a basement tank, up four flights of stairs. This modest single source had to heat all the rooms in his family's apartment, and Caizzi recalls his older brother had tricked him into assuming this onerous daily chore when he had been barely big enough to pick up its weight.[9]

Landlords couldn't borrow funds to fix up their units because of redlining, the practice of withholding loans from neighborhoods because they had, or might someday have, blacks and other minorities; that was a particularly pernicious problem in this era. With increasing number of units occupied by low-income elderly and new black residents just in from the South, many parts of the city would be at risk for abandonment, arson, and brutal demographic change in the coming decades.

The decline of Boston was not just a result of natural economic forces. All across the United States there were public policies that in retrospect seem cruelly designed to destroy cities. These housing, transportation, and tax programs drained economic vitality from urban neighborhoods and provided financial incentives for people to move to the suburbs. In the wake of the Great Depression, President Franklin Roosevelt created a number of programs to promote home buying that, even if implemented in a neutral manner, would have encouraged suburbanization, as there was little space to build new homes in cities like Boston. But these policies were not even-handed between urban and suburban as they adopted strict standards for the type of units that would qualify for mortgage subsidies. These excluded multifamily houses and required suburban style single-family homes set out on a minimum 6,000 square-foot lot, impossible conditions for most of Boston except for portions of West Roxbury and Mattapan. So if a family was looking to get a mortgage to purchase a home, they had to move to the suburbs.

Furthermore, these programs were only available to white homeowners, and Jewish borrowers as well faced resistance from lenders. Just as large numbers of African-Americans and Puerto Ricans were moving into the city, they were excluded from these programs. As a result, segregation levels in Boston, as in most other large metropolitan areas, would peak in 1950 and only after that begin a long, very slow decline. This inequity was compounded by the mortgage interest deduction for federal income taxes that, in effect, subsidized an option not available to city residents. The combined effects of racism, inappropriate housing standards, and programs not usable for rental property would push development to the periphery of the metropolitan area and accelerate Boston's economic malaise.

Another major policy that would harm cities across the country was the building of highways. In the hands of engineers and politicians in Massachusetts, and elsewhere, it quickly became a program that enabled more middle and upper-income residents to live in the suburbs and commute by car back into the city; it also allowed them to avoid paying city taxes while still benefiting from jobs and services in the central core. What made these programs particularly egregious was that while vastly subsidizing highways and automobiles, they could not be used to fund mass transit. In essence, they used tax dollars to reduce the cost of cars while leaving transit systems to fend for themselves. The side effects of the highway program included inner city disinvestment, arson, lead poisoning, and global climate change.

Confronted by gloomy current conditions and the prospects of an even worse future, Boston politicians turned on each other. The 1909 city charter had given the mayor immense power at a time when Yankee business interests were angrily pitted against Irish ward bosses. But this backfired when the Irish cemented their hold on the mayor's office. Plotting to recapture city hall, business leaders and their reformer allies sponsored a 1924 referendum that created a twenty-two person council, one from each ward. But that system also failed to prevent graft, and there was large scale corruption as council members shook down anyone they could: transit operators, parking lot owners, residents seeking permission to pave a driveway, and even carnival owners.[10] And as much as business interests and reformers seethed under the corrupt system, they were about to be even further assaulted by the city's voters.

Into this scene of decline and change enters James Michael Curley, three-time mayor of Boston, who has been waiting for the opportunity to re-take the office. Powered by revenge, a need to vindicate himself, and a lust for power, Curley sought an unprecedented fourth term as mayor in 1945. Born in the South End on Northampton Street, he had been a newsboy and a delivery man before settling into his true calling: politics. Curley dominated Boston for most of the first half of the twentieth century: beginning with his first election to the Boston Common Council in 1904 to his final defeat in the mayoral election of 1954. He served one term as governor, four as mayor, two in congress, and two in jail, the first for taking the civil service exam in someone else's name and the second for mail fraud in conjunction with bribery and other political shenanigans. Ironically, his rise to power was facilitated by the Yankee establishment that had sought to obliterate the old ward bosses they thought were ruining the city. Taking advantage of the reformers' voting system, Curley successfully supplanted the bosses with his own political machine. Curley had not been mayor since 1934, despite several attempts to regain the office, and had spent the intervening years dreaming of a comeback. Now, 1945 was his time, as he proclaimed in his loud lilting voice that captivated many in the city.

Curley's detractors, and there were many, were so agitated by him that they lost all perspective and blamed every single problem in the city on this diminutive man with a giant grasp. Whenever he ran for office, his foes rallied around a candidate to defeat him, making Curley the central pivot point in a region obsessed with politics. But Curley gathered energy from the hatred he generated. To bait the anti-Irish business class, he played up his florid complexion, exaggerated his accent, and sharpened his cutting wit; his every mannerism and movement was meant to convince friend and foe alike that he was an unpredictable and unstoppable Irish demagogue. Curley's both melodious and odious anti-Yankee rhetoric successfully unhinged his opponents who treated him with open contempt. One critic, for example, introduced him at a public event as the "convict candidate for mayor." Another called him the "Huey Long of the Bay State."[11]

Mayor Curley. Passionately loved or hated, he was the central pivot point of Boston politics for the first half of the twentieth century.

His opponents' most serious charges were that Curley bankrupted the city and ruined its economy. But, as described above, the decline was regional and its causes were rooted in large scale economic changes and the ossification of Boston's investment community. Curley did not cause the textile mills in Lowell or shoe factories in Lynn to close, nor did he have anything to do with how family trusts invested their money. Furthermore, at this point he had been out of the mayor's office for thirteen years and would later permanently leave public service in 1950. Yet, as will be seen, the city's economy did not begin to revive until the late 1970s. If the problem was Curley, why couldn't the next three mayors fix the city's finances?

Even more flimsy was the charge that Curley drove the Yankees out of the city with his rhetoric and governing policies.[12] Some scholars have even compared Curley to Robert Mugabe, the African dictator who worked to emasculate his opponents by forcing them into exile.[13] In reality, Yankees began to leave the city as far back as the 1840s with the building of street cars and commuter rail roads; in fact, the South End was developed in the 1850s in the vain hope that a new residential neighborhood might keep Yankee families in the city.[14] Curley did not consolidate his power until after World War I when the city was overwhelmingly Irish, Italian, and Jewish. Yankees were just scapegoats that Curley used to scare his supporters to go out to the polls, as there were few Yankee voters left in Boston.

It was Curley's epic later races for mayor that strongly colored his legacy. In these elections, he ran against Maurice Tobin, John Kerrigan, and John Hynes, middle-class Irishmen that Curley had to mobilize his poor Irish base against in order to outpoll them.[15] These were battles between poor immigrant Irish in the lower numbered wards versus middle-class American-born Irish in the higher-numbered wards, angry contests that would drive Boston politics even up to the 2015 election. Capitalizing on his opponents' inability to match his vitriolic rhetoric to make them seem less Irish and more out of touch with low income voters, Curley was a political genius.

Curley campaigned as the mayor of the poor and he governed as one. So his priorities were the concerns of low-income neighborhoods: finding residents jobs, providing relief to the indigent, and building public works. He expanded City Hospital, built the wonderful amenities along the South Boston beaches, and helped feed the hungry. This directly contrasted with the agenda of the well-off who wanted to cut city jobs in order to balance the budget, saw alms as immoral coddling of the poor, and demanded new investment downtown. Curley's agenda also took funds the city didn't have, so he repeatedly tried to extract money from the city's commercial property owners. He raised the assessment on the Statler Hotel by $1 million and Filene's Department Store by $950,000, for example. Each year about 30-40 percent of downtown properties appealed their assessments with many settled through court action or negotiation at a fraction of what the city was counting on.[3] It didn't matter, the city used these initial estimates to present a balanced budget and then carried the resulting deficits forward into future fiscal years, adding to its debt.

But Curley was a scoundrel, purposely maddening his opponents. He proposed to use the Public Garden for housing for low-income veterans, enraging the elite on Beacon Hill. And he was corrupt. In election after election, he would hire men to bait his opponents, pose as supporters, and beat up critics. He bullied those he did not like and held grudges for decades. He paid hecklers to interrupt his speeches to sow sympathy and once employed a man to impersonate a survivor of the Grand Army of the Republic and attend campaign events as a way of earning the gratitude and votes of veterans. Another time he bought an old lantern from a junk shop on Washington Street. A close associate then dressed as Diogenes and walked the streets of South Boston and Newspaper Row, searching for an honest man among Curley's opponents. In his autobiography, Curley bragged that he was so angry that the First National Bank would not loan money to the city he called up its president to tell him "there's a water main with the floodgates right under your building. You'd better get that money up by 3 P.M. or those gates will be opened, pouring thousands of gallons of water right into your vaults."[11] There were suggestions that Curley had used city hall to amass a personal fortune. He claimed he was poor and kept a modest lifestyle, but he regularly visited Europe and built himself a lavish mansion in Jamaica Plain.

In the 1938 and 1942 races, it appeared the opposition had finally destroyed Curley's political ambitions when they successfully ran Maurice Tobin against him for Mayor. Tobin had his start in politics as a protégé of Curley's, so his triumph and Curley's anger over it proved a savory victory. Once out of city hall, Curley plotted his comeback as he occupied a Congressional seat during the World War II years. Then Tobin, afflicted with the disease of ambition for higher office that ran epidemic among Boston politicians, was elected governor in 1944. Seeing an opening, Curley wanted another term as mayor as the 1945 election season began.

He had been written off as irrelevant and at first it appeared that Curley was a longshot. There was no primary and anyone who could collect enough signatures was on the ballot in the November election. One opponent, John Kerrigan from South Boston, was young and good looking and so politically adept he had been elected Acting Mayor by his colleagues on the City Council to replace Tobin. As thoughts turned towards how to restore prosperity once the war ended, Kerrigan was a fresh face against the corrupt politics as usual Curley. But then Kerrigan disappeared for several months, setting off a very public mystery in a city that demanded that its politicians attend every wake, neighborhood meeting, and public hearing. When Kerrigan resurfaced in New Orleans, professing love for a show girl, his chances of becoming mayor were substantially reduced.[6]

The other major candidate, William Arthur Reilly, had baggage of his own. He was a protégé of Tobin, so Curley was able to tie him to Tobin's twin weights of austerity and burdensome taxes. These policies were so disliked that Tobin would be swept out of the Governor's office in a landslide election that was a triumph for Republicans in 1946. In addition, Reilly had been Fire Commissioner when the tragic Coconut Grove nightclub fire killed 490 people in 1942. In the investigation that followed, both Tobin and Reilly barely escaped being indicted for bribery, and many blamed Reilly for his department's failure to enforce safety codes.

Despite his rivals' weaknesses, it was a tough election. Curley faced withering public opposition and was taunted by the press with the major papers taking every opportunity to burnish his opponents. He had to rely on his radio addresses and his well-oiled machine to deliver his votes. To complicate matters, federal prosecutors indicted Curley for mail fraud in connection with a scheme that collected bribes from construction companies hoping to secure contracts to build public housing.

In those days before opinion polls, no one knew who had the advantage but it seemed to observers that Curley's support was slipping away. Then his son Paul died at the age of 32. He had been fragile for many years with a heart condition that kept him out of the war and a constant battle with alcohol that usually bested him. Curley reacted with a mixture of grief, relief, and political analysis. He was heartbroken but surmised that the sympathy vote would ensure his victory.[12]

The Purple Shamrock, as he was known to his supporters, still had some fight in him. Defying his opposition, Curley won the 1945 election carrying nineteen of twenty-two wards in the biggest landslide the city had ever seen. He beat second place Kerrigan by over 51,000 votes and, for the first time in twelve years, Curley was back in charge of city hall. It's not clear that Curley had a vision to remake the city or a plan to revitalize it, however, attracting development and investment were not his priorities. Instead he sought to reward his supporters with public jobs while relishing the hatred of his enemies.

That the three candidates for mayor were Irish was no surprise. As the largest ethnic group in a city known for its tribal neighborhoods, the Irish hold on Boston was at its zenith. The Irish began to arrive in Boston in large numbers in the 1830s and then poured in as the Great Famine of 1845 and its aftermath decimated Ireland. After the mid-nineteenth century, immigration increased and decreased as economic, political, and social conditions improved or deteriorated. Even as late as the 1980s, a series of economic crises produced another wave of Irish immigration into Boston.

As their numbers grew, the Irish faced tremendous animosity from native-born Protestants. In words and deeds, Yankee Bostonians sought to contain and humiliate them, forever searing into the memory of the city's Irish a resentment of their treatment and social status. But the Irish came to dominate the city, and after generations of discrimination, they had a lock on municipal employment, utility company jobs, and access to the building trades. Many used this economic power to move to the suburbs, but others opted to remain in the city, either staying in the old immigrant neighborhoods or moving to the more suburban-like outer wards. The more upwardly mobile proudly sent their sons to the new Boston College High School at Columbia Point (moved out of the South End in 1948) and then on to Boston College in Chestnut Hill. A few lucky families boasted of a son who was a triple eagle: attending both and earning a Boston College law degree as well. Not all the Irish approved of these new middle-class families. Some resented these "lace curtain" or "two toilet" Irish, and powerful class conflicts fueled the political divide between the poorer Irish of Boston's lower-numbered wards and the middle-class Irish in the higher-numbered wards.

Despite these differences, the two groups shared a tremendous commitment to the Catholic Church. The power of the clergy was immense. It was more than just political influence: over 80 percent of Catholics attended Mass weekly, many young people met their spouses at church-sponsored dances or youth events, and thousands of Bostonians participated in Catholic organizations. Large families provided sons for priests and daughters for nuns, and when Catholics took ill, they went to Catholic hospitals. If they needed assistance, they turned to Catholic charities, and after receiving last rites, they were buried in Catholic cemeteries.[16] The faithful of all income levels flocked to the schools and churches revitalized by the beloved Cardinal Cushing (a South Boston native who was Archbishop of Boston from 1944 to 1970), and many, when asked where they were from, replied with their home parish, not their neighborhood or town.

The Irish were a majority in Charlestown, Dorchester, Brighton, Jamaica Plain, and other sections of the city, but the proudest Irish neighborhood in the city was South Boston. The distinct Irish-American culture of the neighborhood had solidified in the thirty years after the Civil War. At its best this emphasized faith and obedience to the Catholic Church, a strong family value system, and a robust sense of community that brought people together. At its worse it created a suspicion of outsiders, a rigidity of beliefs, and a fierce opposition to changing societal values.

Thomas O'Connor, one of the greatest Boston historians, credits the Boston police strike of 1919 as cementing the "us against world" attitude of South Boston. In his view, it convinced residents that they could rely only on themselves for security, and all interaction with outsiders was to be, at best, politely tolerated. In this context,, even intermarriage with Italians was met with disapproval, and because few blacks worked in the neighborhood and none lived there, many in

South Boston, 1971. The area had a mix of very poor to well off households.

South Boston grew to "maturity without ever having seen or spoken to a black person."[17]

Yet even South Boston was touched by change as World War II and the post-war era intruded upon it. Many young people, exposed to the larger world by military service, left the neighborhood while others who might have wanted to remain were forced to the suburbs by redlining. Neighborhood ties were also eroded by changing social tastes that caused attendance at local institutions to drop. Some returning servicemen, many now going to college on the GI bill, looked down on the older way of life. They wanted nicer housing, better jobs, and cleaner government than what Boston had been providing. Also affecting South Boston's social cohesion, there were substantial differences inside the neighborhood by midcentury as well. Wealthier families lived by the beaches while poorer households clustered in the Lower End. The neighborhood had three large public housing projects: the Old Colony and Mary Ellen McCormack developments were more likely to have working families and more integration into their neighborhoods while, in contrast, the D Street projects were poorer and apt to have whites from all across the city as residents.

For many, opportunities for advancement were still limited as the Boston public schools in the late 1940s were too often a dead end. If a child was stuck attending South Boston High School, a boy could hope for little more than a job on the docks or at the Edison, as everyone called the local electric utility. A girl, if she didn't marry young, at best might go to Boston Teachers College. So in 1948, an ambitious four-teen-year-old William Bulger decided that to get ahead he needed to go elsewhere for high school. Assessing his chances, he chose Boston College High School as a safer alternative than Boston Latin. For those less talented or ambitious, there were other options. For the South Boston petty criminal class, for example, the preferred way of making money was nonviolent theft from trucks or the docks or helping run the illegal lottery.

All of this overlooks the many joys of living in the neighborhood. Young men didn't need a lot of money to have a good time with their girlfriends in Southie in the 1940s and 1950s. A local pol might score the couple some free tickets to the ferry to Provincetown or they could walk along Mayor Curley's well-landscaped beach strand. Everyone could visit Castle Island, shop along Broadway, and get fried clams at Kelly's.[18] The neighborhood seemed stable and secure.

Residents of that era recall both the poverty and the good times. It was not uncommon for triple deckers in South Boston and elsewhere to have only one bathroom, located in the basement, which could lead to uncomfortable walks on cold winter nights from third floor apart-ments. The better apartments were advertised as having "improve-ments," which meant they had hot water, but many could not afford such a luxury. Even so, most families were intact and parents worked to create a nurturing environment for their children and provide food on the table. A traditional Saturday night dinner was beans and franks with brown bread. Sometimes the beans came from a can, the brown bread always did. Another well cherished tradition was the New En-gland boiled dinner: smoked ham, cabbage, potatoes, and carrots all simmered together. The neighborhood was alive with peddlers, fami-lies, and others, and even into the 1960s, South Boston had a rag man who would go up and down the streets in a horse drawn cart shouting

"Rags! Rags!"[19]

Though their numbers were small compared to other cities, Boston always had an important black community. From Crispus Attucks, shot by British soldiers in the Boston Massacre, to William Monroe Trotter, who courageously fought against segregation, Boston's black population has made major contributions to the country's history. But Boston lacked industry and its accompanying jobs, especially its dock work and domestic labor positions, were heavily reliant on Irish labor; for these reasons, the economic attractions that pulled blacks to other cities did not exist here. Adding to its political powerlessness, the community was divided between Black Brahmins, a relatively well-off and educated elite, Caribbean Blacks, who began to arrive in large numbers after 1900, and blacks with roots in the South, the most diverse group who were often poorer and ostracized by the others.

The first important center for blacks in the city had been on the back side of Beacon Hill, but after 1890, the population shifted to the South End, particularly to the areas between Columbus Avenue and the rail road tracks, the corner around City Hospital, and the tenements of Lower Roxbury. However, blacks were not a majority even in these areas. It was only during World War II that Boston's black population began to rapidly increase. In 1940, there were only 23,675 Blacks in the city, but by 1950 there were 40,057, a nearly 70 percent increase, and the next several decades would see similar growth. Blacks came to Boston because of wartime opportunities, Boston's educational institutions, and its liberal reputation. Martin Luther King, Jr., for one, moved to Boston to study for a Doctor of Theology degree at Boston University. During his stay in the city, he met and married Coretta Scott, a native of Alabama who was attending the New England Conservatory of Music.

The stretch of Massachusetts Avenue near Columbus Avenue became a nationally known center of jazz and nightlife in the years after World War II. Stars including Duke Ellington and Dinah Washington came to perform in the nightclubs, and area restaurants were known as some of the few places anywhere that served both whites and blacks.[20] Malcolm Little, who would later change his name to Malcom X after converting to Islam, was a teenager when he first came to Boston, living with his sister in Roxbury. The wild nightclubs, the flashy fashions (Malcolm would boast of his sky blue zoot suit), and the abundance of women kept him in Boston. It was the first place he had been where black and white couples walked hand in hand without notice.[21] Boston seemed to be a better place than elsewhere, though Malcolm complained about the inflated self-importance of many Roxbury blacks. He noted how blacks living along Humboldt Avenue looked down on their brethren living in Lower Roxbury and the South End, and those born in New England considered themselves better than those from the South. "It didn't make any difference that they had to rent out rooms to make ends meet," he said of the African-American community, "Foreign diplomats could have modeled their conduct on the way the Negro postmen, Pullman porters, and dining car waiters of Roxbury acted."[22]

Unfortunately, most blacks found in the city many of the same hardships and barriers they were fleeing from. Boston was safer, it did not suffer from the white on black violence that plagued Detroit, Chicago, and the South, for example. But their employment opportunities were extremely restricted as municipal jobs, union memberships, and even maid positions were under the tight control of the Irish.[23] If a black man without a college education didn't succeed in getting a porter or wait staff job with the railroads, there was little available to him.

Housing discrimination was even worse. Though there were integrated blocks in the South End, most blacks were funneled into an ever-expanding ghetto that began in Lower Roxbury and relentlessly moved south towards Franklin Park. As World War II began, Seaver Street was the southern edge of the ghetto. But much of Roxbury was still integrated with many Jewish families remaining even during a time of racial change. Then, after the war, racial change accelerated, and white families left as fast as they could sell or rent elsewhere with most moving to the suburbs.[24] Year after year, white flight combined with new black residents resulted in what was once a Jewish, Italian, and Irish neighborhood becoming predominantly black.[25] The city often purposely neglected or withheld services from areas with large black populations, and housing codes were not enforced, trash was not picked up, and parks were abandoned.

Of course the nightclubs were not for every black city resident.

Boston's strong network of black churches, fraternal and women's organizations, and settlement houses played a large role in many black families' lives. Though at least one church, Union United Methodist, catered to all three groups of Boston blacks, most were attended by one group or another with Southern Blacks, Black Brahmins, and Caribbean Blacks all organizing their own places of worship. For the most part, segregation was dealt with as a fact of life, opposed when possible, angrily put up with when not. To many whites, the 1940s were a time of racial harmony; to many blacks, it was a decade when the community began to organize to fight oppression.[26]

Black Roxbury was poor, yet its residents were resourceful. There were few supermarkets anywhere in Boston at the time, and residents would go store to store to buy food for the week at small groceries, meat markets, and vegetable sellers. Because no one had a car, shoppers relied on delivery boys who would load up their metal wagons with a number of clients' purchases and then walk them up the many flights of stairs to the apartments. One woman recalls always hearing the clack of metal wheels throughout the day as the boys made the rounds. She also remembers not locking the door so that the delivery boys could just leave the purchases on the kitchen table for when they came home from shopping.[27] No one could have predicted the tremendous changes to the community that would come in the ensuing decades.

Many Yankees felt tethered to a city they were increasingly growing to dislike. As they became alarmed by the decay around them, Boston's business community organized itself to reassert their control over the city government taken over by Curley. In the process, they would create what is known as a growth machine, a coalition of businessmen, developers, union leaders, and others that prioritized strong pro-development policies over other municipal functions. The group would dominate the city for the next seventy years. Boston's post-war business coalition had three goals: devise a new council election system that would minimize neighborhood input, create a new bureaucracy to promote redevelopment, and reform taxation to reduce costs.[5] To implement this agenda, they sought to connect with the city's Irish middle class which was increasingly embarrassed by Curley's boorish behavior and angered by the ever higher taxes he imposed.

Within days after Curley's election, the city's business elite, including the Chamber of Commerce, the Greater Boston Real Estate Board, the First National Bank of Boston, Gillette, New England Telephone, John Hancock Insurance Company, and Boston Edison began to meet to figure out a way to work against the mayor. But efforts to reform the city's urban renewal program and change the city's tax structure were stymied at City Hall and the State House.

More successful was the push to transform city elections. A coalition of business interests and good government reformers succeeded in placing a charter amendment on the ballot for the 1949 election that would change the twenty-two member, ward-based City Council to a nine member body elected at large. This successful initiative would have profound effects on Boston over the next three decades as it increased the power of downtown interests and developers who used their control over campaign donations to influence elections. Similarly, it helped reduce the strength of voters in the central poorer wards as these were the places that were most rapidly losing population, and it tipped the balance of power in favor of the middle-class Irish wards. Finally, it eliminated the possibility of any black representation just as their numbers were growing and their anger over racism increasing. It would take nearly twenty years to elect one black city councilor, and over thirty before there would be two serving at the same time.

Business interests also helped set up and fund a good government coalition that pressed to end corruption, support reforms, and elect alternatives to Curley and neighborhood ward bosses. Led by Jerome Rappaport, a young attorney, the group was primarily made up of young veterans and their wives. They would play an influential role in the 1949 election.

Another important, yet often invisible, group in postwar Boston was its lesbian, gay, bisexual, and transgender (LGBT) population. Boston had a flourishing gay community in the late 1940s and 1950s even though it was tightly hemmed in by social discrimination. This was not unique to the city, most people in the United States did not talk about gays or lesbians at all during this era and had never conceived of the idea that anyone might be transgender or questioning their sexuality. When they did attract public attention, gays were thought to be criminals, communists, or sick. Many thought they were security risks and dangerous.

In Boston as elsewhere, it was illegal for men to dance with men or women with women, so bartenders would flash the lights to warn patrons that the police were about to sweep in and couples would separate or dance with the opposite sex. It was also against the law for men to wear women's clothing. The College Inn, for one, found itself fighting to keep from being closed down because its waiters dressed in drag.[28] The police hit gay bars for kickbacks while lesbians had to fear sexual assaults by uniformed officers who were confident that no one would complain out of fear of being outed.

With no legal protections, gay men and lesbians could be easy targets for robbery, and gay men never knew when a potential pickup might demand money or turn violent. For example, one young hustler was an attractive blonde teenager named James "Whitey" Bulger. "According to survivors of the era, Whitey worked out of a couple of gay bars on Stuart Street, primarily a joint called Mario's, which was also known as the Sail Aweigh. As a young male hustler, he quickly became adept at rolling his tricks—his police record indicates an arrest for "unarmed robbery." Another of his favorite pickup spots was the Punch Bowl, which was frequently raided by the Vice Squad."[18]

Yet not all was bleak and furtive. Much of gay social life consisted of parties in private homes, or men would cruise for sex partners outdoors. Right before World War II, an unpublished manuscript described how there were those who preferred to pick up partners in the Public Garden but who would never deign to meet men on the Common, while others had an equally strong opposite preference. It reported that though they tended to avoid any public involvement with the straight community, gays and lesbians fell in love, had careers, and maintained close friendships with each other.[29] Gay men tended to live on the back side of Beacon Hill. Lesbians were more dispersed and other queer people even more invisible due to the oppression of the day.

Boston's LGBT people faced less overt discrimination than elsewhere. Though the police sweeps of bars must have been traumatic for everyone present, these tended to be shakedowns of owners, and patrons were usually left alone as long as they could show identification to the police. Prescott Townsend, a descendent of a signer of the Declaration of Independence, Yankee blueblood, and a well-known advocate for gay rights in the 1940s and 1950s, attributes this relative freedom to the fact that the first gay bar after the end of Prohibition was started by the head of the Liquor Dealers Association and his wife.[30]

Townsend took advantage of his homosexuality to transcend boundaries of class and race, inviting one and all to share his two homes on Beacon Hill and his beach shack in Provincetown. Some stayed in spare bedrooms, some in Townsend's bed. He helped found the Boston chapters of the Mattachine Society and One, Inc., two organizations dedicated to fighting for political rights for gay and lesbian people at a time when such advocacy took courage. Year after year, Townsend would go to the State house, usually alone, to lobby for the repeal of sodomy laws.

Activists would gather in Townsend's basement at 75 Phillips Street on Sundays to discuss the status of gay people. Later, these gatherings moved to the Parker House. Many of the attendees went there to meet others, which annoyed the more politically minded. "The purpose of the group was for public education, not for assignations," complained one anonymous critic who also didn't like that many of the attendees flaunted conventional gender roles. "Prescott was defending his screamy-meamy, bubble-headed faggy types."[31]

Eventually, the flamboyant Townsend was ordered out of the group because he didn't fit in with its goal of proving to the world that gays could be conventional, next door neighbor types. This is an early example of a split that would run through the LGBT community in Boston (and elsewhere) for the next sixty years: there would be those who would openly refuse to comply with social norms for sexuality, gender, and behavior, challenging straight society to accept them on their own terms, and another group that would stress their conformity with these norms as they campaigned for equal rights.[32]

The Mattachine Society lasted into the first years of the 1960s, though the group was asked to stop meeting at the Parker House "because each and every meeting would turn into . . . well, I won't say an orgy, but we'll stop just short of that."[33] By 1960, the Boston Mattachine Society was sending out 1,200 copies of its monthly flyer. Yet the group was timid. When asked by Townsend to cosponsor repeal of anti sodomy laws in late 1959, it declined, saying it could not take so public a role.

Many turned against Townsend, complaining of his need to dominate the various groups he founded and the unselfconscious manner in which he lived his life. Most other men and women had far too much to lose by being so open at the time. This points out another critical facet of LGBT life in the postwar era. Boston could be tolerant of LGBT people but only if they agreed to keep their behavior out of public view. Townsend had crossed this line decades before and had been effectively erased by proper Yankee society. It wasn't so much that he was gay but that he was so open about it that led to him being ostracized. Townsend "would have done less damage to his reputation by making a pass at his hostess's son than by waving a banner and tooting his one note," suggested one longtime friend.[31] Long before anyone came up with the term, Boston was dominated by a strict policy of "don't ask, don't tell."

In the 1940s, the group that was most rapidly leaving the city were its Jews, then Boston's third largest demographic block. Blue Hill Avenue was the central spine of one of the country's most important Jewish neighborhoods, one that rivaled New York's Lower East Side or the Bronx Concourse, and as the war ended perhaps over 100,000 Jews lived along the Avenue from Roxbury to Mattapan. Blacks were moving in from Lower Roxbury and the Irish were thickly settled to the east, but to friend and foe alike, "Jew Hill Avenue" with its delicatessens, synagogues, stores, and throngs of people provided everything residents needed. It had "fruit stands, herring hawkers, and floating chicken feathers from kosher butcher stores."[25] The area had eighty credit unions to provide the services banks would not.

The Jewish history of Boston dates back to the nineteenth century as many from central Europe began to settle in the blocks around Park Square and the Common. Many Jews moved to the South End and then Roxbury and Dorchester as they were joined by thousands more from Eastern Europe. There had once been strong Jewish neigh borhoods in the West End and the New York Streets area in the South End, but by World War II, most Boston Jews lived along Blue Hill Avenue.[34]

Blue Hill Avenue and Quincy Street, 1948. At one time, Boston had one of the most prominent Jewish communities in the United States.

The buckle of the Avenue was the G&G Delicatessen at the corner of what is now Ansel Road. Inside, "there were glass display cases and steam tables resplendent with smoked meats and kosher-style prepared dishes over which customers shouted orders to aproned countermen."[25] It seemed that almost everyone in the neighborhood showed up at some point during the week: young men sat by the windows to look at passing girls, businessmen preferred the booths, and policemen, cab drivers, and many more stopped by for lunch. It was the sound level of the deli that outsiders noticed: there was a cacophony of Yiddish and English that bordered on deafening. Jews were not the only visitors to the G&G. Perhaps inspired by Franklin Roosevelt's motorcade drive down Blue Hill Avenue during the 1936 election, when he was mobbed by adoring crowds, Dwight Eisenhower campaigned for President at the G&G, and John Kennedy ate there as he sought a seat in Congress. Other politicians sought out support more quietly in the back room of nearby Levine's Funeral Chapel.

Former residents were nostalgic for the neighborhood's peculiarities. For reasons unknown, for example, residents preferred to walk in the median of the Avenue rather than on the sidewalks. There were also tensions between the observant, who would scowl at anyone driving on the Sabbath, and secular Jews who prided themselves on their struggles to learn Hebrew. In the summer, so many families went out to Nantasket Beach that a section was called Little Israel.

Yet the neighborhood was changing as Jews, particularly middle-class and American-born ones, had been leaving Boston for the western suburbs for decades, and Brookline was seen as the place to be. Other families elected to stay on in the city and would soon be buying new ranch houses and capes in Mattapan, a few miles south, but far from the action at the G&G. So there was a whiff of sadness in the blocks along Blue Hill Avenue in the late 1940s. It was a world that was ending.[25]

Curley, meanwhile, barely had time to govern the city. In December 1945, he went on trial in Washington despite the intervention of a large number of politicians to have the charges dropped. The judge was accommodating, suspending proceedings in order to enable Curley to be sworn into office in January 1946. But Curley was convicted and, appeals exhausted, he went to prison in June 1947.

Curley's temporary replacement was the mild-mannered City Clerk, John Hynes, a safe choice as he had never been elected to public office and was so bland as to be almost invisible. In the five months that Curley was in prison, Hynes purposely kept a low profile and did not implement any new initiatives. So when Curley's sentence was commuted by President Harry Truman, Hynes was ready to quietly return to the City Clerk's office.

Then, in what may have been the worst blunder in twentieth-century Boston politics, Curley publicly humiliated Hynes on the first day he resumed mayoral duties. After signing a few minor pieces of legislation, Curley announced that he had just accomplished more in one day than Hynes had accomplished in months. Hynes was furious, shouting to his family, "I'll kill him! I'll bury him!" and vowed revenge. The stage was set for the pivotal mayor's race of 1949.[6]

It was easy to see why Curley had dismissed his temporary replacement. Hynes was born on East Lenox Street in the South End to a railroad worker. He was a devoted family man and Catholic, attending mass daily, and by the time he ran for mayor, he was living in Dorchester with his five children. "Hynes was a short, slight man who was always impeccably dressed in a banker's suit. He wore rimless glasses under wavy hair that made him look like a kindly country doctor."[6]

But he was smart and connected, and he reached out to former Mayor Tobin and people in the business community to finish off Curley's career. He also enlisted the support of Jerome Rappaport and his good government coalition who were trying to boost the turnout for the city council charter amendment and who strongly disliked Curley. Though Curley was still very popular, particularly among elderly voters, the generation nurtured on the resentment of Yankees was dying off, and Hynes was able to capture enough younger voters and people tired of corruption and the old ways to defeat Curley. Yet even in his twilight, Curley received more votes than ever, 126,000, but this was not enough to best Hynes' 141,000. Charlestown, South Boston, East Boston, the North End, and the West End went for Curley, but the middle-class outer wards, home to the upwardly mobile Irish, were Hynes territory, and that was where a majority of votes was now located. In a rematch two years later, necessitated by a successful charter reform vote, Hynes beat Curley 108,000 to 77,000.[6] Then Hynes beat Curley again in 1954. The Master never won another election.

No one knew it at the time, but 1949 marked the end of conservative Irish dominance of the mayor's office in the city. There would be an unbroken string of Irish mayors for the next 44 years and then another Irish mayor after 2014, but these would be the more moderate or liberal candidates in fields that often featured a conservative candidate that drew on older Irish voters for support. Hynes would also mark the start of a long series of mayors who favored downtown development interests over neighborhood concerns. For the next thirty-four years, mayors would be more or less distant from the people they governed.

1.   Linscott S. Boston becomes bedlam of jubliant demonstrators. *Boston Globe.* August 15, 1945; p. 1.
2.   Ross L. Joyous, friendly crowd surges through streets. *Boston Globe.* August 15, 1945; p. 18.
3.   Kennedy L. *Planning the City Upon a Hill: Boston Since 1630.* Boston: University

of Massachusetts Press, 1994.

4. Allen DG. *Investment Management in Boston: A History.* Boston: University of Massachusetts Press 2015.

5. Horan C. Organizing the "New Boston": Growth policy, governing coalitions & tax reform. *Polity.* 1990; 22.

6. O'Neill G. *Rogues and Redeemers: When Politics was King in Irish Boston.* New York: Crown Publishing Group, 2012.

7. Levin MB. *The Alienated Voter: Politics in Boston.* New York: Holt, Reinhart and Winston, 1966.

8. Melnik M. *Demographic and Socio-economic Trends in Boston: What We've Learned From the Latest Census Data.* Boston Redevelopment Authority. 2011.

9. Caizzi C. *Just So You Know.* Boston, 2013.

10. Marchione WP. The 1949 Boston charter reform. *The New England Quarterly.* 1976; 49: 373-98.

11. Curley JM. *I'd Do It Again.* Salem, NH: Ayer Company, Publishers, 1957.

12. O'Connor T. *Building a New Boston: Politics and Urban Renewal 1950 to 1970.* Boston, Massachusetts: Northeastern University Press, 1993.

13. Glaeser EL and Shleife A. The Curley effect: The Economics of shaping the electorate. *The Journal of Law, Economics, & Organization.* 2005; 21: 1-19.

14. Lopez R. *Boston's South End: The Clash of Ideas in a Historic Neighborhood.* Boston: Shawmut Peninsula Press, 2015.

15. Beatty J. *The Rascal King: The Life and Times of James Michael Curley (1874-1958).* Reading, MA: Addison-Wesley Publishing, 1992.

16. Lawler P. *The Faithful Departed.* New York: Perseus, 2010.

17. O'Connor T. *Bibles, Brahmins and Bosses: A Short History of Boston.* Boston: Trustees of the Public Library of the City of Boston 1984.

18. Carr H. *The Brothers Bulger: How they Terrorized and Corrupted Boston for a Quarter Century.* New York: Grand Central Publishing, 2006.

19. Donovan MA. I Married into South Boston. City of Boston, *Born Before Plastic: Stories from Boston's Most Enduring Neighborhoods.* Boston: Grub Street Inc., 2007.

20. Hentoff N. *Boston Boy: Growing Up with Jazz and Other Rebellious Passions.* Philadelphia: Paul Dry Books, 2001.

21. Marable M. *Malcolm X: A Life of Reinvention.* Nwe York: Viking, 2011.

22. X M and Haley A. *The Autobiography of Malcolm X.* New York: Random House, 1964.

23. Lukas A. *Common Ground: A Turbulent Decade in the Lives of Three American Families.* New York: Vintage Books, 1986.

24. Motti TL. *Social conflict and social movements: An explanatory study of the black community of Boston attempting to change the Boston public schools.* Doctoral Thesis, Brandeis University, 1975.

25. Levine H and Harmon L. *The Death of an American Jewish Community. A Tragedy of Good Intentions.* New York: The Free Press, 1992.

26. King M. *Chain of Change: Struggles for Black Community Development.* Boston MA: South End Press, 1981.

27. Haskell KB. Saturday Scenes. City of Boston, *Born Before Plastic: Stories from Boston's Most Enduring Neighborhoods.* Boston: Grub Street Inc., 2007.
28. The History Project. *Improper Bostonians: Lesbian and Gay History from the Puritans to Playland.* Boston: The Beacon Press, 1998.
29. Bernstein A. *Millions of Queers (Our Homo America).* Unpublished Manuscript, 1940.
30. Wicker R. Boston's Bohemian Blueblood: An Immodest Interview with a Happy Old Man. *Magazine-Unknown Title,* 1969.
31. Cathcart A. *Unpublished memoir,* 1995.
32. White E. *States of Desire: Travels in Gay America.* New York: Dutton, 1980.
33. Biography. Beans, Cod, and Libido: The Life of Prescott Townsend 1894-1973. *Manifest Destiny.* 1973.
34. Sarna JD, Smith E and Kosofsky S-M. *The Jews of Boston.* New Haven, Connecticut: Yale University Press, 1995.

Chapter 2

A Rocky Beginning: 1950-1959

WHEN JOHN HYNES was sworn in as Boston's 49th mayor on January 2, 1950, much of the excitement of the day focused on his clothes. This was the first time the event was televised, and the new mayor sported a jaunty fedora and a well-tailored gray suit rather than the now outmoded silk top hat with stodgy formal clothes that mayors (particularly Curley) had traditionally worn. Through his wardrobe and use of new media, Hynes demonstrated to the city that a new era was at hand. But there were also signs of troubles. Hynes devoted most of his speech to the city's dire fiscal problems and the cutbacks and tax increases he needed to balance the budget. Also ominous, the ceremony included the swearing in of just twenty-one of twenty-two city councilors in the final iteration of the old system. The one unsworn, Lawrence Banks, should have been the city's first black councilor. But the racist white power structure was against him and had used illegal ballots to block his election. Banks was forced to sue to get his seat and the case took so long to be settled in his favor, he would not be sworn in until almost the end of the term. Then with charter reform in 1951, the council was changed to a nine-member body, elected at large; there would not be another black city councilor until 1968. As blacks sought to politically assert themselves, the Irish political structure conspired to shut them out.

The reputation of John Hynes's administration was greatly enhanced by virtue of his being the anti-Curley, earning the gratitude of the hundreds of thousands inside and outside the city who despised his predecessor. To a whole generation of those reacting against the former mayor, Hynes was the man who saved Boston from decay. But from a perspective fifty years later, Hynes's administration was hampered by a combination of fiscal problems and bad policy decisions and ultimately did little to revive the troubled city.

Hynes's spent much of his time trying to manage the city's finances, but as revenues stagnated and expenses rose, there was little room to maneuver and no ability to launch new initiatives that required city money. Publicly, Hynes's tried to cut expenses, but the only way to do that was to lay off employees, which he was reluctant to do, so city employment would drop by just 2 percent by 1957. As a result, Hynes's had to keep going hat in hand to the legislature and the bond markets, and the conditions imposed by them further squeezed the city.

At least Hynes had the downtown business coalition supporting him. Business leaders believed that addressing Boston's problems required them to organize, and they met regularly: 4 PM sharp every other week in the conference room just outside the vault in the basement of the Boston Safe Deposit and Trust Company. The group was small and limited to the leaders of Boston's major banks and private companies, but it was very influential and strongly shaped development policies during the several decades following. Officially, the group was known as the Boston Coordinating Committee, but most referred to it as the Vault. In its first major initiative, it worked with Hynes to try to stem the red ink strangling the city's budget.

The city's budget problems were no more Hynes' fault than they were Curley's, and in the thirty-four years spanning 1950 to 1984, the city ran deficits in twenty-eight of those years. There were some improvements over time because the city was able to shift some of its expenses to the state including welfare, courts, and other costs generally covered by the commonwealth for other cities and towns, but not Boston. But in general, Hynes's budgets were little better than Curley's. Though Hynes reduced bonded debt from $75 million in 1949 to $59 million in 1956, he increased outstanding short-term borrowing to $28 million by that same year. This was the result of his using Curley's practices of hiding deficits by over estimating property tax revenues or collecting them in one year and then rebating them the next. Hynes also continued the longstanding tricks of borrowing off of anticipated state revenues and remortgaging city properties. As with his predecessor, Hynes had few alternatives; during his term the local economy declined while new construction averaged less than $15 million a year. The result was that in the first five years of his tenure (1949-1954), city assessed values fell by $100 million while the tax rate increased by 60 percent. Then to make matters worse, in 1957 a new fiscal crisis forced the state to bail out the city once again.[1]

Thus the years between 1950 and 1958 were not good for Boston as the post-war decline continued and the decay of the city was visible to all. "Raggedly dressed children still play between wooden tenement buildings rotting with age and neglect," noted one observer in 1957.[2] Wartime needs and a housing shortage had temporarily boosted the city's population to an all-time high of 801,440 in 1950, but in the next decade, the city population declined by just over 100,000, a quarter of them children. If it hadn't been for 23,000 more blacks entering the city, the population loss would have been even greater. Yet many felt Hynes was promoting progress where Curley had retarded it, and voters rewarded the new mayor with a strong majority when he ran for reelection.

Hynes left a lasting physical presence on the city, though most of his projects are now considered to be problematic. In the context of his time, however, they were thought to be state of the art measures to modernize decaying cities. In perhaps his most lasting legacy, there was a vast expansion in the region's highway network. Planning for the highway system in the greater Boston area had begun in earnest in the early 1940s, an era when faith in the ability of automobiles to move populations and the efficacy of highways to facilitate mobility was at a high point. Automobile production, thanks to new manufacturing efficiencies pioneered by Henry Ford and others, began to rise rapidly in the years before World War I. In the years after that war, total annual car produced jumped into the millions and cities such as Boston found themselves choking on traffic. A particular problem was how to connect affluent suburban homes with center city jobs, shopping, and entertainment. The answer, pioneered by visionaries such as Norman Bel Geddes, designer of the Futurama exhibit at the 1939 World's Fair, was to build an extensive system of highways across metropolitan areas. Enthusiastically adopted by planners in Massachusetts and a series of governors who saw them as job producers in the 1940s, most of this highway construction would be completed in the 1950s.

Planned, built, and funded by the State, Hynes was not directly responsible for the new roads or the benefits and devastation they produced, but as a true believer that they were part of the answer to the puzzle of restarting growth in the city, he did not oppose their construction. He limited his involvement to requests for minor alterations in their routes in order to spare specific blocks or particular buildings. Hynes wanted these highways and considered them worth the cost in disruption and displacement.

William Callahan, father of the man for whom they would name a tunnel to East Boston, created the highway network in and around Boston. As Commissioner of Public Works for Massachusetts from 1934-1939 and 1946-1953, and then the Chairman of the Massachusetts Turnpike Authority from 1952 to 1964, the elder Callahan had a hand in planning and building every major highway in the city. Most of these roads were included in the very influential 1948 Master Highway Plan for the Boston Metropolitan Area that Callahan commissioned and implemented. He had owned a dredging company and then built dry docks and other port facilities, but he had no training in civil engineering, urban planning, or transportation. His power came from his ability to get complex projects constructed on time and within budget.

The very gruff Callahan was involved in a number of scandals over his time as a public servant. Most famously, when attacked for giving insurance commissions to members of the legislature he said, "It is only natural that you give this business to your friends rather than your enemies."[3] He also drew controversy after he granted construction contracts to the firm owned by his son-in-law. Despite having had his larynx removed because of cancer, he was not afraid to confront governors, reporters, and others who stood in the way of his roads. His mission was to get his highways on the ground, and he saw opponents as objects to be moved or demolished.

Storrow Drive opened in 1951. First proposed decades earlier, it was the most controversial of this first wave of highways because it involved the taking of parkland on the Esplanade and cut off Back Bay from the Charles River. Storrow was a Harvard-educated Yankee who was, for a brief time, head of General Motors. He ran for mayor in 1909, losing to John "Honey Fitz" Fitzgerald as the electorate cemented the Irish hold on the city's mayoralty. Storrow also unsuccessfully tried to negotiate an agreement to prevent the great Boston police strike of 1919, but he is most well-known today for his role in creating the series of parks along the lower Charles River, some of the most used and cherished greenspaces in the region. Planners saw these parks as cleared land that could be easily paved over for roads, and in the 1930s there was a proposal to reconfigure the Esplanade with a remade park and highway. But opposition from James Storrow's widow Helen, and others, scuttled the proposed road. In the 1940s, the highway plan was revived and as Helen Storrow had passed away, the opposition was unable to stop the legislature from voting to authorize the new road.

Initially less controversial but ultimately more disliked, the new Central Artery would become a symbol of the problems posed by urban highways. Today, we think of elevated highways as dreary, deadening pollution generators, but when the Central Artery was first proposed, elevated highways were rooted in the dream of engineering technology with the potential to transform outdated cities into modern automobile focused power centers.[4] The idea of an elevated highway slicing through the heart of Boston originated in 1930 as a solution to the city's congestion problem and it included building a tunnel to the airport and extending highways north, south, and west from downtown. Nothing happened, though, until Callahan lobbied for the project at the behest of Governor Robert Bradford in 1948. Then, in 1949, a new Democratic majority in the legislature joined with incoming Governor Paul Dever to pass a $100 million bond bill to fund the new road. The man to build it was Callahan, back at the state Department of Public Works after a ten-year absence.

Individual property owners, merchants, and others were against the Artery, but no unified opposition coalesced to stop it, though controversy regarding the southern portion resulted in that part being buried below grade. It was only after it was completed in 1959 that the city reacted in horror to the new road. "Rising high over the Charles River, running elevated over the North End, and dipping below Dewey Square, the dull green ribbon of steel and concrete displaced residents, bisected neighborhoods, and gashed a dirty barrier through the heart of downtown Boston," would be how *The Boston Globe* described it later.[5] It quickly became noted for the horrendous traffic on both the Artery itself and its approach roads.[6] The Artery would blight a stretch of otherwise prime land for almost fifty years until it was torn down in the 1990s.

Creating approaches to the Artery was also problematic. The Southeast Expressway was carved out of the Dorchester waterfront causing the collateral damage of separating that diverse neighborhood from the Harbor; sadly, in the process the state destroyed historic Chester Park in the South End in order to create better traffic flow from the Expressway to Back Bay. Further south, construction of the Expressway caused the Old Colony Railroad to shut down, forcing its 10,000 daily riders to find new ways of getting to the city.[7] To the north, the Tobin Bridge, named after Curley's nemesis, was to divide Chelsea and create a tremendous lead poisoning problem in that troubled little city as paint chips rained down on the blocks surrounding the road.

One of the most important highways in the region was constructed about a dozen miles outside the core and does not even reach Boston at all, Route 128. When the first sections opened in 1951 it was derided as the "highway to nowhere" and critics suggested that the whole project was a boondoggle.[8] By 1957, however, there were 17,000 jobs within one mile of the highway; by 1959 there were 30,000. In that year, 38 percent of the total business development in the metropolitan area was in the Route 128 corridor. The area was most heavily invested in manufacturing with 72.6 percent of its employment in that sector. In what was to become critical to the revival of Boston decades later, few financial service jobs moved there, but most of the manufacturing in the corridor had been relocated from Boston with companies seeking the parking, horizontal layouts, and access to highways they could not get in the city. Many also went in search of lower land costs and lower taxes.[9]

The new road greatly facilitated suburban development around Boston. In these new subdivisions, residents could go to school, work, shop, and find everything they needed without visiting the city. It also enabled them to ignore Boston's economic and social problems as it helped hasten the city's decline. One special feature of Route 128 that set it apart from those of other cities in the country was that it was built on the periphery of a ring of old established towns. It lies on the edges of Newton and Waltham, for example. This might explain why, along with the area's heavy reliance on industry rather than office services, Boston never developed full fledge "edge cities," or nodes that rival downtown financial districts in density and diversity of land uses. This uniqueness would have profound implications when Boston began to revive in the 1970s.

A crucial ingredient of the Route 128 economy was that its companies focused on research and development. These were mostly small in the 1950s, many of them were related to MIT and Vannevar Bush's efforts to foster innovation and new technologies. An electrical engineer by training, Bush cofounded Raytheon Corporation in the 1920s and then ran the country's military research operations during World War II. But he is perhaps most famous for his role in launching the Manhattan Project that would produce the world's first atomic bomb. Convinced that the country's security and economic prosperity rested on its science and engineering prowess, Bush promoted new companies and expanded research along the Route 128 Corridor throughout the 1950s.

The Hynes years also saw the last large scale construction of family public housing. There would be additional units for low income residents built in later decades, but most of that would be housing for the elderly or units built and owned by private developers with the assistance of public subsidies. For the most part these public housing developments were owned and operated by the Boston Housing Authority (BHA) and were funded under the Federal Housing Act of 1949. There had been large-scale construction of public housing in the city before the war that used both state and federal housing programs. Then in 1949, President Harry Truman signed new legislation that authorized a large scale new program of housing that in Boston culminated in Bromley Heath, Columbia Point, and Cathedral in the first half of the 1950s.[10] In subsequent years, these developments were both demonized as poorly designed warehouses for the poor and cherished as having once been desirable communities for stable families.

In reality, there never was a golden age of Boston public housing, and as soon as they opened, projects were distinguished by their problems. Some of these related to their design: most of them were ugly and terribly different from the neighborhoods around them. Other problems stemmed from their financing. Cheaply built because of strict limits on construction costs, they tended to have poor heating systems, leaking roofs, and drafty windows from the start. Worse, the entire public housing program was based on the belief that rents would be sufficient to pay for maintenance, management, and capital improvements. But the developments needed repairs as soon as they opened, and rents would never be high enough to keep them from becoming ever worse.[11] By the mid-1950s, the developments were seen as failures, and Boston's experiences helped convince the federal government to stop funding additional conventional family public housing.

Nor did the developments succeed as safe temporary launching points for striving families. The new middle class wanted to move to the suburbs and live the suburban dream. So almost as soon as they opened, the developments were havens for those with few other options: the poor, unemployed, and split families. By the late 1950s, the BHA paved over open spaces to reduce maintenance costs, and within a decade almost a quarter of the public housing units in the city would be vacant.

Perhaps Hynes's largest legacy, and his greatest failure, was urban renewal. The program was launched by the City Planning Department in 1940 and focused first on demolishing and replacing the city's vast amount of substandard housing. Then the Federal Housing Act of 1949 set up a process for cities to undertake renewal using federal and state funds. The act's requirements included the designation of a local agency to implement renewal; in the case of Boston, this would be the BHA. The new legislation allowed the Authority to use federal funds to replace blighted housing with non-residential uses, and with Hynes's approval, the city moved to create a plan that involved clearing neighborhoods for new housing or manufacturing. It was vast in scope, promising to demolish nearly a quarter of the city's housing stock while displacing nearly 200,000 people. South Boston, Jamaica Plain, East Boston, Roxbury, the South End, and other inner neighborhoods were to be made over in the image of the modern city: broad avenues, superblocks, concrete garden apartment blocks, and strict separation of land uses.[12] Inner Boston as it had evolved over the centuries was to be torn down and destroyed. Downtown business interests were excited by the plan, but most residents never knew it existed nor did they know what it would mean for their homes and neighborhoods. Hynes believed it would save the city.

From its beginning in the 1940s through its final death throws in the 1970s, a major goal of urban renewal in Boston was to replace its low-income residents with the middle class and the wealthy. The proponents of renewal wanted to rid the city of its poor, or at least reduce their numbers and contain them. The poor were a burden and an embarrassment to the growth coalition dominating the city; the aim of renewal was to produce a new city, one affluent and modern. So they had to go. The human cost of this goal would be enormous.

Fortunately, the BHA proved unable to implement Hynes's city-wide renewal plans because it lacked the necessary staff and expertise to do so. Instead, it concentrated renewal efforts on two projects on the edge of downtown: New York Streets (NYS) and the West End. The first neighborhood to be scraped clear by urban renewal was the New York Streets area of the South End, built on filled land in the first half of the nineteenth century. Mel King, a former resident and later a candidate for Mayor, recalls a neighborhood of small ethnic grocery stores:

> On the corner of Seneca and Harrison there was an Armenian store with olives in barrels out front, and a fish market next store. The next block down on the corner of Oneida was Leo Guiffri's bakery, I think. There was a synagogue on Oswego. Bikofsky's bakery was on the corner of Lovering and Harrison, and Saroka's Drug Store a block down on Davis Street.

King remembered the close proximity of other businesses and destinations to be a positive part of his childhood:

> We used to play ball in the area between Albany Street and Fort Point Channel, which was also a great place to

watch the drawbridges and the tug boats. We would swim at the Broadway Street or Dover Street bridges. The lumber yards, also between Albany and Fort Point Channel, provided some of the best fires a kid could ever hope to see.[13]

Former residents fondly recalled the Catholic Our Lady of Pompeii Church, established to serve the area's Italian residents. Others worshiped at the Church of All Nations, one of the few integrated congregations in the city.

Throughout the 1940s there were extensive studies of the demographic, housing, social, and economic conditions of the neighborhood. The area had a mix of races and ethnicities—Italians, Jews, Blacks, Greeks, and Syrians—and a city analysis of the population in 1940, based on a census tract that was larger than NYS, reported that 506 or 12 percent were African American, 2,369 or 56 percent were native-born whites, and 1,312 or 31 percent were foreign-born whites.[14] As early as 1901, observers of the neighborhood remarked at how an individual building in the neighborhood often had people of different races, most often Jews and blacks, living in the same tenement building. One author, in condemning this close proximity, reassured readers that despite the close living conditions, the races did not truly mix.[15] In 1950, city hall was deeply troubled by this integration. Perhaps if it hadn't been redeveloped, NYS might have provided an alternative model for race relations, one that emphasized harmony and friendship, but outside forces feared and disliked this community.

Another concern was that the neighborhood had a mix of land uses and was not strictly residential. Though the non-residential land uses were not noxious, they were considered to be inappropriate, and their presence contributed to the perception that the community needed to be cleared and rebuilt. Maps of land use and building owners from 1948 show that most of the neighborhood continued to be used as housing, but Washington Street had theaters and stores while the land along the southern edge of the neighborhood was mostly warehouses, lumberyards, and auto repair shops. A number of electrical supply, hardware wholesalers, and automobile garages were scattered

New York Streets after redevelopment. This was the first neighborhood to be demolished by urban renewal.

among the residential blocks, and there were churches, boys and girls clubs, and social service providers in the neighborhood as well.[16] The BHA warned that these mixed-use blocks were unacceptable for a healthy city.

In 1952 the city proclaimed the neighborhood to be a "menace to housing and a barrier to proper business development." Studies pointed out that there were problems with "outworn and outmoded residential buildings together with the encroachment of business uses and the concomitant truck traffic [that] has rendered the area undesirable for anything except business and industrial uses in the future."[17] The BHA wanted the area to be completely rebuilt.

The first plans, including one by the newly-arrived Bauhaus architect and German refugee Marcel Breuer, called for replacing the area with modernist housing placed on superblocks. But then city planners decided that the New York Streets area would be the perfect location for an industrial park. Cleared, the acres would have good utility service and close access to highways, rail, and the airport.[18] The city saw it as an opportunity to reverse the decades long decline in manufacturing; residents would be displaced to save the economy of the city.

The city began land takings and demolitions with little notice to those who lived there. Confronted by shut off street lights and eviction notices, residents were stunned and unable to stop the destruction of their close-knit community, and though a few building owners sued to stop the takings, they lost in court. Other property owners complained that the long lead time between when the takings began and concluded left them saddled with high tax bills as tenants left and rents ceased. The people who lived there were mostly on their own, relocation assistance was a failure, and most moved to equally squalid, but often more expensive, housing nearby because the city spent less than $2 a family on relocation assistance.[19] Cheered by the ease of taking a neighborhood and blinded by optimism that the project would revive the city, Hynes happily presided over a ceremony launching the city's first urban renewal project in 1956.

It was a failure. *The Boston Herald* built a new printing plant, keeping a few hundred jobs in the city, but otherwise the blocks remained vacant or were only used by warehouses and other low employment businesses. The problem of manufacturing in the city was not a lack of space but insufficient demand. The redeveloped area had broad streets, vacant land used for parking, and a drab, empty feeling for the next fifty years. It was an "industrial no man's land" created by city efforts and funded by federal dollars.[20]

Hynes struggled to launch other renewal projects and closely co-operated with the Vault to promote investment, but nothing worked to get private development built in the city. Even as workers demolished homes in the New York Streets area, another residential neighborhood next to downtown was targeted for destruction, the West End. One of the first areas to be filled in during the large-scale expansion of Boston in the nineteenth century, for generations the West End had welcomed new comers to the city. It had once held a substantial black population, and in the 1920s, it was the stronghold of one of the city's grandest Irish ward bosses, Martin Lomansey. Nicknamed "The Mahatma," Lomansey was "an impressive figure with handlebar mustache, penetrating gray-blue eyes behind gold-rimmed spectacles, and conservative clothes." He favored a yellow straw hat and always wore a batwinged tie.[21] But Lomansey died in 1933, and the neighborhood's predominately Italian residents had no influence over the Irish political establishment and Yankee businessmen eyeing the land under their homes. The pro-urban renewal machine was at the height of its powers.

Italians immigrated to Boston later than the Irish, not arriving in large numbers until the final decades of the nineteenth century. They mostly came from southern Italy and Sicily, the country's poorest region, and in Boston they crowded into some of the city's worst housing. Italians first settled in the North End, but they soon had important numbers in East Boston, the West End, and other parts of the city. They were Boston's second largest ethnic group in the 1940s before urban renewal, gentrification, and increasing affluence led many to depart for the suburbs.

We know a lot about what life in the West End was like and how terrible were the effects of renewal on its displaced residents because of a series of studies by sociologists before and after the neighborhood was destroyed. Herbert Gans wrote a book, *The Urban Villagers*, which revealed that rather than being a wasteland, the West End and other poor urban neighborhoods provided warmth and moral sustenance to their residents that was lost when demolished.

The West End, North End, and other Italian districts—NYS had an important Italian population as well—were characterized by close-knit groups of immigrants and their children who could trace their connections back to specific villages in Italy. Sometimes, an entire block or street would all be from one village, and residents could distinguish the Italian dialect on one block from that of another. The men formed tight, but transient, groups that hung out at particular street corners or bars. As they grew older, married, and had children, the men used these bonds for support, help finding jobs, and social activities.

The West End c. 1948-1950. Once a poor but thriving Italian community, it was completely demolished by the city.

Women were more closely watched by their families, but they too relied on a close network of relatives and friends for sustenance. So important and intense were these social connections, the ties of religion and family, and the sense of history and experience of place that many residents rarely needed to leave their neighborhoods. The city's smaller Italian communities tended to be more integrated with their neighbors and include immigrants from across Italy, but these often more middle-class areas also had an important ability to nurture family ties and group solidarity. Most of Boston's Italian neighborhoods would vanish over the next several decades: the West End and New York Streets in the 1950s, the North End in the 1980s, and much of East Boston after 2000 would all see their Italian immigrant communities displaced.

As urban renewal loomed, 68 percent of working people in the West End held unskilled or semiskilled occupational jobs, another 17 percent were skilled manual workers. Professional, semiprofessional, and business people together made up just 6 percent of the neighborhood's working people, most of whom were employed by nearby Massachusetts General Hospital. Only 78 percent of male heads of households were regularly employed (in a sample that excluded people over 65) and 54 percent earned less than $75 a week.[22] Though this was before the establishment of federal poverty guidelines, researchers estimated that 23 percent of the non-elderly households were poor and another 32 percent had marginal financial status. In twenty-first century nomenclature, this would be called a high-poverty area—but it did not suffer from concentrated poverty.

The social conditions were similar in the neighborhood next door. One longtime resident called the Italian North End "a happy ghetto." According to her fond memories, people were poor but there were a few differences in income so that everybody felt as if they were in similar circumstances. She recalled having what was known as a stack heater in her kitchen that provided hot water so she didn't have to go to the old bathhouse like other folks as one of the few class distinctions during her youth. Many of her classmates went on to college and very few people went hungry, even during the Depression. As in other urban neighborhoods, there were many good times. The feast of Saint Anthony, for example, was a celebration including a parade with confetti thrown from rooftops. Children would play in the confetti as if it was snow and end up being covered in it.[23]

To outsiders, however, these neighborhoods were foul tenement districts responsible for Boston's economic problems. Even William Whyte, the author of an important work documenting the vitality of the North End, subtitled his book, *The Social Structure of an Italian Slum;* he and Gans acknowledged that outsiders were often afraid to visit these neighborhoods.[24] Non-Italians thought they were dangerous, full of untrustworthy foreigners, and breeding grounds for crime, vice, and social problems. This prejudice and racial animosity made the West End an easy mark for destruction, and its Italian residents and political leaders would find no compassion from Yankee businessmen and Irish politicians.

The city announced its final decision to clear the West End in 1953, and for the next several years, residents passionately marched, pleaded to reporters, signed petitions, begged politicians, filed lawsuits, and demonstrated to save their homes and way of life. When eight hundred people packed a hearing at the State House in 1957, the Capital Police had to step in several times to restore order.[25] Most of the local Italian elected officials–Mario Umana, Michael LoPresti, Christopher Ianella, and others–opposed the project. But the pro-renewal forces were stronger and supporters for the project included the Massachusetts General Hospital, the Museum of Science, the Central Labor Union, the Eye and Ear Infirmary, Boston Medical School, and other business and civic leaders. When the project was first proposed, Joseph Lund, Chair of the BHA, said that to reject the project would "constitute a body blow to Boston's attempt to revitalize itself economically and socially through urban renewal."[26] Years of opposition did nothing to change the mind of City Hall.

The replacement plan for the West End called for a dramatically different cityscape. Instead of small blocks lined by a jumble of tenements, small commercial buildings, and one of a kind structures that had been built over decades (what would now be called an organic streetscape), planners called for a few large apartment buildings set apart from a few redesigned streets surrounded by plantings, plazas, and parking. The prevailing architectural trend in the United States in the 1950s was Modernism, a European theory that was heavily based on a severe separation of land uses, an extreme aesthetic of rationalism, and a dislike of ornamentation. It was supposedly rooted in science but in reality was simply the slavish acceptance of the personal tastes of its acolytes.[27] Housing units were supposed to be "machines for living," but as Catherine Bauer, an important midcentury advocate of public housing and a noted critic of Modernism pointed out, people did not want to live in machines.[28] Just as problematic were the rents for these new units. Expensive and beyond the reach of existing residents, the buildings were designed for and marketed to middle-class and wealthy households looking to live in the city but who were otherwise afraid of its grit and crime. The entire neighborhood was transformed into an antiseptic version of urban living.

Despite the opposition, the push for renewal was relentless. A few of the blocks near Beacon Hill were thought to be in relatively good condition and were initially to be preserved, but pro-renewal advocates convinced the BHA to tear them down as well because of fears they would harm the abutting new development. The expanded project was approved in 1956 and land takings formally began in early 1958–in fact the BHA had been quietly buying buildings and demolishing them for years, using the growing deterioration and population loss as further arguments that the entire neighborhood needed to be bulldozed. By November 1958, 1,200 of 2,700 households had moved and "by the summer of 1960, only rubble remained where two years ago had lived more than 7,000 people."[29] As one observer noted, "It was never much except home and then it was gone, pulverized brick and drywall ash to the wind." [30] Many of the displaced people were overcome by grief and some would visit and sadly walk the barren streets where they, their friends, and families had once lived. It would take years, but the experiences of West End residents would help activists across the country put an end to the national program of urban renewal.

The development that replaced the West End, Charles River Park, sits on the side of central Boston like a sore that can never heal. Despite promises made to residents, there was no replacement housing built for them, and residents were mostly displaced out of the city to the north. The urban renewal process was carefully proscribed by the federal government with the end steps in the process calling for the city to sell the land as a highly reduced cost to a private developer. In what many thought was a sham, the Hynes administration created a public bidding process that ended up awarding the lucrative deal to Jerome Rappaport, who had now moved on to a private law practice after spending several years as Hynes's personal secretary. Though both Hynes and Rappaport swore there was no special deal, the public never ceased to believe the process was fixed. The corruption increased the bitterness of displaced residents, and the obvious disaster of the project would haunt the city for the remainder of the century. After it was demolished, whenever a major development initiative was proposed anywhere in the city, opponents almost always brought up the experience of the West End.

During his time in office, Hynes had two other urban renewal priorities that were very public failures: Government Center and the Prudential Center. Both were launched by Hynes, but neither could be brought to fruition by his administration. The most prominent project was a new Government Center, conceived as a vast remake of the area between the North End, downtown, the West End, and Beacon Hill. Proposed to include new landmark facilities for city, state, and federal offices, it was to be a showcase of new architecture built on the bulldozed blocks of Scollay Square. Just as with the redevelopment of residential areas, the Scollay Square remake was characterized as a modern rebuilding of a troubled area, and Hynes presented his Government Center proposal to the public as the solution to the problem of a squalid area of moral decay that needed to be bulldozed out of existence. This masked a more nuanced reality of residential, commercial, and other uses.

City planners and their business allies wanted to demolish Scollay Square because they were convinced that its dive bars, cheap restaurants, and bawdy shows were a drag on the rest of downtown. They were reacting to the fact that the city's economic decline was affecting its premier shopping district. At the end of World War II, downtown department stores were major assets in what was the retail center of New England and included Filene's, Jordan Marsh, Gilchrist's, Raymond's, RH White's, and RH Stearns. In 1949, "Boston was not glitzy but it held thousands of places to shop and eat. Variety was the word for most streets in downtown . . . dusty, dark . . . a bit tacky . . . but oozing variety from every brick and beam."[31] But Boston's decay was evident in the blocks around Winter, Summer, and Washington Streets.

At first, department stores opened new outlets in retail districts such as Wellesley, Newton, and Medford. But then they began to open in the new malls ringing the city: Chestnut Hill, South Shore Plaza, and others. As a result, from 1948 to 1954 retail sales declined by 8 percent in the Central Business District while increasing by 30 percent in the rest of the metro area. Downtown shopping sagged, and after 1956, stores began to close rapidly. The city tried to shore up the district by building parking garages and renovating buildings to accommodate more modern stores, but the decline continued. In reality, it was the falling population of the city, new suburban shopping centers, and the increasing concentration of poverty inside Boston that was hurting sales. In hindsight, the demolition of urban neighborhoods for renewal and highway construction would be counterproductive, reducing the number of people who were most inclined to shop downtown.

Not everyone wanted to see Scollay Square demolished. Though the area was much shabbier than it had been in the 1920s, or even during World War II, on the eve of its destruction it continued to be a meeting place sheltering dance halls, lunch spots, after work bars, and a variety of businesses that catered to people from around the metro region. It was more than just vacated theaters and bars serving the down and out, "like Marseilles, Panama City, and Shanghai, it is known to sailors all over the world, a brash honky-tonk tenderloin."[32] It also had a number of bars and restaurants catering to the city's LGBT community[33] and was the place a young man would gravitate to in order to meet other men.[34]

Despite his best efforts, the project stalled, and though Hynes succeeded in getting commitments for new state office buildings and the funding of a city hall, nothing could go forward without the cooperation of the federal government. Unfortunately, it wanted to build its new office building in the Back Bay where the Hancock Building is now located and refused to negotiate a new location. So when Hynes left office in 1959, it was doubtful that anything would be built in the area.

A proposed new Prudential project on the site of the Back Bay railyards was also at a standstill. Insurance companies began moving into the Back Bay in the 1920s, part of a national trend that saw them leaving congested downtowns for adjacent office districts. In Boston, there would be four major companies located within a few blocks of each other: New England Life, John Hancock, Liberty Mutual, and the Prudential. The city hoped to solidify the role of the Back Bay as a major national center for insurance, but wildly changing assessments and uncertain tax bills were a major barrier to development. When the twenty-six-story Hancock Building opened in 1947, its assessment jumped from $6.5 to $24 million.

The Prudential Center project was first conceived in 1945 when the Newark-based company decided to restructure and decentralize itself with Boston selected as one of seven regional headquarters cities, but the company took years to find a suitable site. When Prudential chairman Carrol M. Shanks unveiled the plan for the project at a Chamber of Commerce meeting on January 31, 1957, his investment in Boston was seen as an endorsement of the city's business environment after so many years of decline. The site spread outside the rail yards to include enough land to make up thirty-five acres total, the total office space would be twice that of Rockefeller Center, and the central tower would be Boston's tallest building by far. Designed as a "city within the city," it used a series of plazas and walkways to connect to the surrounding areas and included retail, apartments, a hotel, and a city-built auditorium. But there was a major sticking point: the company would not go forward without a guaranteed long-term property tax break from the city.

The Hynes administration was thrilled, but the mayor could not figure out a legal way to guarantee a tax agreement and the project was at a standstill. Complicating its construction, by the time the Prudential publicly announced its $100 million project, the Turnpike Authority was eyeing the rail line as the best route to connect its highway to the Central Artery downtown. Once again, the city seemed to be incapable of hosting new development, and nothing broke ground at the site while Hynes was in office.

Hynes succeeded in implementing one important urban renewal change that would have lasting impacts on Boston. To help jumpstart renewal, the business community worked with the mayor to change how renewal was administered in the city. Currently under the jurisdiction of the BHA, they proposed to have a new city agency, the Boston Redevelopment Authority (BRA), manage all renewal activities. This required authorization from the legislature because of federal rules governing urban renewal funds. Working together, Hynes and city businesses successfully lobbied the legislature in 1957 and for a few months it looked that the city might finally speed up redevelopment. But the legislation resulted in simply transferring the urban renewal department of the BHA along with its existing staff into a separate authority. The hopes for the launching of delayed projects were dashed.

So as the Hynes era ended in 1959, he had little to show for his renewal plans other than two bulldozed neighborhoods and two stalled projects, and from the point of view of his contemporaries, the desperately wanted New Boston was yet to be born. With hindsight, this may have been a good thing as the shortcomings of Hynes's plans loom large today. Even in their own time there was widespread consensus that the New York Streets project failed to create jobs or spark reinvestment in the city while the West End project was ugly, unaffordable for most current city residents, and revealed the horrendous human cost of neighborhood change. Worst of all, neither project had reversed the accelerating decline of the city. The city lost over a hundred thousand residents in the 1950s, and the municipal budget situation continued to deteriorate. As a result, Boston looked hopeless, and a decade after they had defeated Curley, the Yankee business establishment was forced to look for other reasons why no one would invest in the city. A sense of panic that the decline was irreversible began to set in, and many thought something drastic was needed to save Boston.

Paradoxically, the very freedom that Boston blacks enjoyed up to the late nineteenth century set the stage for their political problems in the twentieth century. In earlier times, blacks were not seen as a threat by the Yankee Protestant establishment, and they were given unparalleled access to education and freedom to participate in civic life, allowing for the development of a small black elite.[35] These were not years free of racism; Yankees could speak of and treat black people just as cruelly as others in this era often did. But the status of blacks in Boston contributed to the perception the city was a welcoming place to live.

This all changed as the Irish began to assert their dominance over Boston politics. The first Irish Mayor, Hugh O'Brien, was elected in 1884, and by the 1920s, the hold of Irish Democrats on the city was nearly absolute. Blacks, responding to local Yankee liberalism as well as the Republican Party's support for abolition and the growing repression led by white Southern Democrats, were solid Republican voters in Boston. So as the Irish consolidated their hold on the city, it was easy for them to exclude, ignore, and punish blacks. With the election of Roosevelt in 1932, many blacks moved to vote Democratic, and while Mayor Curley incorporated black voters into his machine via the South End's Taylor brothers, he was careful to stingily parse out jobs to them as rewards.[36] The small size of the black community helped render them powerless as well.

As their numbers grew rapidly in the 1950s, blacks in Boston began to be influenced by civil rights activism in the South. No longer content to negotiate for small rewards from a system that was systematically oppressing them, they began to openly challenge racism in the city. Boston activism in the 1950s was built on the founding and expansion of institutions in previous decades. It was rooted in the NAACP, the Urban League, the Robert Gould Shaw House, and churches such as Twelfth Baptist and Peoples Baptist. Freedom House, organized in 1949, was also a major center of activism as Boston's black community began to demand equal rights. Working together, they pressured businesses to hire blacks and began forging relationships with people and institutions outside the community.

The two issues that would dominate the agenda of black community leaders for the next several decades were education and housing. After World War II, Boston schools began to lose white students at a rate of about 2,000 per year, but an influx of black students kept overall enrollment steady. Yet conditions deteriorated in the 1950s, and along with rapidly increasing segregation, blacks were shunted into older dilapidated schools with the worst teachers. Still, many black students went on to college, contributing to what became a core of academics and activists in the 1960s who would work for change. The opening of middle-class and professional jobs to blacks after 1950 put additional pressures on the schools as parents began to question an educational system that did not provide a good pathway to higher education. Decent jobs required decent education, but just as the need for quality education became acute, Boston's schools were becoming more conservative, more racist, and less able to give students the education that black parents were demanding. This ended up alienating the small middle-class black community who became radicalized during the 1950s. Parents and grandparents who had attended integrated schools were angry that the current generation was now confined to segregated schools. Yet their primary goal would not be integration, it would be to improve their children's education.

Led by representatives of the NAACP and others, in the 1950s black parents began to visit the schools and document the substandard conditions they found. Appalled, they organized. One of the hardest-working black parents of this era was Ruth Batson, a Boston native who sent her children to the public schools. Her education activism began humbly: when she contacted the NAACP to ask about their stand on local educational issues, she was appointed chair of its education committee. Eventually Batson became the first black to run for the school committee in the twentieth century; in 1951, she ran on a platform that included curriculum reform, better working conditions for teachers, and the lack of hot lunches for elementary students. She finished sixteenth out of thirty-six with 15,000 votes. Unable to influence policy at the ballot box, the first parent-organized protests occurred in the late 1950s, but these were easily ignored by the School Committee that did nothing to issues the problems Batson and others were raising.[37]

The school crisis that exploded in the 1970s began in the 1950s. The all-white School Committee could have taken black interest in the public schools seriously and used it to implement reforms that would have benefited all students, perhaps even slowing or reversing white flight out of the schools and the city. But instead they chose to ignore the demands of black parents and double down on maintaining segregation and substandard schools. As a result of these willful policies, conditions in the schools would continue to deteriorate and black anger would grow.

Exhausted by ten years as mayor, Hynes declined to seek another term in 1959. In an election dominated by the decline of the city and its inability to jumpstart urban renewal, the two main contenders to replace Hynes were John Collins and John Powers. Once again it would be a contest between an Irish representative of the low-income central wards (Powers) and a middle-class Irish contender from the outer wards (Collins). As the race began, no one thought Collins had a chance. He was born in Roxbury to a father who worked as a mechanic for the Boston Elevated Railroad. In 1955, he almost died from polio, but his wife Mary campaigned for him for city council even as three of her four children also struggled with the disease and its aftermath.[30] Collins had a following inspired by his determination to overcome his debilitating illness, but it was small compared to Powers' strong organization.

Hynes had defeated Powers in the 1955 mayor's race, but many had been impressed by his losing campaign. So Powers was thought to have the advantage four years later. The son of a streetcar motorman who had died in an accident, Powers had grown up poor before turning to politics. He first ran for state representative in 1938, then for the state senate in 1946, and he had a strong base in South Boston. His 1955 loss to Hynes was his first political setback.

Taking the election seriously, Powers campaigned hard and earned many major endorsements. Both United States senators backed Powers while Cardinal Cushing was the guest of honor at a $100 a plate campaign dinner for him at the Statler Hilton. With the backing of the Vault, Powers sought to expand his base, and he courted Republicans, Syrians, Greeks, and Jews. He claimed that all the "Negro ministers in the city supported him."[38]

Though five men ran for mayor in the 1959 preliminary election, Powers' supporters boldly predicted he'd get 60 percent of the vote in the primary. He received 34 percent while Collins squeaked into second place with 22 percent, only 2,500 more votes than third place finisher Gabriel Piemonte, who had strong support in Italian wards. Demonstrating his dominance of the electorate, Powers had carried sixteen wards to Collins's one.

In the run up to the final election, however, nearly every move that Powers made worked against him. The more money he raised and the more endorsements he gathered, the more he solidified the perception that he was the product of the corrupt establishment, beholden to bribery, and unable to reverse the city's decay. In contrast, Collins was able to communicate that he was an independent, not tied to any interest group with the intelligence and competence to change the direction of the city. A coincidental federal raid on a bookie in East Boston that included a photograph of a Powers campaign poster behind a man in handcuffs just before Election Day didn't help. Losing by more than 24,000 votes, Powers won only four wards: two in South Boston and Wards 8 and 9 in the South End. The people of Boston had delivered a powerful mandate for change.

1. Slavet JS and Torto RG. *Boston's Recurring Crises: Three Decades of Fiscal Policy.* Boston: John M. McCormack Graduate School of Policy and Global Studies 1985.
2. Fuchs L. Presidential Politics in Boston: The Irish Response to Stevenson. *The New England Quarterly.* 1957; 30: 335-447.
3. William Callahan Profile. He Always Remembers His Friends. *Boston Globe.* March 6, 1962; p. 11.
4. Finstein AD. *Lofty visions: The architectural intentions and contrary realities of elevated urban highways in America, 1900 – 1959.* Department of Architectural History.

University of Virginia, 2009.

5. Turner L and Tuite L. The elevated Central Artery. *Boston Globe*. June 28, 2013; p. 1.

6. Plotkin AS. No Immediate Relief in Sight For Overloaded Central Artery. *Boston Globe*. Sep. 27, 1959; p. 10.

7. Lewis W. Yes, Old Colony's Gone. *Boston Globe*. July 1, 1959; p. 1.

8. Herwick EB. *Route 128, Once Known As 'Road To Nowhere,' Had A Traffic Jam The Day It Opened*, https://news.wgbh.org/post/route-128-once-known-road-no-where-had-traffic-jam-day-it-opened, 2015.

9. Manners G. Decentralization in metropolitan Boston. *Geography* 1960; 45: 276-85.

10. Vale L. *From the Puritans to the Projects*. Cambridge MA: Harvard University Press, 2000.

11. A. van Hoffman. A study in contradictions: The origins and legacy of the Housing Act of 1949. *Housing Policy Debate*. 2000; 11: 299-326.

12. Boston City Planning Board. *Workable Program for Urban Renewal*. 1955.

13. King M. *Chain of Change: Struggles for Black Community Development*. Boston MA: South End Press, 1981.

14. Boston City Planning Board. *Rehabilitation in Boston*. 1943.

15. Woods RA. *The City Wilderness: A Settlement Study*. Boston: Houghton, Mifflin and Company, 1898.

16. Sanborn Fire Insurance Company. *Map - Boston, Massachusetts*. 1948.

17. Urban Redevelopment Division - The Boston Housing Authority. *The New York Streets Project (Preliminary)*. Boston, 1952.

18. Urban Redevelopment Division - The Boston Housing Authority. *Expressways to Everywhere*. Boston, 1955.

19. South End Project Action Committee. *Special Housing Committee Report*. Boston, 1975.

20. Kennedy L. *Planning the City Upon a Hill: Boston Since 1630*. Boston: University of Massachusetts Press, 1994.

21. Curley JM. *I'd Do It Again*. Salem, NH: Ayer Company, Publishers, 1957.

22. Fried M. *The World of the Urban Working Class*. Cambridge, MA: Harvard University Press, 1973.

23. DeMinico A. Memories of a Happy Ghetto. City of Boston. *Born Before Plastic: Stories from Boston's Most Enduring Neighborhoods*. Boston: Grub Street Inc., 2007.

24. Whyte W. *Street Corner Society: The Social Structure of an Italian Slum*. University of Chicago Press, 1955.

25. Opposition. West End Renewal Project Stirs Tumult at Hearing. *Boston Globe*. April 15, 1957, p. 21.

26. Hanreon R. West End project could be spark to revitalize Boston. *Boston Globe*. December 20, 1950, p. A14.

27. Lopez R. *Building American Public Health: Urban Planning, Architecture, and the Quest for Better Health in the United States*. New York: Palgrave Macmillan, 2012.

28. Bauer C. Redevelopment: A Misfit in the Fifties? In: Woodbury C, (ed.). *The Fu-*

ture of Cities and Urban Redevelopment. Chicago: University of Chicago Press, 1953.

29. Gans H. *The Urban Villagers: Group and Class in the Life of Italian-Americans*. Glencoe, NY: The Free Press, 1962.

30. O'Neill G. *Rogues and Redeemers: When Politics was King in Irish Boston*. New York: Crown Publishing Group, 2012.

31. Shopping days. *Back to School in 1949 Retro Boston*. http://shoppingdaysinretroboston.blogspot.com/search?updated-min=2011-01-01T00:00:00-08:00&updated-max=2011-09-04T05:40:00-07:00&max-results=19&start=5&by-date=false, 2011.

32. Gilbert D. "Why dwell on a lurid memory?": Deviance and redevelopment in Boston's Scollay Square. *Massachusetts Historical Review*. 2007; 9: 103-33.

33. The History Project. *Improper Bostonians: Lesbian and Gay History from the Puritans to Playland*. Boston: The Beacon Press, 1998.

34. O'Hara F. *The Fourth of July*. Unpublished. UC San Diego: Special Collections and Archives, Donald Allen Collection. 1951.

35. Fox SR. *The Guardian of Boston: William Monroe Trotter*. New York: Atheneum, 1970.

36. Travis T-M. The unfinished agenda. *Psychiatric Services*. 1986; 19: 610-7.

37. Motti TL. *Social conflict and social movements: An explanatory study of the black community of Boston attempting to change the Boston public schools*. Dissertation, Brandeis University, 1975.

38. Levin MB. *The Alienated Voter: Politics in Boston*. New York: Holt, Reinhart and Winston, 1966.

CHAPTER 3

Renewal and Chaos: 1960-1967

COLLINS BECAME MAYOR just as the placid 1950s were giving way to the turbulent 1960s, and the city's experiences during his two terms in office reflect this. In Boston, the turmoil that resulted from civil rights demands and anti-war protests would be compounded by the trauma stemming from the urban renewal program that Collins and his administrator of the BRA, Edward Logue, imposed on unwilling residents. The resulting chaos would stalk Boston's neighborhoods until the mid-1970s while the fallout from the era's politics haunts the city to this day. The tactics that residents learned while defending their neighborhoods in the battle over renewal, in protesting for civil rights, and while fighting an unjust war would be adapted by antibusing demonstrators and used in ways that would tarnish the city's reputation. To make matters worse, Collins' renewal program failed, for the most part, and his inability to solve the problems that exploded as he left office would be his real legacy. Perhaps the most important failure was that Collins and other elected officials in this era ignored the growing crisis in the public schools, setting up the tragedy of 1974.

Yet there were some benefits from these battles that raged across Boston neighborhoods; they arose from a passionate desire by residents to keep their homes and preserve their communities. Many protagonists would go on to work in health centers, neighborhood associations, social service organizations, community development corporations, and other institutions that would be the real saviors of the city and launch its true renewal at the end of the 1970s.

Most of the country would recall the beginning of the 1960s as a time when optimism for the future and faith in the economy peaked, as a time when the United States committed to going to the moon and incomes had been rising for almost two decades. Nationally, inflation would only begin to be a problem after 1964, and unemployment did not rise until 1968. But in Boston, the economy stubbornly continued to decline. Despite the best efforts of Hynes and Collins, little new investment was made in the city, though the business coalition that had put the two mayors into office had promised otherwise. As a result, the city would be poorer in 1968 when Collins left office than it was in 1960 when he was first sworn in as mayor.

During the Collins administration, total assessed valuation in the city dropped by $20 million despite the pickup in inflation near the end of the 1960s. Collins brought some fiscal stability during his first term, and total expenditures dropped through a reduction of about 9 percent in the city workforce and a curtailment of some of the worst budgetary excesses. As a result, the tax rate dropped by 5 percent, total indebtedness went down by 7 percent, and, in 1962, Collins presided over the first net cash surplus since 1947. But after Collins was reelected in 1963, and began to prepare for his 1964 senate bid, the city's financial position again deteriorated. Expenditures increased faster than revenues, total municipal employment rose, and the structural deficit reappeared. Once again, the tax rate climbed.[1]

Boston's economic malaise was made worse by the prosperity of its suburbs. In the area around Route 128, federal defense and space spending reached a high point, and the many companies along the highway prospered through government contracts. Cold war competition with the Soviet Union, efforts to land an astronaut on the moon, and the escalating war in Vietnam prompted large-scale investment in new technology companies founded by people associated with MIT and Harvard. Yet these enterprises failed to have much effect on the economy of the city itself, and few of their employees or owners lived in Boston. Middle-class and wealthy households preferred to stay out of Boston altogether, and developers built a ring of shopping centers around the city that siphoned off retail sales from downtown. The metropolitan area was hollowing out.

Perhaps the only consolation was that Boston was no longer the only major city in the United States that was visibly declining. The unique problems of Boston in 1945 had become a nationwide urban crisis in the 1960s. In older large cities across the country, jobs and white residents fled to the suburbs while poor black newcomers fought the remaining whites over control of decayed housing, shabby neighborhoods, and bankrupt city halls. Hundreds of cities would see destructive race riots in the 1960s with brutal struggles over the right to live in neighborhoods and angry demands to integrate schools and other institutions. Over the course of the 1960s, there would be a large-scale increase in programs targeted at inner cities and their poor residents, culminating in President Lyndon Johnson's Great Society Program and a series of important new civil rights laws. Then, as the country turned conservative, these programs would be reduced and eliminated.

Boston lost 50,000 residents during the 1960s as its white population declined by over 100,000–an influx of blacks, Latinos, and Asians kept the population from falling more than it did. The number of children in the city was stable, but the 1960s was the only postwar decade where the number of occupied housing units fell. As will be seen, the causes of this continued population loss were complex. Some of it was the result of demographic trends that had begun decades before, but it was also prompted by the large-scale land takings across the city that displaced residents as their homes were torn down for highways and urban renewal.

In the 1960s, the stage was being set for the busing crisis of 1974. Black parents, students, and activists struggled to find a strategy that would make the schools better, and the NAACP considered filing suit against the schools as early as 1961. But at first, most blacks tried to work with the School Committee. Otto and Muriel Snowden were two prominent leaders of the school desegregation effort. Muriel was the daughter of a New Jersey physician and began her lifetime of activism in Newark. Moving to Boston, she sought to revive and improve Roxbury as it decayed and transformed from white to black. Together with her husband Otto, she founded Freedom House, an organization dedicated to solving issues of concern to Boston's black residents. Along with others, the couple fought for integration in all aspects of life, particularly in the schools where segregation was growing as rapidly as the black population. A pivotal event in the struggle for better education was a meeting at Freedom House on March 20, 1963, when Paul Parks reported on how the schools were systematically failing black children. Soon Parks, the Snowdens, Ruth Batson, Mel King and others were trying to engage the School Committee in vain efforts to improve education.

The schools were horrendous. Jonathan Kozol spent the 1964-65 school year working as a substitute teacher in a black school and subsequently published a harrowing account of the conditions he found there, *Death at an Early Age*. Unruly fourth graders, and even abused children with emotional problems, were routinely whipped with bamboo canes. One disciplinarian advised the teachers to soak the canes overnight in vinegar to make them sting more. Teachers called students niggers and complained that first graders were impossible to teach. Kozol's school was filthy, smelled of urine, and so overcrowded that his class of thirty-five met in a corner of the auditorium cordoned off by torn dirty drapes–the noise from other classes in the room was often overwhelming. The space was decorated with "scrap lumber-bits, peeled paint, torn curtains, and cardboard windows."[2] The schools would not hire black teachers, counsellors, or administrators; in 1963, there were less than forty black teachers in a system with 2,800 teachers. There were no black secretaries, lunch ladies, or custodians. Though the problems were worse in black schools, the rest of the system was little better. So white parents with the economic means either moved out of the city or sent their children to private schools, and enrollment in the public schools dropped from 137,500 in 1933 to 89,000 in 1962.[3] By 1963, one third of Boston's children attended private schools.

The forces against reform were captained by Louise Day Hicks, a major figure in Boston politics for almost fifteen years. The daughter of beloved South Boston judge William Day, she was devoted to him, and his death when she was fourteen was a major influence on her decisions to attend college and run for political office. Hicks could have moved to the 'lace curtain' wards or the suburbs with her husband and two sons but chose to stay in South Boston–she was loyal to the neighborhood and its people. Though her high-pitched, nasal voice and dowdy dress led some liberals to dismiss her, others admired her self-driven success and behind the scenes efforts to keep some of the worst violence she unleashed at bay. Mayor Kevin White was most grateful to her for keeping him informed of antibusing actions through informal back channels, and he appointed her to the Retirement Board.

As Boston's black population expanded, segregation only became worse, meaning that the School Committee's refusal to address problems early on made it more difficult to find solutions later. In the twenty years before Judge Arthur Garrity would rule in 1974 that the schools were illegally segregated, the School Committee repeatedly refused any suggestions to improve education in black schools, preferring instead to stick with alternative policies that made segregation worse and left conditions unchanged. In 1961, for example, a study by the Harvard School of Education warned that the schools were becoming increasingly segregated and suggested a program of strategically sited new schools to integrate the system. It was rejected by the School Committee. Almost every year saw a new proposal to advance integration, yet the School Committee refused them all.

The School Committee balked at admitting there was any segregation, and Hicks tried to deflect the demands of black parents by saying the problems were system wide, not just focused on black students. But black parents were not easily deluded and sought to insert themselves into a system that was adamant to contain them. Mel King, for example, ran unsuccessfully for School Committee in 1961, 1963, and 1965, and though a 1961 reform slate that included King succeeded in placing one liberal on the School Committee for one term, they made little headway in promoting improvements as the conservatives were deeply entrenched. With the backing of the teachers' union, for example, Hicks topped the race with 38 percent of the vote in 1961. The obstacle was that with at-large elections, where each voter could pick five candidates, blacks and liberals lacked sufficient votes to capture one of the five top positions. As the run up to busing accelerated, white politicians saw no need to compromise.

In 1963 there a brief moment when the busing disaster might have been averted. Trying to negotiate, the NAACP Education committee invited Hicks to a meeting at Freedom House. It was cordial enough and some were optimistic; the NAACP drafted a fourteen-point agenda that included hiring more blacks and teaching black history. In recognition of this perceived opportunity, Hicks hinted she might agree to the agenda. But at a June 12 follow-up meeting, the School Committee refused to even consider that segregation existed in the schools, and their position began to harden. Still there was hope that an agreement might be reached, and while a crowd of more than three hundred protested outside, a more private set of negotiations went on behind closed doors that included Mel King, Ruth Batson, and Paul Parks.

Another negotiating session was held on June 15 where the School Committee made some concessions, though it still refused to acknowledge there was segregation. Then the negotiations collapsed, and the chance to avoid confrontation passed. So on June 18, over 3,000 students walked out of their classes to participate in a boycott to protest conditions in their schools. The School Committee did not back down, but on June 21, Mayor Collins went on television to acknowledge that the Boston public schools were segregated. The school year ended without a resolution.

On August 19, 1963, the state Board of Education declared the Boston school system racially imbalanced, but as the school year began, there was still no reaction by the School Committee. Black students, however, were inspired by the national civil rights March on Washington and 6,000 turned out for a March on Roxbury on September 27 to protest conditions in the schools. Unfortunately, the public demonstrations prompted a reaction from those in favor of segregation, as the conservative incumbent slate won the School Committee elections in the fall of 1963 by a large margin citywide, though losing heavily in black precincts. The city was splintering.

Frustrated, black parents tried to use the power of the state and federal government to force change. In February 1964, the NAACP filed six bills in the legislature to reform the schools but none of them passed, prompting a new wave of activism. Finally, advocates introduced the Racial Imbalance Act of 1965 that declared any school more than 50 percent minority was imbalanced and mandated local authorities to address the imbalance. The lobbying effort was boosted by the heroic vigil of Pastor Vernon Carter who lived, prayed, and slept on the sidewalk in front of the Statehouse for 118 days to persuade lawmakers to act. Others, including clergy from a variety of faiths, white liberals, and suburban residents, joined in the effort to pass the bill, and on August 18, 1965, Governor John Volpe signed it into law.

The reaction of the School Committee was harsh. Calling the law undemocratic and unworkable, it banned the use of school funds to bus black children to any vacant seats in the white part of the system (the schools were already busing thousands of white and black students to schools where they made up a majority in an effort to maintain segregation). The committee refused to comply with the law or make any changes to enrollment boundaries to move schools into balance. These were critical actions as they turned a problem of de facto segregation (resulting from housing patterns) into a case of de jure segregation (caused by government action), in this case the School Committee's refusal to implement a state law. Federal courts had been ordering busing to address de jure segregation since the famous Brown versus the Board of Education decision in 1954 but had consistently ruled that de facto segregation was outside their jurisdiction. If the School Committee had complied with the Racial Imbalance Law, it would have avoided court ordered busing. But instead it openly defied the law, and the School Committee made the crisis of 1974 inevitable by its actions in 1965.

The schools' strong segregation policies, coupled with declining white enrollment, created many empty seats in white schools. Hoping to use these vacancies to advance the education of black students, Ellen Jackson and other parents started Operation Exodus in September 1965 to bus black students to white schools that had empty seats, an option the School Committee had made possible years before in order to allow white students to escape black schools. Jackson had grown up in Roxbury and attended Boston State Teachers College. She left school in 1954 before graduating and raising five children, all of whom attended Boston public schools. By early 1965, she was working to organize parents, serving as a liaison between the Northern Student Movement and the community and then as a social worker in Jamaica Plain. The immediate trigger for Operation Exodus was a plan to double session students at Roxbury schools to accommodate overcrowding. As just one example, the Garrison School, built for 690 students, had 1,043 attending, and one of Jackson's children had been in a class of 44 students. Fed up, she and other organizers sent out word of a meeting and 250 parents met at the Robert Gould Shaw House to agree to enroll their children in schools outside Roxbury.

The catch in the transfer policy was that parents and students had to get to their new schools on their own because the School Committee refused to pay for this voluntary desegregation program (another action the court would use to establish there was de jure segregation). So parents used private cars and chartered buses to transport their children to their new schools despite the cost and inconvenience. Furious whites acted as if they were being invaded. Some principals turned students away in violation of the policy and many pulled desks out of classrooms while others simply lied about vacancies (all more evidence for the court finding of de jure segregation in 1974). Rather than support this modest attempt at desegregation, Mayor Collins went on television to ask black parents to stop sending their children to white schools, though he proposed no alternative to Roxbury schools' overcrowding beyond promising construction of new schools in the neighborhood – something that would have taken years to implement and not have prevented double sessions at the time. Though Hicks called Operation Exodus illegal and did her best to stop it, 475 children took part in the program in its first semester.[4] For black parents, the program was critical even though paying for private busing was difficult. Parents used fashion shows and dances to raise money, which was always very tight, and staged a suburban event that featured singer Eartha Kitt.[5]

This small step towards integration set off a strong political backlash. In the 1965 School Committee elections, incumbents sought to mobilize white voters by suggesting they were all that stood between their children and busing. Committee member Thomas Eisenstadt mailed a busing questionnaire to parents to scare them, even though none of the black school advocates had called for citywide busing. The race baiting worked and the pro-segregation slate of incumbents and allies crushed the progressive alternatives. Activists were bitterly discouraged and some decided to abandon the public schools altogether and formed a network of alternative schools.

Outside pressure continued. In 1966, citing that forty-nine schools in the city were now imbalanced, the state withheld funds from the city, and for the next several years, state and federal agencies sought to compel the School Committee to end segregation through a combination of reports, technical findings, and withholding of funds. But the School Committee continued to resist change. In 1966, for example, it submitted a desegregation plan that was rejected by the State Board of Education. So the Committee submitted the same plan a second time that was again rejected, but these actions bought it more time. When the plan was rejected once again, the Committee sued the state and the court then ordered the state to reconsider the rejected plan one more time. So the Committee successfully fought off integration another year. But these actions solved nothing except in 1974 when they would be used by lawyers to prove de jure segregation and would help convince Judge Garrity that he should not delay his busing order. Meanwhile, tensions continued to rise. In June 1966, when Hicks was the commencement speaker at a black junior high school, her presence set off a riot by the students.

Giving up on Boston, some black parents created a program to enroll their children in suburban schools. METCO (the Metropolitan Council for Educational Opportunity) began in early 1966 when the town of Brookline invited ten black students to attend its schools. By the fall, it included 7 communities and by the time the busing crisis exploded in 1974, 1,900 black students were being bused to 28 communities. Altogether, by the end of the decade nearly a quarter of black children in Boston were participating in non-standard programs. But most of these children came from middle-class or intact working-class homes. Poorer and more fragile students were less likely to be involved, and so advocates continued to press for reforms.

As the Collins years ended, black parents were stalemated. The system remained highly segregated, and the School Committee had successfully stymied black demands for another decade. But black anger was rising, problems were continuing, and parents began to consider suing the School Committee. Once in court in the 1970s, the School Committee's actions in the 1960s would be found to be evidence of illegal segregation. The ultimate cost of remedies was rising.

As he took office, Collin's major priority was jumpstarting renewal, by then widely considered to be a failure. He faced strong pressure from the Vault and others to make renewal work, as many of the city's business leaders were in a panic over Boston's economic decline. In 1960, as its first wave of projects stalled or failed to spark a revival, Boston was the tenth largest city in the country but twenty-third in the amount of federal renewal money received.[6] Collins aimed to change that. The disenchantment with the BHA's oversite of renewal had led to the establishment of the BRA late in the Hynes administration, but it continued to be staffed by the same people responsible for the West End, Government Center, and other stalled and failed projects. The solution, in Collins's opinion, was a strong leader to take over the BRA: Edward Logue. Credited with implementing New Haven's renewal program, thought at the time to be the best in the country, Logue was the first choice of Collins's prodevelopment supporters who believed he would save Boston. Years later a reassessment of Logue's work in New Haven would reveal vast shortcomings and a city devastated by his policies.[7] But his failings would be not publicized for another decade and the faith in Logue's abilities were as yet unquestioned. As Collins worked to justify his appointment to a public suspicious about renewal, the World War II veteran and lawyer appeared to be progressive minded and attuned to the concerns of residents the neighborhoods about to be redeveloped. Encouraged by his business allies desperate to remake the city, Collins lured Logue to Boston with the promise of a salary higher than his own.

There was a barrier to hiring Logue posed by the existing staff of the BRA: the legislation creating the agency protected Kane Simonian, the current Executive Director, from being dismissed. So initially, Logue was hired as a consultant with orders to draw up a new citywide plan for urban renewal. Released in 1960, it was breathtaking in extent. About one quarter of the city's land area was included in various urban renewal projects along with nearly half the city's population. Altogether, it was projected to cost $90 million of federal money, ($718 million in 2015 dollars) and promised to remake the city into a strong economic engine for the region. Residents would get new housing and jobs, businessmen would receive new office buildings and tax relief.

Excitement over the plan, along with careful courting of business interests, newspaper editors and reporters, union representatives, and leaders of the city's churches, universities and other important institutions, created strong pressure to hire Logue. The advocacy on his behalf included the strange sight of a large demonstration of bankers, developers, and real estate lawyers, dressed in conservative suits, protesting outside city hall in favor of redevelopment. Pressured by editorials and personal lobbying, the BRA Board appointed Logue Administrator while keeping Simonean as Executive Director.

Once in power, Logue micromanaged all the various renewal projects, leaving Simonean and the BRA Board to rubber stamp minutia. The Board oversaw each check paid to property owners and approved all employee vacation requests, for example. But mindful of its place, the board never critiqued or modified redevelopment plans or refused land takings, even when desperate residents pleaded to save their homes. There was no way to appeal any part of Logue's plans; only by packing public hearings and launching demonstrations in the streets could opponents make any headway to save their neighborhoods. Hired to make renewal happen, Logue knew he only needed to keep Collins happy and maintain the Vault's support.

Full of energy, Logue vastly increased the amount of federal aid and the size of the Authority: in 1960 the BRA had 80 employees, by 1967 it had 498. Among the innovations that Logue implemented was that the city now coordinated economic development along with its capital plan. In addition, the BRA absorbed the city's planning department, a situation that continues to this day and is unique among major United States cities. He also persuaded the federal government to accept the city's capital improvement expenditures as Boston's contribution for renewal projects to comply with the 1949 urban renewal law's mandate of a local match for federal funds. Just after Logan left Boston, the federal government prohibited this practice, and the resulting funding crisis contributed to the collapse of the city's urban renewal activities in the early 1970s.

Logue implemented renewal through a difficult to counter combination of speed, control of the media, and political domination of any opposition. The urban renewal process established by the federal government included community, BRA Board, and city council approval steps, so Logue needed to use all his power to maintain momentum in the face of near certain opposition. He constantly goaded his staff to speed up their planning activities, carefully screened his community advisory members, and intimidated the city council to rubber stamp his proposals. The result would be slipshod plans that often only vaguely corresponded to existing conditions, promises that could not be kept, and a decade of near constant conflict between city hall and Boston residents. For example, his ideas regarding demolition would cause hundreds of South End row houses, no more rundown than those preserved, to be demolished. In Allston, his proposals to bulldoze blocks of housing were met by bewilderment as their occupants did not live in substandard conditions. In Charlestown, families were told they would be evicted in order to stop their neighborhood from declining. Furious residents vowed to stop any and all actions by the BRA in their communities.

With a few exceptions, urban renewal was extremely unpopular. Residents were desperate for better housing, but they were more afraid of displacement and losing their homes. They could see the damage caused in the West End and New York Streets areas; many had friends and relatives displaced without assistance, and most easily understood that the New Boston that Logue and Collins were promoting was meant to push them out of the city. Therefore, most people vigorously opposed the city's redevelopment plans.[8]

Logue's autocratic manners and strange ideas regarding renewal didn't help. Confronted by opposition, Logue's natural inclination was to bully, lie, and force his plans to be approved, which in turn further inflamed the neighborhoods against him. What makes these battles even more poignant was that Logue had no training as an urban planner and he had no reason to think his ideas would work other than his immense reserve of self-confidence. For example, without any evidence whatsoever, Logue's instinct told him that the best way to revitalize a community was to demolish 20 percent of its existing housing because he thought this was the ideal balance between a project that was too small to make an impact and one so large it would ignite too much protest. But residents reacted to any demolition with horror. Furthermore, his rehabilitation plans for the remaining housing stock lacked sufficient safeguards for existing residents. Most rehabilitation would be privately financed and result in what had been affordable housing for low-income occupants being turned into units that could only be rented and owned by middle-class or wealthy households. So existing low-income residents had to fight these proposals or be displaced. There was a small federal loan program for rehabilitation loans, but these would also produce unaffordable units while the replacement housing program would be plagued by underfunding, delays, and poor administration. In reality, the urban renewal program had nothing to offer low-income people.

Not surprisingly, as specific neighborhood plans were released, turmoil gripped the city. Residents packed meetings alternatively threatening BRA representatives and pleading to be spared from displacement. Some appealed to the Mayor but he never overruled the BRA administrator. Others begged the City Council or BRA Board to intervene but they rarely listened. Yet despite his tremendous power, Logue had many defeats, particularly in white neighborhoods that had greater political muscle. Eventually, Logue was forced to abandon renewal programs in South Boston, East Boston, Jamaica Plain, and the North End. He was forced to vastly downgrade the project in Allston, and his large residential programs were restricted to Charlestown, Roxbury, and the South End.

In the late 1950s, Irish Charlestown was not as poor as other neighborhoods targeted for renewal, but because of the construction of highways along its periphery and the blighting influence of the Elevated, it was perceived by city hall as being a community that was in major need of redevelopment. So even before Logue came to the BRA, it had been the site of a large-scale planning process. Planners found a neighborhood trying to cope with the forces of decay attacking other communities, yet stable at is core. Like other city neighborhoods, many of its young and upwardly mobile families had moved to the suburbs while among those who remained, about 70 percent of the men worked on the docks or in the factories and warehouses the surrounded the community. A small neighborhood, Charlestown had three parishes serving this overwhelmingly Catholic community, and there was a longstanding network of family ties that both united and split residents.

The formal planning process began with the appointment of a BRA project director and the establishment of a community group, Self-Help Organization-Charlestown (SHOC) to support renewal. At first everything seemed to be going well, though the process was slow as SHOC sought to create a consensus for what should be done to stop the creeping deterioration. Then Logue came to the BRA with a mandate to speed up renewal, and he quickly imposed his ideas on the planning process. He replaced the project manager with one who had less interpersonal skills and demanded that a plan be quickly finished to demonstrate Logue's ability to make renewal happen.

There was a plan that called for the demolition of 60 percent of the neighborhood's housing stock that was never released; it would have created intense opposition because rather than a remake of the neighborhood, residents wanted a renewal program that would enhance the existing social and physical environment of Charlestown without disruption or demolition. Though scaled back, this plan formed the basis for Logue's proposal. As Logue changed the process from an unstructured collaboration to a formal centralized one, he demanded that the program demolish a significant portion of Charlestown's housing, thus angering the neighborhood. Pushing for quicker action, Logue replaced SHOC as the formal community group involved in the process with a new group, the Federation of Charlestown Organizations (FCO), that included SHOC as just one member entity among many. Logue carefully picked who was on FCO and how it would vote to ratify his plans; as a result, FCO was dominated by representatives from Charlestown's three parishes who saw renewal as an opportunity to revive the church's dwindling congregations and whom Logue could control through his close relations with the Archdiocese hierarchy.

Without community support, the process broke down. When the BRA presented its ideas for renewal at a public hearing on January 7, 1963, over 1,000 people showed up with an estimated 85 percent opposed to the BRA plans. Determined to stop the plan, they attacked speakers with "booing, catcalls, and complete chaos".[9] As was Logue's practice, three plans were presented that contained varying percentages of demolition with the BRA hoping the public meeting would ratify Logue's preferred plan that called for 19 percent demolition. But all were unacceptable, particularly to SHOC, which had packed the meeting and came with a jaundiced eye because they felt they had been smothered by the change in the process. Another problem was that the BRA's plans, because they were rushed, were very unclear and glossed over issues of major concern to the neighborhood such as the timing of relocation and the location of the replacement housing. Residents attacked everyone associated with the plan, and because church leaders strongly supported large-scale demolition, the turmoil prompted an action never seen before in Irish Catholic Boston: at several community meetings parishioners openly booed their priests. Renewal did not just change the built environment, it demolished the old social order as well.

The BRA was forced to regroup and spent nearly two years developing a new plan. Presented in 1965, this one was even more strongly opposed. In the end, Logue had to further reduce the scope of his plan, displacing only 525 families in the neighborhood. Charlestown was saved and residents learned that loud organizing could defeat all opposition.

The BRA's largest initiative, the South End Urban Renewal Project would have lasting negative psychological impacts on the city as it transformed a large multiethnic lodging house district into an elite haven for the well-to-do. The BRA prepared a plan in 1959 which called for the complete demolition of the neighborhood with its Victorian row houses replaced by modern concrete garden apartments and its tight street network remade into large superblocks.[10] It was never released. When Logue was appointed administrator, he was confronted by the need to jumpstart South End renewal, and he ordered his staff to prepare a new plan, giving them a deadline of only a couple of weeks. They took six months and incorporated many of the elements of the 1959 proposal. While the new renewal program preserved most of the existing housing and street network, many legacy elements would spark tremendous protest as the plan was implemented. Once again, Logue's need for quick planning would contribute to the problems of renewal.

Despite this 1962 plan's promise to preserve more housing, it was very controversial. Most disliked was a proposal to create a large greenway about where Shawmut Avenue runs that would have demolished hundreds of buildings and destroyed the neighborhood's important Syrian community. Though the BRA had carefully cultivated a network of middle-class homeowners, they angrily rejected the plan and Logue was forced to develop a new one.[9]

Released in 1964, this plan further reduced the amount of demolition. It eliminated the green strip and prioritized rehabilitation of most of the central row house district. This plan was better received, though it continued to contain problematic elements from the 1959 plan that would haunt its implementation. Learning from protests in Charlestown and Allston, Logue took no chances that his revamped plan might be rejected by residents, and the required public hearing was heavily policed with promises that protestors would be arrested. The front of the auditorium was stacked with supporters and BRA staff while most of the opposition was forced to listen to an audio broadcast of the hearing from another room.[11] Logue was successful in ramming through this version of the plan, and it was approved by the federal government in June 1966. The six-hundred-acre South End renewal program was on.

One of Logue's major achievements was the launching of the long-stalled Government Center project, which has very mixed reviews today. In the context of its time, however, Government Center represented advanced planning and architectural ideas. It was situated on top of public transit, prioritized pedestrians, incorporated mixed uses, and sought to create unified access to local, state, and federal agencies. The Government Center plan included the ongoing preservation of Faneuil Hall, the Old State House, and Beacon Hill as part of its larger extant; thus it could boast of its inclusion of both old and new, though these wider boundaries were just a vehicle for Logue to demonstrate his commitment to preservation—there had never been plans to bulldoze these blocks or use urban renewal there. By having just three streets replacing a chaotic twenty-two streets, the plan banished automobiles from most of the area and connected Faneuil Hall to Government Center in a pedestrian-friendly manner via a bridge over Congress Street.[12]

The BRA used the services of some of the greatest architects of the era on the Government Center project. Walter Gropius, founder of the Bauhaus and then chair of the architecture department at Harvard, was the lead designer of the John F. Kennedy Federal Building. I. M. Pei, the architect of the Kennedy Library at Columbia Point and the once controversial but now iconic glass pyramid entrance to the Louvre, was in charge of the master plan for Government Center. He designed it with Walter Muir Whitehill, the head of the Boston Athenaeum, and Kevin Lynch, an influential designer from MIT, also contributed to the site plan.

Most controversial was the design for City Hall itself. Collins and Logue had wanted to make an architectural statement about the forward-thinking qualities of Boston and the potential beneficial power of government. So they held a design competition that was won by Gerhard Kallmann, a Columbia University professor, and Michael McKinnell, a Columbia graduate student, then relatively unknown. They beat out over 250 alternative designs. The groundbreaking for the $26.3 million ($197 million in 2015 dollars) City Hall occurred in 1963, and the building opened at the beginning of 1968.

Using a style known as brutalism (from its use of raw wooden forms to shape its concrete), City Hall has a large city council meeting room and a dramatic space for the Mayor overlooking Faneuil Hall known as the Eagle Room. But for the most part, the building is terribly dysfunctional. On all four sides of the building, the first floor is mostly blank; much of the side facing Faneuil Hall is taken up by loading docks and a several hundred-foot-long featureless brick wall. The main entrance is from the plaza on the third floor, bewildering visitors who once they get into the main lobby see broad steps that go nowhere; elevators to the upper floors are hidden to the right, while escalators to lower floors are invisible to the left. Each floor is uniquely laid out as an incomprehensible maze with mysterious twists and turns that even long-term municipal employees cannot navigate. Most offices are too hot in the summer and unbearably cold in the winter; overall, the building's energy use is a scandal.

Yet architects love City Hall. From the moment it was unveiled as the winning design, Boston City Hall has been praised by architects and hated by the public.[12] Ada Louise Huxtable, architecture critic for the New York Times, called the building "magnificently monumental"[13] while Mayor Collins reportedly gasped in horror when the winning design was unveiled. Architects see the building as a strong articulation of theory, a complex response to ideas and history, and perhaps the best building in the city since Trinity Church. The public evaluates it from the perspective of users and sees a cold ugly building that is threatening and unusable.[14]

The diametric difference between Boston City Hall's professional and popular reception attest to the wide gulf that had opened in the United States by the second half of the 1960s between the culture of experts and ordinary citizens. While the architectural elite hailed the Prometheanism of the design gesture, and municipal leaders and businessmen saw the rebuilding of a seedy and antiquated downtown district as a boon for commercial development, most Bostonians felt alienated and angry.[15]

The building is a perfect monument to the disconnect between the 1960s elite that supported urban renewal and the public who fought it with all their might.

In the reassessment of urban design in the wake of 1960s urban renewal, Government Center contains many failed design ideas. It was not truly mixed use, almost every building is single purpose, large, and monolithic with a showcase plaza that is vast, windswept, and lifeless. The new streets and pedestrian paths were too large grained to be effective as it replaced a lively Scollay Square with a stark unloved streetscape while Congress Street is a speedway that separates Faneuil Hall from City Hall. The pedestrian bridge was never built, which in retrospect was a good outcome as these types of infrastructure rarely work. Excluding Faneuil Hall, the project area is a dead zone between historic Beacon Hill and downtown.

There was other collateral damage that derived from the Government Center project. Scollay Square had many undesirable features such as crime, open drunkenness, and tawdry businesses, but bulldozing the area simply caused these problems to move elsewhere. The problem of public alcoholism, for example, shifted to Dover Street, harming the South End. Sex-related businesses ended up on Washington Street, contributing to what was already known as the Combat Zone.

Logue had similar mixed successes with smaller commercial projects elsewhere downtown. Along the waterfront, for example, he would shepherd through a hotel on Long Wharf, a new aquarium, and the interesting, if also controversial, Harbor Towers, designed by I. M. Pei. Though some saw the last to be another great example of concrete Modernism, in the 1980s BRA Director Stephen Coyle suggested that the US Navy use the twin towers as target practice.[16] Still, Logue was more successful downtown than he was in the neighborhoods.

Not all new development activity was the direct result of federally-funded urban renewal. An industry that would contribute much to the revitalization of the city, medical services, began to grow in the 1960s, fueled by new technologies and research. But with this, Boston also began to experience problems associated with institutional expansion, particularly in the neighborhoods around the Longwood Medical Area. Unlike other centrally-located neighborhoods, Mission Hill had been built for working-class families rather than the wealthy or middle class. Over the years, waves of Irish, Canadian, German, and Jewish families moved into the area, and in the 1960s it attracted significant numbers of blacks and Hispanics, many of whom moved into the large Mission Main and Mission Extension Projects. Because of its proximity to jobs, the neighborhood was heavily developed and housing density was high.

In the 1960s, the Lahey Clinic, New England Baptist Hospital, and Harvard University and its teaching hospitals repeatedly encroached on Mission Hill.[17] Harvard's push was unique. It was privately funded and had no city backing because the new development was exempt from property taxes and was blocked, in part, by student activists working with neighborhood residents. As a consequence, the BRA sought to contain Harvard's expansion rather than encourage it.

Founded in Cambridge in 1782, Harvard Medical School moved to its present location in 1900 to be close to the hospitals already located there. By 1962, Harvard's expansion planning was underway with the goal to combine a number of independent hospitals into one new facility, Brigham and Women's Hospital. An initial idea to grow across Huntington Avenue using federal renewal funds was abandoned in the face of BRA and community opposition. This led to a concentration of expansion efforts on the working-class district to the south where 230 families lived in 128 buildings. Harvard's master plan did not include any discussion as to their fate.

Harvard Medical School bought the land for the new hospital with the intention of leasing it back to the facility, and through sham purchasers, by 1969 Harvard owned all but two of the residential properties. Harvard spent over $3 million to buy the houses, and they turned their management over to a company that had no experience with low-income properties. The company favored students over families, and the properties deteriorated. Finally ready to clear the area, in February 1969 the university mailed 182 eviction notices and neighborhood opposition exploded. Residents reached out to students at Harvard who made their cause a priority, and when students took over the Harvard University administration building as part of an antiwar demonstration in April 1969, saving Mission Hill was one of their demands. They kept up the pressure, and by 1970, the BRA and Boston City Council were investigating Harvard's actions.[18] Eventually Harvard agreed to limit is footprint and worked with a group called Roxbury Tenants of Harvard to create a new mixed-income development on the land the university purchased. This was just the first battle in the wars between expanding institutions and their neighbors that would recur over the next several decades.

Across the city in East Boston, another battle between residents and a powerful institution played out as the Massachusetts Port Authority (Massport) sought to expand Logan airport, thus pressuring the neighborhood. East Boston had been slow to develop because of a lack of transportation to Boston and the mainland. Then in the mid-nineteenth century, with the help of road connections and ferries, the community began to grow rapidly as it became a center for shipbuilding and maritime activities. The first people to live in the area in modern times were the Irish followed by Jewish and Russian immigrants. Italian residents arrived in large numbers after 1900, and within a few years it was the largest Italian neighborhood in the city.

Logan Airport began operations in 1923 and was vastly expanded in the 1940s to accommodate passenger traffic. Massport was created by the legislature in 1956 to run the airport, but it was the appointment of Edward King as Executive Director that set off more than a decade of disputes with the neighborhood. King was feisty and determined to implement his vision for a modern airport despite opposition from people in East Boston. Proudly conservative, King would defeat incumbent governor Michael Dukakis in the 1978 gubernatorial primary on a platform of being tough on crime, against abortion, and fiercely opposed to taxes to pay for social services.

King and airport planners wanted new runways, expanded terminals, and large freight operations at Logan, putting them into conflict with neighbors. The airport already had a tremendously negative impact on the environment of East Boston. In its decades of operations, it was responsible for the demolition of a thousand units of housing, and the blast from approaching jets "not only knocked down television antennae but stripped the leaves off trees."[19]

Over the opposition of residents, Massport paved over the beloved Wood Island Park, designed by Frederick Law Olmsted, and demolished houses on Neptune Road. Residents went to court to stop these actions, but the legislature had given Massport strong legal power to take land by eminent domain, and there was nothing that East Boston or the city could do to stop them. A showdown occurred when large numbers of trucks carrying fill to expand the airport began to rumble through residential streets.

Blocked from legal redress, neighbors took to the streets and stopped trucks; mothers, pushing children in strollers, battled a man who fancied himself to be like Winston Churchill in his World War II bunker. From 1968 on, residents had the backing of Mayor White, and they began to block King's expansion plans. After 1975, Dukakis appointed a majority of the Massport board who promptly fired the controversial King; he would get his revenge in the next election. Again, the lesson was that community action could stop outsiders from harming neighborhoods.

There have been many factors credited with the responsibility for the revitalization of the Boston economy: the defeat of Mayor Curley, urban renewal, special events such as First Night and the annual Fourth of July concert on the Esplanade, Mayor Kevin White's strong pro-development policies, and so forth; but perhaps the program that most deserves credit for the great downtown office boom that began in the 1970s–and later attracted a hundred thousand or more middle-class and wealthy residents into the city–was the 121A property tax agreement. By setting out what a property owner would owe the city in the long term, it made new projects immune from the manipulations in assessments favored by Curley and other mayors and locked in very low tax payments. This facilitated development by vastly lowering the cost of occupying new buildings and came about just as downtown businesses were seeking to expand to service the financial, legal, and consultant needs of companies on Route 128. The result was that renting new space was cheaper than leasing old space. These 121A tax agreements were for forty years, meaning that in 2015 agreements signed by Kevin White in his second term of office were just expiring.[20] The Prudential Center was the first development to be granted a tax break, and though it took almost a decade to be approved, it set the standard for these agreements that continue to be granted to this day.

When Collins took office, the Prudential project looked highly unlikely to be launched. However, there were powerful forces working to make it happen as William Callahan made it a priority of the Turnpike plan to accommodate both the Extension and the Prudential development. The Turnpike Authority had been created by the legislature in 1952 with a mandate to end the road in "the vicinity of Boston," and the 127-mile-long turnpike had opened in 1957, taking cars from New York State to the western edge of Newton. Callahan was determined to bring it into the city with a direct connection to the Central Artery. But Governor Volpe wanted to end the Turnpike at the Inner Belt, a problem because construction of that other road was not planned to begin until more than ten years after the Extension was complete. Regardless of the route, the State was going ahead with raising bond money to pay for a new road, and Callahan, seeing an opportunity, connected his Extension to the fate of the Prudential Center.

The roadblock to building the Prudential was the lack of legal authority for the city to grant tax agreements; it needed new legislation giving it the power to do so. The first attempt was struck down after the State Senate asked the Supreme Judicial Court for a ruling on whether the city could grant a long-term abatement under its current urban renewal powers. The proposal involved creating a "Back Bay Commission" that would have been the public vehicle for the abatement. But the court ruled this was a private, not a public, purpose and thus violated the state constitution. It declared the project was not slum

Rendering of the Prudential Center. Desperately wanted by the business community, the project's ring road and wind swept arcades eventually had to be replaced.

clearance and that the Back Bay Commission lacked the power to declare the rail yards blighted. Thus there was no public purpose behind the agreement.

Working with the new Collins administration, Callahan proposed that the Turnpike Authority acquire the yards and lease them back to the Prudential. In addition, the Authority would build a 2,500-car garage and ramps for its Back Bay interchange. But again, the court ruled against this, declaring that the Turnpike was promoting nothing more than an identical substitute for the illegal previous proposal. In the court's view, the Turnpike Authority was not an urban renewal agency. But the court did say that, given the need for redevelopment, a public renewal authority (i.e. the BRA) was duly authorized to declare an area blighted, and, with the power of eminent domain granted by the legislature could be a vehicle for providing a tax abatement. Meanwhile, the Prudential applied strong pressure to force an abatement. On August 24, 1960, the company purposely turned off the site's dewatering pumps, flooding the giant hole on Boylston Street. This self-vandalism was meant to demonstrate to the state and the city that either they approve the project on the Prudential's terms or else.

Finally, Logue, Collins, and Callahan submitted new legislation that granted the BRA the power to declare vacant and underutilized areas blighted and granted the Authority the power to negotiate tax breaks to encourage redevelopment. The Back Bay was specifically included in the bill, now known after its location in the law books as Chapter 121A. This legislation passed and the court declined to review its legality, so construction on the Prudential Center could began at last. This was not the end of the relationship between the Turnpike and the Prudential; the company purchased many of the bonds the Turnpike Authority floated to pay for the Extension.

The architects of the Prudential prided themselves as prioritizing and protecting pedestrians. But as built, the Center had a series of plazas rarely used by anyone, two semi-open retail arcades that were wind tunnels of artic air during the winter, and a useless ring road that cut the development off from the street. When the center opened on April 19, 1965, critics already hated it.[21] Though the Center attracted two department stores, most of its retail space was vacant or underutilized until it was rebuilt in the 1990s.

Just as problematic was the destruction caused by the construction of the Massachusetts Turnpike Extension. Homes were taken in Brighton, important buildings were demolished in the South End (including the complex of buildings owned by the Church of All Nations and Morgan Memorial), and a long linear scar was left behind that continues to divide neighborhoods to this day. The trauma of land takings, that included the eviction of his mother, convinced a young transportation planner, Frederick Salvucci, that urban highways were a mistake. Within a few years, he would be in a position to implement his ideas for alternatives to road buildings.

The South End enjoyed at most six months of peace after the urban renewal plan was approved. Then as the BRA stepped up the pace of land takings and demolitions and new middle-class households began to buy up properties and evict tenants, the neighborhood sank into chaotic fighting between low-income residents terrified they were being displaced, longtime landlords who had let their properties fall into disrepair so as to sell to speculators, new homeowners who had just sunk their life savings into buildings that needed lots of work, developers who were busy converting rooming houses into new homes and apartments, and BRA staff who vainly tried to referee disputes while pushing forward what was increasing apparent to be an unworkable plan for renewal.

The problem, as far as the South End's low-income and minority residents were concerned, was that the demolitions, still substantial at 20 percent of the housing stock, heavily targeted their homes, and the BRA had no ability to provide affordable or nearby replacement housing despite its promises and legal obligation to do so. Rehabilitated housing was for new middle-class people coming into the neighborhood, and promised replacement housing, funded by a federal program of subsidized mortgages, was stalled—the first

South End Urban Renewal Protest. Disfunctional from the start, most of the neighborhood turned against the city's renewal program.

new assisted housing was still years away.

The situation was inflamed by a wave of gentrification sweeping through the neighborhood. For the first time, affluent outsiders wanted to move into Boston, perhaps lured into the South End by a combination of new jobs at the Prudential Center and the charm of cheap, attractive red brick row houses. The city administration, of course, welcomed these new comers and assisted them with architectural advice, tax breaks, and low-interest mortgage programs. But the flip side of this was that the existing residents of the South End, many elderly, poor, and minorities, were forced out. The process began in the early 1960s, and by 1967, tenants were organizing to oppose renewal and gentrification. A showdown was coming.

The one neighborhood that welcomed urban renewal, at least initially, was Roxbury that was mostly included in the new Washington Park Urban Renewal project.[22] The neighborhood's population had shifted from 71 percent white and 29 percent black in 1950 to 28 percent white and 72 percent black in 1960; this racial change was accompanied by a 17 percent drop in population. The remaining whites were mostly poor elderly Jews, a holdover from the time when Roxbury had a large Jewish population. Blacks were a mix; the first to move into the area had been relatively well-off families, but as time went on, the newcomers were more likely to be poor with many displaced by the South End urban renewal project.

One of the most prominent black Roxbury residents, Melnea Cass, had moved into the neighborhood in the 1930s. She was deeply concerned about the decline around her, and the designation as a renewal district promised access to city services in an era when city hall did not respond to black concerns. Others agreed with her. The Snowdens, for example, declared, "We decided that you couldn't plant flower boxes and make the community better. You had to have some basic changes: new buildings, schools, streets – plow everything. That's why we supported urban renewal."[23] In the early 1960s, Boston's black middle class lived in upper Roxbury where small successes also brought optimism. Parents were banding together to pressure the School Committee while others were forcing downtown businesses to begin to hire blacks. So there was reason to think that residents could manage renewal to benefit the existing community.

For many, renewal was an opportunity to force the city to pay attention to the needs of black residents. For decades, whenever there were service cutbacks or a retrenchment of operations, the city made these reductions in Roxbury. By the 1960s, the amount of trash in local parks would be so great that activists took to burning piles of rubbish to embarrass the city into cleaning them up. Streets were decaying and houses were falling apart. Logue promised that renewal would solve these and other issues.

Roxbury's problems were made worse by Boston banks' continued reluctance to make mortgages in any urban renewal area, but under pressure from the city, they came together in 1963 to create a pool of Federal Housing Administration (FHA) mortgage money–thus they got credit for loans that were risk free. But the loan-based rehabilitation program in Washington Park was a failure. Many tenants were displaced along with lower-income homeowners. Many participants ultimately ended up borrowing at higher, market rates or turned to unregulated lenders, exposing them to great risks. Some who bought properties with the expectation of receiving low-cost loans ended up abandoning their properties. Others just purchased buildings with the goal of quickly flipping them or burning them down for insurance money. In any case, these sources of capital were not available to black residents. So the city worked with lenders to create the Boston Banks Urban Reinvestment Group (BBURG) program. In this initial phase, BBURG provided a pool of money for subsidized mortgages, but few loans were made at this time.

Initially proposed as a 186-acre project in 1958, the Washington Park project was expanded by Logue to 502 acres so that it could incorporate enough better quality housing to get closer to his desired 20 percent demolition target. But even with the expansion of project boundaries, the demolition rate was high as the plan called for 2,800 out of 8,500 Washington Park units to be demolished with 1,550 to be constructed, a net loss of 1,250. Unfortunately, both demolitions and rehabilitation displaced residents. As of June 1967, there were 2,549 households already in the BRA relocation program with another 2,427 projected to be evicted for demolition. In addition, thousands of others were being forced out of their homes to make way for the new Inner Belt highway. Most would be pushed out of the neighborhood with less than a quarter of these assisted by the BRA relocation program. In addition, these numbers did not include the other displacement in the community as evictions caused by private sales did not qualify tenants for help.[24] Altogether, one third of Roxbury's population was displaced by renewal or highway construction in the 1960-1970 period. Meanwhile, residents waited for the promised improvements of city services.

Under pressure because of land takings for urban renewal and highway construction, Boston's black population was in the middle of a housing crisis. With their numbers rapidly growing, black families found most of the city blocked to them by discrimination; they could not rent or buy in well over 80 percent of the city. In the South End, new housing was years away. In Roxbury, there were a few projects that opened up during the Collins years, but rather than providing quality durable housing, these new units were an ominous foreshadowing of the problems of renewal era affordable housing programs.

The AFL-CIO financed the first phase of Academy Homes (202 units). Unfortunately, the projects rents were unaffordable to the low-income households in the area, and they added to the stream of people desperate for alternative housing. Similar problems resulted from the Charles Street AME Church-sponsored second project, Charlame Park Homes (92 units). A third project was Marksdale Gardens. Completed in 1964, a twenty-five-foot section at the end of one building collapsed on New Year's Day, 1965.[25]

In one of the more problematic consequences of Logue's management style, the planning for the South End and Roxbury renewal projects was kept separate with not even BRA staff aware of what each project was proposing. So South End relocation staff aimed to rehouse people from that neighborhood to Roxbury at the same time Washington Park planners sought to move displaced Roxbury residents to the South End. As a result, there were thousands of people without housing, many of them poor and most unable to move to large portions of the city because of discrimination.[11] This added to the growing trauma of renewal.

There was disconnect from the beginning of the renewal era bcause many of the things residents wanted the most were beyond the abilty or jurisdiction of the BRA: better schools, police protection, trash pickups, and so forth. Along with rehabilitation, that often proceeded in starts and stops, and land takings that resulted in years or decades of vacant land, Roxbury dissolved into anarchy as residents became militarized and organized themselves to oppose Freedom House and the BRA. Angered by the mess the BRA had created, Mel King and the Urban League confronted Robert Weaver, the Secretary of HUD, at an appearance in the neighborhood to tell him that his project to rehabilitate 2,074 units across Roxbury was not going to happen. Rehabilitation was not employing residents, not providing housing, and was often contributing to decline because it aided speculation and allowed shoddy construction. [26] Renewal was fostering rebellion.

Boston avoided the great wave of civil unrest that swept across urban America in the 1960s until almost the end of the Collins era. Then a riot shook Grove Hall in June 1967. Blacks had moved into the area in the 1950s as the local population declined and became poorer. There was less money to spend in the area, but tax assessments were never lowered, encouraging abandonment and rumors that the BRA was planning to make the area a new urban renewal district and take all the properties in the neighborhood further discouraged investment.[27] Angered, blacks saw themselves as being steered into one of the city's least desirable neighborhoods.

The flash point for the riot was the welfare office on Blue Hill Avenue. Poor families found the office staff to be capricious as they harshly treated low-income families seeking assistance. Clients were imperiously summoned to appear at rundown and poorly-staffed offices, benefits could be cut off without warning or opportunity for appeal, and the whole system was on the verge of collapse. At the time, it was one more patronage-ridden city department—Boston administered the welfare program.

Pressing for reform, a group called Mothers for Adequate Welfare (MAW) formed in 1965 and organized a sit in on April 26 at the downtown welfare headquarters. In 1966 they staged a protest at the State House, and on May 26, 1967 they held an all-night sit-in at the Blue Hill Avenue office. As relations deteriorated, tempers grew short.

On Friday June 2, 1967, a group of black and white mothers, along with some college student supports, chained the doors of the Grove Hall welfare office shut with themselves and over fifty staffers locked inside. Police quickly swarmed outside the building. Then a welfare worker hiding in her office reported she was having a heart attack, and Mayor Collins ordered the police to clear the building. They rushed in to break the siege using ladders and brute force and were met by resistance from the protestors. A woman went to a window to scream that demonstrators were being beaten, and rocks and bottles began to pelt officers, who responded with greater force. Witnesses later reported the police beat, kicked, and dragged the demonstrators out of the building while verbally abusing them and calling them niggers. At 6:40 the building had been surrounded by protest sympathizers, and police began to fight with the crowd. Then, as the police secured the building, violence spread into the neighborhood and the police began to arrest everyone they could, including workers trying to calm the protests. They fired sixty to one hundred rounds of shots over the heads of protestors.[28]

By 8:00 the building was empty, but the enraged crowd moved up and down Blue Hill Avenue looting stores, breaking windows, and setting fires. There were forty-four arrests and forty-five reported injuries. The police lashed out at everyone they could reach and even clubbed Thomas Atkins, who was soon to be elected city councilor; Byron Rushing, then an organizer for the Massachusetts Council of Churches, and later a State Representative was arrested twice that evening as many other others were caught up in police sweeps. The city teetered on the edge of a full-scale race riot.

The next night rioting began again as roving groups of young men battled police, snipers shot at police and firemen, and crowds of protestors filled the streets. Sunday night, June 4, saw even greater violence as protestors threw bricks, bottles, and Molotov cocktails and snipers pinned down police. It took 1,900 policemen to restore peace, though there was lesser violence on June 5. Little was done to improve conditions in the community as the Mayor and other white leaders blamed the problems on criminals. [28] The violence subsided but not tension that had caused it.

Hynes's, Collins's, and Logue's ideas for urban renewal, shared by most city planners of the 1950s and 1960s, now seem at best misguided, at worst evil. Their goal was to connect the city to the suburbs via cars and prioritized everything possible to facilitate automobiles. In Boston, this meant the construction of the Southeast Expressway/ Central Artery, the Common Parking Garage, Government Center, and the Prudential Center. Three of the four would eventually be viewed as particularly bad for the city. Furthermore, renewal scared residents who saw it as a potential destruction of their families, neighborhoods, and way of life. Though they were carefully spared the bulldozers that were turned on the Italian/Jewish West End, the multicultural downtown edge of the South End, and black portions of Roxbury, the Irish residents of the inner wards saw renewal as a threat to be opposed by all means necessary.

The experience of displacement throughout the city's renewal areas provided clear lessons to all residents: renewal was bad and city hall was not to be trusted. Furthermore, it told them that the media, business leaders, clergy, and virtually all outsiders were prejudiced against city residents and were out to destroy them. The only way to defend themselves in this environment, residents grasped, was to take to the streets. These lessons would soon be applied on a large scale across Boston.

Urban renewal offered low-income residents nothing. Not jobs, not improved city services or lower taxes, and little viable replacement housing.[29] It seemed only capable of providing sterile concrete monstrosities, and overall, it turned the city into an angry, distrustful place. So the major legacy of renewal was that it radicalized the city. The renewal battles of the 1960s were the practice wars for the busing battles of the 1970s as South Boston and Charlestown learned how to use neighborhood solidarity to fight the city. For Boston's emerging black leadership, battling renewal projects produced the first great victories for civil rights in a generation and taught them the power of the injunction, demonstrations, and organizing.[30]

Collins had staked his political career on revitalizing the city through urban renewal, but by 1966 the city had had enough and the mayor had little political support. Blind to his unpopularity, however, Collins ran for the US Senate against Governor Endicott Peabody. In the backlash against the turmoil caused by the Vietnam War and the civil rights movement, Republicans did very well nationally. In Massachusetts, Collins lost by a landslide and even lost twenty-one out of twenty-two wards in the city. His political career shattered, and he limped through his final year as mayor. After leaving office, Collins became a bitter conservative gadfly, angry with the people of the city he once led and baffled that they did not share his ideals and values.

Lured by the empty office, the 1967 race for mayor was a classic Boston political brawl with ten candidates in the running. It included backroom deals, planted evidence, and mysterious witnesses with even Logue participating in the dirty tricks when his campaign secretly paid for a lawyer to challenge Kevin White's nomination papers. Three prominent candidates almost secured spots in the final. John Sears, a Yankee patrician form Beacon Hill, was one for the few Republicans in the city, and he thought that his core supporters would provide enough votes for him to be one of the top two primary finalists. He came in third. Perhaps unaware of the depth of the anger against him, Logue appeared to have learned nothing from Collin's landslide defeat the year before, and though he initially attracted some business support, the neighborhoods were united against him and he came in fourth. Another prominent candidate who just missed being a finalist was Christopher Ianella, an Italian immigrant who would serve for thirty years on the City Council.

The primary was a battle for second place because the frontrunner was Louis Day Hicks, who ran on a blatantly racist platform. Her "you know where I stand" campaign slogan was meant to tell white voters she would do everything in her power to support continued segregation. Candidates figured they could rally the anti-Hicks vote in the final because of the widespread perception that if she became mayor, it would be a disaster for the city; liberal and middle-class voters along with downtown business interests scrambled to find someone who could beat her in the final. The business people's natural inclination was to rally for Ed Logue, but eventually they came to understand he had no chance of winning and they supported Kevin White, who came in second in the preliminary election.[30]

The fear of Hicks dominated the final election. If she won, would the city burn down? Would redevelopment stop? What would the liberal legislature, vital for providing financial support to close the city's deficits, do if Hicks was in office? Anti-integration represented 100 percent of Hick's platform, and if elected mayor, she had no other agenda. Hicks knew nothing about public administration, and after she promised to increase police and fire salaries by a third, she could not identify where the money to pay for this would come from so she naively suggested she would get Washington to pay for the raises. Senator Edward Kennedy quickly ended that option.

The final election was another battle between the working-class Irish (Hicks) and the middle-class Irish (White), but this time there was a small but critical additional group that would grow in influence with each subsequent election: white liberals and minority voters. Wooing them, White created a new coalition dedicated to stopping Hicks as he peeled off those inner wards that were dominated by minorities and added them to the more traditional supporters of good government: Back Bay/ Beacon Hill and the middle-class outer wards. This was an important change. For generations, Boston blacks had voted for the working-class Irish candidates such as Honey Fitz and Curley, supporting the former, for example, because his opponent, James Storrow, had declared he opposed hiring black schoolteachers. Black wards had gone for Powers over Collins. But now, as Boston slid into the maelstrom of confronting its racism, the old political coalition fell apart and new alliances formed between minorities and middle-class whites, and together they beat the conservative candidate in a hard fought final. White defeated Hicks, 102,706 to 90,154, and it appeared that Boston had dodged disaster.

1. Slavet JS and Torto RG. *Boston's Recurring Crises: Three Decades of Fiscal Policy*. Boston: John M. McCormack Graduate School of Policy and Global Studies 1985.
2. Kozol J. *Death at an Early Age*. New York: Penguin Books, 1967.
3. U.S. Department of Health Education and Welfare. *A Report on the Schools of Boston*. 1962.
4. Motti TL. *Social conflict and social movements: An explanatory study of the black community of Boston attempting to change the Boston public schools*. Dissertation, Brandeis University, 1975.
5. Huang B. *The first educational exodus: A narrative of 1965*. Dissertation, Depart-

ment of History. MIT, 2013.

6. Anderson M. *The Federal Bulldozer.* Cambridge MA: MIT Press, 1964.

7. Jackson MI. *Model City Blues: Urban Space and Organized Resistance in New Haven.* Philadelphia PA: Temple University Press, 2008.

8. Mollenkopf JH. *The Contested City.* Princeton, New Jersey: Princeton University Press, 1983.

9. Keyes L. *The Rehabilitation Planning Game: A Study in the Diversity of Neighborhood.* Cambridge MA: MIT Press, 1969.

10. Barbour WE. *Notes toward a general plan for the South End.* Boston City Planning Board 1959.

11. Lopez R. *Boston's South End: The Clash of Ideas in a Historic Neighborhood.* Boston: Shawmut Peninsula Press, 2015.

12. Crane D. The federal building in the making of Boston's Government Center: A struggle for sovereignty in local design review. *Studies in the History of Art.* 1995; 50: 21-38.

13. Huxtable AL. Boston's New City Hall: A Public Building of Quality. *New York Times.* February 8, 1969; p. 33.

14. Monteyne D. Boston City Hall and a history of reception. *Journal of Architectural Education.* 2011; 65: 45-62.

15. Ockman J. The School of Brutalism: From Great Britain to Boston (and Beyond). In: Pasnik M, Kubo M and Grimley C, (eds.). *Heroic: Concrete Architecture and the New Boston.* New York: The Monacelli Press, 2015.

16. Kennedy L. *Planning the City Upon a Hill: Boston Since 1630.* Boston: University of Massachusetts Press, 1994.

17. Robinson SD. *An urban design and development plan for Mission Hill.* Masters Thesis, DUSP. MIT, 1973.

18. Winkeller M. *University expansion in urban neighborhoods: An exploratory analysis.* Dissertation, Heller School. Brandeis University, 1971.

19. Nelkin D. *Jetport: The Boston Airport Controversy.* New Brunswick, NJ: Transaction Books, 1974.

20. Boston Redevelopment Authority. *Fact Book.* 1972.

21. Rubin E. *Insuring the City: The Prudential Center and the Postwar Urban Landscape.* New Haven, CT: Yale University Press, 2012.

22. Keyes L. *The Boston Rehabilitation Program: An Independent Analysis.* Joint Center for Urban Studies, 1970.

23. Carden L. *Witness: An Oral History of Black Politics in Boston 1920 - 1960.* Chestnut Hill, Massachusetts: Boston College, 1989.

24. Gergen D. Renewal in the ghetto: A study of residential rehabilitation in Boston's Washington Park. *Harv CR-CLLRev* 1967-8; 243-310.

25. Hock J. Bulldozers, busing, and boycotts: Urban renewal and the integrationist project. *Journal of Urban History.* 2012; 39: 433-53.

26. Spiders JH. "Planning with people": Urban renewal in Boston's Washington Park, 1950-1970. *Journal of Planning History.* 2009; 8: 221-47.

27. Poor RM. *White business owners after the riots in Roxbury: Reactions, problems, recommen-*

dations. Masters Thesis, DUSP. MIT, 1968.

28. Tager J. *Boston Riots: Three Centuries of Social Violence.* Boston: Northeastern University Press, 2001.

29. Hartman C. The housing of relocated families. *Journal of the American Institute of Planners.* 1964; 30: 266-86.

30. O'Neill G. *Rogues and Redeemers: When Politics was King in Irish Boston.* New York: Crown Publishing Group, 2012.

Chapter 4

Hope and Despair: 1968-1975

A CASUAL VISITOR to Boston in 1968 might have found the city placid, but it was about to tear itself apart in disputes around race, class, and the role of government in foreign and domestic policy. The city's mix of ancient and recent grudges – Irish against Yankees, blacks against whites, rich against poor – would break into new mutinies in the streets and courtrooms with the resulting violence and bloodshed documented in newspapers and television broadcasts around the world. When it was over, Boston would never be the same.

Economic change was coming, but it was out in the suburbs as the city continued to deteriorate. During the 1960s and 1970s, Massachusetts transformed its moribund economy into a vibrant modern one reliant on education, research, technology, and medicine. Though by now this was having a dramatic impact on Boston's suburban fringe, the city itself had yet to benefit from Route 128 companies' military contracts and new technologies. Two famous companies from this era, Draper Labs and Polaroid, were in Cambridge, for example, but most were at least a dozen miles to the west. Some were even further away from the city; two of the largest firms, Digital Equipment Company and Wang Laboratories, were in Maynard and Lowell respectively. For the most part, this reflected the demographics of these companies' founders.

Most were older Protestant white men (An Wang was a notable exception), and if they weren't exactly traditional Yankees, they shared their disdain for Boston and disliked city living. Few opened facilities in the city, and for the most part, their employees avoided Boston as well, preferring the leafy suburbs. The isolation from the urban core was extreme, Digital employees, for example, seldom ate, lived, or shopped as far east as Route 128.[1]

The anti-urban bias of these companies was reflected in their politics. As one example, though the political arm of California's San Jose area technology companies, the Silicon Valley Manufacturing Group, has been at the forefront of advocating for affordable housing, mass transit, and other urban friendly policies, the Route 128 equivalent, the Massachusetts High Technology Association, focused on tax cutting and was a prime backer of the 1978 property tax limitation initiative that disrupted state and local finance in the 1980s. Again, with the exception of An Wang, most did not involve themselves in city philanthropy, politics, or social activities.

Therefore, the effects of the technology boom on Boston were of a secondary nature. Though many companies hired as much in-house staff as possible, collectively they required large numbers of lawyers, bankers, accountants, and other highly-paid consultants. This fed a downtown office boom which led to the hiring of thousands of construction workers, architects, and others. Then some of these highly-paid lawyers and bankers began to move to Beacon Hill, Back Bay, and the waterfront. The middle-class architects, executive assistants, small builders, real estate agents, and similar beneficiaries of this new economy started to fill up the South End, Charlestown, and Jamaica Plain while the lower-paid construction workers and office support staff went to South Boston and Dorchester. Notably, these new jobs did not go to blacks, Hispanics, or Asians, who for the most part were excluded from all but the most menial jobs. But many minorities came to the city to be hired as janitors, hotel staff, and other low skilled, low paying positions. Also important, for most of the city revival was still at least a decade away, with the exception of a few core neighborhoods, Boston continued to lose population in the 1960s and 1970s, and its housing stock continued to decay. The city's population dropped by 50,000 in the 1960s, and its white population fell by 100,000.

Kevin White, 1978. The "loner in love with the city" hated to campaign yet always dreamed of higher office.

There were several types of urban mayors in the 1960s and 1970s. Many municipalities turned to conservative white leaders, such as Frank Rizzo in Philadelphia and Richard Daley in Chicago. These often openly reactionary mayors helped give a voice to alienated white working-class voters during times of wrenching economic decline and racial transition. Other cities turned to black mayors as racial change promoted new electoral coalitions, Coleman Young of Detroit being perhaps the most famous of these. But conservative white Boston's ability to elect a mayor was thwarted by the racism of its leading potential mayoral candidates and the political power of the new middle class/minority coalition. Meanwhile, the city's demographics were still too traditional to elect a minority mayor. So Boston was led by a white liberal, Kevin White, for the next sixteen years, limiting the political ambitions of both minorities and poor whites. At least during the beginning of his tenure White was thought to be a progressive, enlightened politician. Just 37 when he was first sworn in as mayor, White was Boston's equivalent of New York City's John Lindsay: photogenic, well educated, and competent.

White was a traditional middle-class Boston Irishman, born in Jamaica Plain and raised in West Roxbury but eventually living on Beacon Hill. Politics was in his blood: his father and one grandfather had been city council presidents as was his father-in-law. White's first office was Secretary of State of Massachusetts, a nomination he earned through the extensive help of his family. After seven years, he ran for mayor as his goal was always higher office.[2]

White charged into city hall with an accompanying group of young white college graduates who helped to promote his reputation as a man of ideas and idealism. Barney Frank, Fred Salvucci, Colin Diver, and many others were attracted by White's combination of street smarts and commitment to solving the country's urban crisis.[3] He would need all of this talent as he was forced to address a number of daunting issues.

Even before the 1967 election, the South End was in a meltdown. Urban renewal had demolished thousands of units, displaced even more people, and set in motion a tremendous wave of gentrification that would ultimately clear out all low-income people in the private housing market. But replacement housing was taking years to complete, and low income, minority residents were desperate. Middle-class residents, many of whom were sympathetic to the needs of existing residents, were angered by the slow pace of redevelopment, the inability to improve city services, and the terrible architecture of city-sponsored projects. Low-income tenants were opening challenging the renewal process, middle-income people wanted substantial reforms as well.[4]

Ultimately, as many as 16,000 residents were displaced by the South End Urban Renewal Project.[5] By the early 2010s, the neighborhood would have over 5,000 units of affordable housing (many built with the help of post-renewal programs), but the housing development program that was supposed to be implemented in tandem with renewal proved to be a tremendous failure with most units arriving years after they were needed. The BRA had hoped to work with churches and other non-profit groups interested in sponsoring housing that would contain a mixture of low and moderate income units made affordable through the federal 221(d)3 loan subsidy program. But the nonprofits turned out to be unable to manage development, necessitating BRA staff to step in and then the projects turned out to be financial failures because of underfunding by the federal government.[6] As a result, construction was shoddy and fell apart almost as soon as projects opened. Another problem was that many of the elements of the South End plan simply didn't make sense. The core of the neighborhood, for example, was to be bulldozed to make way for a large park and community facilities including a school and an ice rink. It was a legacy of the original 1959 proposal that Logue had hastily incorporated into the 1964 plan and reflected no community need or demand. The Puerto Rican tenants who lived on these blocks fought to save their homes. Redevelopment was a mess.

Residents were scared. Organizing under the banner of CAUSE (Community Assembly for a United South End), angry South Enders confronted White's new appointee to lead the BRA, Hale Champion, at a packed meeting in January 1968 to demand community control over renewal. Champion refused but would be eventually over-ruled by White whose main goal was to channel and control the demonstrators. The activists were not placated, however, and over the next several months, they occupied the BRA site office, staged demonstrations at City Hall, and most famously, erected a protest camp at the site of what was once supposed to be housing but was now proposed to be a parking garage, Tent City. Across the South End, tenant-based groups demanded a halt to rehabilitation programs, an end to evictions, and the preservation of low-income housing. These groups, which were to have national reputations, included Inquilinos Boricuas en Accion (IBA–Puerto Rican Tenants in Action), the Tenants Development Corporation, and the Tent City Corporation. Using a variety of confrontational, but peaceful, tactics, tenants responded by creating their own alternative institutions, many of which proved more competent at producing housing, identifying community issues, and improving neighborhoods than the increasingly out of touch BRA staff.[7] Mayor White struggled to find a way to accommodate the activists' demands without ceding control over renewal.

These groups inspired similar efforts across the city as they worked to protect neighborhoods against renewal, displacement, and abandonment and fought developers, BRA planners, the media, and others who in turn saw them as irrational opponents of the New Boston. Fortunately for the long-term health of the city, these activists eventually stopped renewal and kept most of Boston's neighborhoods intact.[8]

At the time, however, there seemed to be no end to the conflict, and the South End sank into bedlam. To complicate what had been a fight between low-income residents and the city, a backlash among a few of the new gentrifiers developed. Small in number but strong in voice and influence, they began to challenge efforts to build additional low-income housing in the neighborhood and over the next several years would file lawsuits against several proposed developments. These failed, but they succeeded in slowing and stopping projects. Neighbor fought neighbor and poor administration by the BRA caused most of the South End renewal program to languish for years. However, gentrification and displacement in the neighborhood were relentless, and by 1980, virtually all of the market rate housing in the neighborhood would be unaffordable to the poor. The one-hundred-year era of the South End as a rooming house district for striving immigrants and the impoverished elderly was at an end.[4]

With its many college campuses and liberal outlook, Boston was a natural center for the national movement opposing US military involvement in Vietnam, and as the war dragged on and the casualties mounted, so did the scale of protests in the city and around the region. Several local events contributed to the larger national movement: the organizing of a group at MIT to oppose military-funded research; local hero John Kerry's dramatic testimony in Washington before a Senate subcommittee in 1971 when he asked, "How do you ask a man to be the last man to die in Vietnam? How do you ask a man to be the last man to die for a mistake?" and the federal prosecution in Boston of beloved pediatrician Benjamin Spock, Yale chaplain Sloane Coffin, and three others for counseling men to avoid the draft. Spock, Coffin, and two other men were found guilty, but the convictions were overturned upon appeal.

One of the largest protests occurred on Boston Common on October 15, 1969 when over 100,000 gathered after marches from several area colleges. Other important antiwar events occurred at MIT, Boston University, and other area campuses. The protests were met with anger in South Boston and other neighborhoods where military service was an honored pursuit and where families bore the brunt of deaths in the conflict. Boston antiwar protests were peaceful, but the idea of mass gatherings to oppose government actions would be consciously adopted by antibusing activists a few years later.

There were non-political gatherings on the Common as well as young people smoked marijuana, listened to music, and held impromptu parties. This scene in downtown Boston influenced the LGBT community and others to become more open and helped set the stage for the events to come.

Mayor White did not enjoy a peaceful honeymoon after his election. Barely three months after he was sworn into office, another round of violence rocked the Blue Hill Avenue corridor in the aftermath of the assassination of Martin Luther King on April 4, 1968. The unrest in Boston was mild compared to that in other cities with renewed rioting in Grove Hall and isolated incidents elsewhere in Roxbury, Dorchester, and the South End. Kevin White and Barney Frank claimed they kept the city calm by persuading James Brown to not cancel his performance at the Boston Garden the next night. Brown had been no friend of King, and White had never heard of Brown – he kept calling him Jimmy – but the televised concert, with only 2,000 people in attendance, was said to have so transfixed angry, bereaved, would-be rioters that they stayed home to watch the performance.[6] A more plausible, if less romantic, reason for the reduced level of violence in the city was that for the past year, Mel King and other black community leaders had been creating a network of youth outreach workers to target potential troublemakers and work in advance of troubles to keep the peace.[9] White would take credit for averting another riot a few years later by springing the Rolling Stones from a Warwick, Rhode Island, jail after they were arrested for drug possession.[10]

Kevin White was politically ambitious, even moving from Secretary of State to Mayor was part of his plan for national attention, but seemingly every initiative in the city posed problems that thwarted his dream of higher office. One example of how the mayor's goals were buffeted by local issues was the controversy over the Inner Belt. By the mid-1960s most of the plan for highways in and around Boston had been completed with large highways radiating north, south, and west from the city with another major road circulating about a dozen miles outside. But highway planners still had one major road on their agenda: bringing in Interstate 95 from the south. They couldn't fit the road through central Boston, so their solution was to have it extend to a mile south of downtown and then have it split with one arm going north through Cambridge and Somerville to connect with other highways there and one reaching around to the south to merge into the Southeast Expressway at Massachusetts Avenue.

At first, the plan was to build the highway through Boston along the eastern edge of Blue Hill Avenue, but in the late 1940s, the route was changed to go from Readville, the very southern tip of the city, up along the railroad tracks to about Ruggles, where it would split in a spectacular six level interchange. A major problem with the route was that it was a densely populated area, and as land taking began in the 1960s, opposition to the highways began as well. Up to this time, there had been few successful anti-highway movements anywhere in the country, and the prospects of fighting this highway, which had the backing of Governor Volpe, William Callahan, Mayor Collins, and major downtown interests, showed little chance it might succeed.

The neighborhoods fighting against the highway were at the time working class, Irish, and Italian along with other white ethnics who had sunk their life savings into older one, two, and three family houses. The area in Roxbury was heavily black and under pressure from urban renewal. Many of the families along the route had sons in Vietnam, many were also closely watching the growing demonstrations against the war or had other children participating in the protests. Local groups from Hyde Park to Somerville learned from these rallies and began to talk to neighbors, hold meetings in church halls and other neighborhood venues, and complain to their elected officials. By 1968, these protests against the highway were reaching a loud climax, yet the land takings and plans continued to go forward and it appeared that thousands were going to be displaced. Mayor White didn't know whether to support the project or oppose it.

Technically not part of the federal/state highway project but essential for it to work was the South End Bypass, a road that would take traffic from the Inner Belt to Copley Square along the railroad tracks that separated the South End from Back Bay. Without this connector, cars would not be able to reach the Back Bay and traffic would back up for miles. Highway planners were depending on the city to construct the road, which would have had six lanes in an either elevated or below grade position. A small group of residents, most of whom had only moved into the South End in the past few years, looked at the looming bypass and saw their beloved new neighborhood at dire risk. First calling themselves the Tubman Area Planning Group and later the Transportation Committee of the South End Project Action Committee, the group realized that without the bypass there was no point to building the highway. If they could stop the bypass, they could stop the entire project. But how?

Their leverage was Kevin White's ambition to become governor. To make his case for his nomination at the state convention, White wanted the support of every Democratic ward committee in the city. As an access road, the bypass did not qualify for federal funding, and the state had never included it in its budgeting process. The road had to be funded by the city, and so the anti-highway group targeted the mayor. At first, White was noncommittal about opposing the project, perhaps because in his initial political assessment there seemed to be no benefit to him coming out against it and lots of potential pushback if he did. The area in the South End that abutted the bypass was in Ward 4, so the Tubman group, along with their allies, stacked the Ward 4 Democratic Committee with anti-highway activists. In their genius analysis, they saw that White's road to the statehouse ran through getting an endorsement from the Ward 4 Committee, and the price of its support was White opposing the Bypass. The mayor considered his opposition worth the endorsement and came out against the entire Inner Belt project. When White said the city would not fund or build the bypass, the Inner Belt was technically dead, though it would take a few months for the project to die.

The incumbent governor, Republican Francis Sargent, was no great highway booster either. This final Boston highway had been proposed by his rival and predecessor, John Volpe, and Sargent was trying to outmaneuver White during the run up to the election. The more liberal votes he could coopt in the inner core neighborhoods, the more difficult it would be for White to beat him. So to outdo him, Sergeant called for a moratorium on new highway construction in 1970 while he appointed a commission to analyze plans. Unions and pro-highway interests screamed, but without the bypass, the project could not be built. Sargent ended up calling a halt to the entire highway and Inner Belt project. The neighborhoods were saved.

For all his plans and maneuvering, however, White was unable to capitalize on his hold on Boston to reach higher office. White barely captured the Democratic gubernatorial primary in 1970, winning fewer votes than his running mate, Michael Dukakis, who was in a larger field. In the final, White even lost Boston to Sargent in a landslide defeat. White's liberalism faded as he blamed blacks and good government liberals for his loss, and he came to believe there was nothing to be gained from championing their issues or pandering to their concerns. Instead, he concentrated on maintaining his hold on the mayor's office and enjoying the perks of the job. Over time, his team of young liberals departed, and his innovations in governing were twisted into supporting his reelection campaigns. For example, White had won nationwide acclaim for his systematic moving of city staff and programs to the neighborhoods through what he called Little City Halls. But residents learned to treat these offices with suspicion. They made it easier to get problems fixed, but they were being used by White to keep an eye on residents and they were the local outposts of his political machine. Residents soon learned that to cross the mayor meant isolation at best or an inability to get streets cleaned, development proposals vetted, or fires put out. Over time the slights accumulated and more and more people were exiled.

The upheaval over race, renewal, and the Vietnam War had a profound impact on the LGBT community. Energized by the 1969 riot outside the Stonewall Inn in New York City where a spontaneous reaction to a police raid by an impromptu group of drag queens, gay people of color, and others launched the gay rights movement in the United States, Boston activists organized a parade on the anniversary of the riot in 1971. Led by John Mitzel, Charley Shively, Diane Travis, Laura McMurray, and others, the loose coalition of activists carefully planned a march to highlight four of the major issues affecting the LGBT community. The parade, which began at the corner of Tremont and Boylston Streets, first stopped in front of Jacques, a bar in Bay Village. One of the few drinking establishments where lesbians could gather, protestors complained about ill treatment by bar staff, the filthy bathrooms, and the unsafe conditions inside the bar. The second stop was on Berkeley Street in front of police headquarters where there were protests against entrapment and enforcement of loitering, lewd conduct, and other laws against gay men and lesbians and demands that the police protect LGBT people against harassment. Marchers called for a meeting between the police department and protestors. The third stop was in front of the statehouse where there were calls for the repeal of laws used against LGBT people and the passing of anti-discrimination protections. The fourth stop was in front of the Episcopal St. Paul's Cathedral in protest of religious bigotry against LGBT people.[11] The march was small but would grow in size each subsequent year. LGBT people were no longer invisible.

Into the city's crises over renewal, integration, and war, a new group began to be noticed. Distant from Mexico and lacking close connections to Latin America, Boston had not been known for its Latino population, but in the 1960s, this began to change. The first to arrive were Puerto Ricans, some by way of the tobacco farms of the Connecticut River Valley, others indirectly from New York. They were joined by Cubans, some fleeing the repressively corrupt Batista dictatorship, others coming later after Fidel Castro rose to power and brought his own political agenda to the island. There were also a few Mexicans, mostly the American-born children and grandchildren of immigrants, moving to Boston to go to college and Dominicans, economic and political refugees from the chaotic rule of dictators and United States military intervention. At first, Latinos mostly settled in the South End, particularly in the area known as Parcel 19, already targeted by the BRA for demolition. Soon they were living in Jamaica Plain and Dorchester as well.[12]

Latinos were socially and politically isolated. Though Puerto Ricans and many of the Mexicans were United States citizens by birth and Cubans were eligible for citizenship, their share of the vote was small, and in the battles between low ward and higher ward Irish and between blacks and whites, they were easily ignored. Though Alex Rodriguez had run unsuccessfully for State Representative in 1968 and several social service organizations were in full operation for several years, many in Boston first became aware of its Latino population in 1973 when the police charged the crowd at the annual Festival Puertoriqueno in Blackstone Park, setting off several nights of melees. Kevin White, always eager to control any and all community-based organizations, eventually found a strong ally in IBA's Jorge Hernandez and employed Micho Spring, who had fled Cuba as a child, as one of his top deputies. For the most part, however, Boston's social, political, and economic establishment was closed to Latinos.

As the 1971 city elections approached, it seemed that Boston had been lucky, narrowing escaping the meltdowns destroying other cities across the country. It was not that conditions in the city were improving, rather it was that Boston was now deteriorating less rapidly than other places, many of which were now in freefall decline. Yet the city was in turmoil, and five candidates opposed White in the primary including Thomas Atkins, the city's only black city councilor. He came in fourth but still captured 11 percent of the vote. In third place was Joe Timilty, also a member of the city council. But for the final, it was to be a rematch between White and Louise Day Hicks. She stuck to her old strategy of focusing on her core white voters as race relations grew more tense. In the context of poor Irish against middle-class Irish aligned with minorities and white liberals, her strategy failed, and despite the seemingly growing strength of antibusing forces, Hicks garnered 20,000 fewer votes than she had four years earlier and lost to White by a larger margin. It was impossible to know if White's success was based on the city's changing electorate, White's growing political powers, the city's satisfaction with his performance as mayor, or that people were becoming tired of the polarization.

White's dreams for higher office almost came true in 1972 when George McGovern briefly considered him as a vice president candidate before Senator Edward Kennedy vetoed the idea. White cried himself to sleep and never forgave Kennedy for thwarting his ambitions, though Kennedy was merely repaying White for supporting John Mc-

Cormack in the 1962 senate primary. After that brief moment of national prominence passed, White gave into his presidential ambitions and as 1972 waned, he began to plot a 1976 campaign for the White House.[2]

Unfortunately for a man who wanted to be on the national stage, White's second term was marked by more turmoil than his first, and any hopes of higher office were ruined by Boston's meltdown over race. The decades of stalling by the School Committee had solved nothing. Black parents continued to contest the horrendous education their children were being offered, conditions in the schools grew worse, and segregation increased. But Hicks's hold on the schools was as tight as any urban boss at any point in the nineteenth or twentieth century as she and her fellow committee members controlled hiring and promotions. There were two requirements to get a job in the Boston schools during her tenure: Irish ethnicity and contributions to political campaigns. This did not mean Hicks personally benefited from the corruption, on the contrary, she lived as modestly as her South Boston neighbors. But it resulted in school department employees, janitors, nurses, teachers, lunch ladies, and principals, contributing to the political campaigns that Hicks and her colleagues suggested or else their careers as school employees would be over. This gave Hicks access to hundreds of thousands of dollars in each election cycle, a power that she used to cement her influence. It also created a symbiotic relationship between Boston's Irish and the public schools: the schools provided stable employment for Irish constituents who in turn supported conservative incumbents. Yet despite this seamless self-serving system and their dominance of the city's political life for nearly eighty years, the Irish felt powerless. They saw any black advancement as a pointed attack against themselves and the system they benefited from.[13]

Their insecurity was justified; any change in this patronage system threatened thousands of well-paying jobs and the position of the people at the apex of this corrupt system. It induced a rabid support for the status quo across neighborhoods in the city long after business as usual became untenable due to minority ambitions and state and federal pressure. This closed system survived into 1974 intact, even Kevin White couldn't overthrow it, and coupled with Hick's brilliant ability to communicate with her constituents, it made her a nearly invincible politician as long as no outside force was brought to bear against the system.[2]

Part of the tragedy of the busing crisis was that the city might have desegregated its schools with less conflict if only options that required less busing and disruption had been considered. But every compromise had been rejected by the School Committee because of its racism. Hicks was not the most rabid anti-black in office in Boston at the time. Her fellow committee member, John Kerrigan, was a "loutish and lecherous race-baiter." At one point he went after a black television reporter, "offering him a banana, then mimicking a monkey's crouch and scratching his armpits, ending his pantomime by proclaiming the reporter a generation away from swinging in the trees."[2] He was one of the key people responsible for managing the system at a time it needed to adjust to its growing black student population. Some whites say busing destroyed once cordial race relations in the city. However, racial tensions soared when City Councilor Dapper O'Neill showed up at Hyde Park High School in 1972 (two years before Garrity's ruling) to say, "I'm not going to stand by and let those niggers take over this school."[14]

The School Committee could have addressed the problems in black schools by working to improve them because the goal of parents and students had been better education, not desegregation. But every proposal had been rejected. For example, as time for a peaceful solution was running out, the School Committee briefly considered busing black children out of three overcrowded schools, but white opposition to any integration resulted in a plan to buy and renovate an abandoned Hebrew school instead, providing more evidence of illegal actions to promote discrimination that would come back to haunt the School Committee. By the 1972 school year, Boston had seventy-five imbalanced schools.

The School Committee's strategy was three pronged: overturn the Racial Imbalance Law, stall solutions, and deny problems. So the Committee began open warfare with the state when it tried to force the city to desegregate. It might have integrated new schools such as the Lee, built in what was once a mixed part of Dorchester with state money that had only been granted with the promise of a multiracial student body. But it opened as the neighborhood became mostly black and the School Committee balked at redrawing attendance boundaries to include white students. This was another critical act; federal courts had held that adopting and then repealing integration plans constituted de jure segregation. So by this action alone, the School Committee had made busing inevitable. Moderates on the committee such as James Hennigan warned that they were increasingly vulnerable to a court challenge, but the vehemently racist majority ignored them. No one knew it in 1972, but busing was impossible to avoid.

Only after trying every other path to remedy the problems in the public schools did black parents go to court. Their lawsuit, filed on March 15, 1972, was called Morgan vs. Hennigan after a black mother of three and the School Committee president. The case was assigned to Arthur Garrity, who if not for this case might have ended up with an anonymous, yet respected, judicial career. Garrity came from an Irish Catholic family from Worcester. His father was also a lawyer and had been a member of the NAACP in the 1940s and 1950s. A graduate of Holy Cross and Harvard Law School, the younger Garrity was known for his intense self-discipline and strict sentencing.

As the case slowly went through the courts, the School Committee continued to stall for time. Other politicians sought solutions, but these were either ineffective or rejected by the School Committee. Running for reelection in 1974, for example, Governor Sargent suggested leaving white students at their current schools while busing black children to newly built magnet schools on the edge of the city. His proposal was ignored. Meanwhile, because the School Committee did not want any integrated schools even as the number of black students increased, it had to redraw assignment boundaries to keep the races separate – more de jure actions.

Waiting for the judge's decision in 1974, the atmosphere was tense as predictions regarding the judge's verdict varied greatly. Would the plaintiffs prevail and force a busing plan rabidly opposed by whites? Or was the School Committee justified in their optimism that they had beat back the forces of change? If they lost, how would Boston's black community react? If the judge sided with the plaintiffs, what would white neighborhoods do?

On June 21, 1974, Garrity ruled that the Boston School Committee had willfully and unlawfully segregated the city's schools through its actions over the previous several decades. His decision rested on the differences between de facto segregation, caused by historic housing problems, and de jure segregation, the result of race-based public policies. Multiple courts had ruled that de facto segregation was not actionable, so if the problem had simply been segregation in the Boston housing market, there would have been no legal authority for Garrity to require it be remedied and he could not have ordered any busing. But Boston's plaintiffs successfully argued that the School Committee had created the segregated system and therefore de jure segregation existed. By this finding, Garrity's hands were tied, he had to order busing and other dramatic measures to integrate the schools. There were no other possible solutions and no realistic way to slow his order.

Betrayed by the pandering of their elected leaders who had committed illegal acts on their behalf, Boston's white parents had no way to overturn the ruling because for an appeals court to have done so would have invalidated all civil rights litigation since 1954.[15] Garrity based his findings on the history of actions of the School Committee, and his reasoning and proposed remedies were well centered on how federal law had evolved to address government-mandated segregation. In this sense, his orders were conservative.

Yet up to the ruling, most white ethnic Bostonians believed that busing would never happen. In part this was because their elected officials told them it would never come to pass. But just as important, the people in the neighborhoods had convinced themselves that the current race-based policies could continue forever. They knew that schools were segregated because they demanded it. But their hold on the schools was thought to be strong enough to stop any attempt at integration, no matter how small. Even after the judge's ruling many thought that the city might avoid desegregation or implement it on its own terms and schedule, but the time for compromise, long ignored by pro-segregationists, was over. The busing order shocked the city. City-wide phase one desegregation was to begin in three months.[16]

Some whites held out hope that busing might be pushed off to later years, but Garrity was against delaying implementation of desegregation because he feared it would give the opposition more time to work against it, and he was sympathetic to the black complaints of twenty years of stalling and delays. There was only one plan for integration at the time, developed by the State Board of Education in response to state court orders. It was flawed and it would have been much better if the School Committee had developed its own plan, but it refused. So Garrity was forced to use it as a basis for a court ordered plan.

During the summer of 1974, there were regular meetings at City Hall to discuss busing and how to deal with potential violence. In Roxbury, frantic parents called Freedom House to ask how they might protect their children, while in South Boston and other white neighborhoods opposition increased over the summer and a systematic plan of resistance was put in place. The School Committee provided only minimal cooperation, refusing to do much beyond mounting failed appeals to higher courts. Nearly everyone feared that busing would tear the city apart.

As the city prepared for the start of school, tensions were high. About 18,000 out of the citywide total of 80,000 students would be bused and opponents gasped at the numbers, vowing protests. On September 1, Cardinal Medeiros announced that he would not allow the city's Catholic schools to accept students leaving to avoid integration and many Boston Catholics felt betrayed – many never forgave the Cardinal. On September 7, a large motorcade paraded through South Boston protesting busing. The next day, a smaller group of cars drove by Judge Garrity's Wellesley home to protest there. Then, in what was the first sign of the violence to come, on September 9 a crowd of antibusing protestors attacked Senator Edward Kennedy when he tried to address a rally outside Boston City Hall. They screamed insults and chased him across Government Center Plaza into the federal building named after his late brother, President John F. Kennedy.

Classes began on September 12 with 80 of the city's 200 schools included in busing. As the day opened, Louise Day Hicks pleaded for peace even as she defended parents who were keeping their children home out of protest.[17] At first it seemed that the city might have accepted desegregation. Schoolwide attendance was at about 65 percent, though it was lower at South Boston and Roxbury High School, and most schools opened without incident. But then, in South Boston, a crowd of 200 or more attacked the buses, throwing rocks and chanting racial slurs as 10 children were injured and several buses damaged. All across the United States, the violence was the lead story on the nightly news. Boston's reputation would never recover.

Even after forty years, the violence of the antibusing protests is jarring: enraged crowds attacking buses filled with scared children and adults, crying children covered in blood, flying rocks and bottles, police lines walking in lock step down streets to clear out rioters, and adults and adolescents screaming racial epitaphs and calling for more violence. Centered that first year in South Boston, violence and hatred were in the air across the city: Hyde Park, Roxbury, Dorchester and other neighborhoods saw an almost complete breakdown in social order, sometimes for days at a time.

Despite pleas for peace by elected officials and clergy, white ethnics in the city erupted in fury. Draconian policing at one point included a squad of policemen beating up the patrons of a Southie bar, yet the support by Garrity and the courts for busing was unflinching. Though some of the violence inside the schools was spontaneous or the result of black frustration and retaliation, most of it was orchestrated by adult and student members of the anti-busing forces who used it as a means to advance their protests and keep other students from attending class. Fights were instigated whenever attendance began to approach normal levels, and on December 6, 1974, for example, adults from the South Boston Information Center entered the high school to "incite a frenzied rally of white students."[14]

The public face of antibusing was the group Restore Our Alienated Rights (ROAR) organized by Hicks, several months before Garrity's ruling, under the name Save Boston Committee. With the initial goal to overturn the Racial Imbalance Act, ROAR's first chairperson was male. But it was mostly made up of women activists who borrowed their tactics from the antiwar and civil rights movements. "Self-proclaimed 'conservatives,' the ROAR women used radical strategies to maintain what they saw as 'traditional' maternal values."[18] One boost for the antibusing movement was the sense that whites were being pushed out of the city by rising rents, gentrification, and the growing minority population. It reflected a community that was put upon by more than just busing. In any case, ROAR was very powerful. It turned out 20,000 protestors against the Racial Imbalance Act on April 3, 1974.

One theme underlying this opposition was a nostalgia for an earlier time, perhaps the 1940s or 1950s, when there was a satisfying social order: the Irish controlled the city, the respect and authority of the Catholic Church was absolute, and everything was understood as immutable. That's how many looked back to the calm neighborhoods just before and after World War II – as a golden era. Then the protests against the Vietnam War and marches for racial justice shattered this peace. The downward spiral of the Boston economy was apparent to all, and the old ways–playing sports at the local high school, using family and political connections to secure a job with the city, a building trade, or a local utility, and affordable rents in the old neighborhood – were rapidly disappearing. This rear guard action for the past, much more than any class-based causes of the antibusing crisis that some have suggested, may have been what sparked the racial animus that drove the opposition to busing.

White Boston was not monolithically opposed to busing. Most liberals supported it, as did many poorer whites. Many were against it but complied with the court order. Others were frightened by the violence into keeping their children home as they were intimidated by the vehemence of the anti-busing forces. Many joined parents' councils or quietly tried to find a way to accommodate busing even as the city was consumed by bloody anger. A 1975 poll of Boston residents found that 87 percent opposed the anti-busing violence, just 10 percent approved of it.[14]

As they fought the busing order, whites suggested alternatives that were unworkable. For example, some proposed to extend busing to the suburbs. But the Supreme Court had ruled against large scale geographic busing and there had been no finding of de jure segregation against suburban towns that would put them within reach of Garrity's power. Others suggested that black students should all be bused to the suburbs in a massive expansion of METCO, but a program that bused only one race of children would have been patently illegal. Many called for delays, but this ignored the twenty-year struggle that preceded the filing of the lawsuit. The forces segregating the schools had run out of options.

Some of the protestors repeatedly complained that Roxbury was unsafe and they cited the horrific murder of Evelyn Wagler, age 24, who had just moved into an apartment in Roxbury in 1973. Having run out of gas, she was walking back to her car with a can of gasoline for the station near Grove Hall when she was attacked by a group of youth who beat her and set her on fire.[19] But most white residents had never been to Roxbury and had no idea of the racism, economic redlining, and the city's race-based withholding of city services that had created the ghetto.[20]

As the people against integration had no viable alternative to busing, their strategy was to create so much noise and chaos that Garrity and the pro-integration people would surrender and let things return to the old ways. What they failed to understand was that despite his Wellesley manners, Garrity really was just like them, and when confronted by opposition, he would not back down or change tactics. He was tough and determined so that the more Southie and other white neighborhoods howled, the more adamant he became to force his will on them.[21] Furthermore, there was an immense outside power that doomed the busing protests: the public in the rest of the country. By this point, much of the United States was unsympathetic to the civil rights movement, but it was even more against the blatant racism of the segregation of Boston's schools and found the protestors embarrassing and wrong. While some politicians voiced sympathy to white complaints, no mainstream office holder would dare overturn the court order even if they could.

Still the protestors held out hope. For much of the fall of 1974, mothers held prayer vigils outside South Boston High School as the maelstrom swirled inside the school and throughout the neighborhoods. Then, the stabbing of a white student by a black student at South Boston High on December 11 marked a turning point for Hicks. White students walked out to join a growing mob outside the school while black students huddled in the back classrooms as authorities tried to formulate a plan to get them out safely. Hicks pleaded with the crowd to let the students go, asking them to believe in her, but the crowd had grown angry, shouting racial epithets, and calling for blood. It took four hours to get the students out. The police used decoy buses at the front of the building to attract the demonstrators while 125 scared students were sneaked out to buses in the back of the school. Hicks was shocked and began to distance herself from the protests.

In her place, Pixie Palladino of East Boston began to lead the anti-busing forces. The shift from Hicks to Palladino reinforced the take-over of the antibusing movement by working-class women as Palladino was the daughter of a shoemaker. In contrast to Hicks, Palladino did not shy from rough tactics. She was rumored to have punched Senator Kennedy and cursed a priest who was not allied with her cause.[18] She talked about her dislike of niggers in front of Melnea Cass and the Reverend Michael Haynes of the Twelfth Baptist Church, prompting Ellen Jackson and other black leaders to walk out of a peace meeting arranged by Mayor White.[22] The antibusing activists wanted no com-promises.

As events spiraled around him, White concentrated on reviving the city. But the federally-funded urban renewal program collapsed in the early 1970s. Part of its demise took place on the national level: as city after city erupted in protests against displacement, political support in Washington faded. In Boston, the faults of Logue's and Collins's pro-gram created additional problems. The federal government challenged their local financing strategy at a time Boston had no other resources to commit to paying for its local match, individual project components were so delayed that it appeared that they would never be completed, and the entire program was hated by the voters. Kevin White soon realized that rather than force an ineffective program on residents, he could turn his attention to downtown, which had the space for new projects he could push forward without provoking opposition. Urban renewal petered out. It never formally ended, however. Even in 2016 the BRA voted to extend the program for another seven years.

White had two brilliant ideas that would eventually help solve Boston's long saga of troubled finances. In his early years as mayor, White convinced the legislature to assume the city's welfare costs as part of a deal to help a legislative leader make the jump to statewide office. This saved the city millions of dollars annually. Then he helped pass a referendum to allow city property taxes to be at a higher rate for commercial than for residential properties. Though many of the

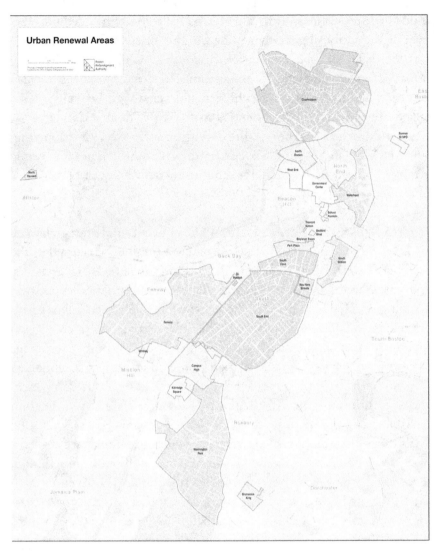

Urban Renewal Zones. Adopted in the 1950s and 1960s, most of these projects were still legally in effect in 2015.

new office building received decades long tax breaks, such as had been granted to the Prudential Center, as these began to expire in the 1980s tax revenues would grow and the city would become solvent in the 1990s.

Though his ambitions for higher office were now impossible, White survived busing for three reasons: it was perceived as a school committee problem and the mayor had no control over the schools, anger was directed against Judge Garrity and not at White, and the mayor focused his busing related actions on ensuring the safety of children. He was the calm at the center of a horrific storm.

Another dramatic success was White's success in promoting new office development downtown. No one dared build anything in Boston in the Kevin White years without first seeking the approval of the mayor, and unless he supported the development, it would never get vital zoning variance approval nor the tax breaks necessary to keep rents competitive with other buildings. This made White's control over building absolute, and the mayor reveled in his power. Almost intoxicated by the adulation of developers seeking his support, White presided over a dramatic change in the city's skyline.

The Custom House tower had opened in 1915 with the next tall building, the Old Hancock Tower, not constructed until 1947. Despite progrowth policies, no new significant towers opened during the Hynes administration while Collins and Logue successfully oversaw just two: the Prudential Center and a new building for State Street Bank. But White shepherded the construction of millions of square feet of new building. In his first term these included new towers for the Bank of Boston, New England Merchants Bank, the Boston Company, and significant buildings at One Beacon Street and elsewhere downtown. In his second term there was a new building for Shawmut Bank and other towers were approved. Thousands of employees were now downtown, and from the outside at least, the dramatic height of the new buildings made the city look prosperous.

White didn't get everything he wanted. The State put a stop to the controversial Park Plaza project proposed by Mortimer Zuckerman, for example. The project would have included a group of high rises and a hotel, but preservationists and environmentalists feared it would cast shadows in the Public Garden and Common and vigorously opposed it. White lost the battle but won substantial support from labor unions and developers.

For most people in the city, however, there was no prosperity. Adding to the decline, the city's navy yards shut down. After President Nixon closed the Charlestown Navy Yard in 1974 in retaliation for the state being the only one not to vote for him in his 1972 landslide victory over George McGovern, the federal government sold the 133 acre site to the city for $1.[23] The yard, once vibrant with thousands of jobs, was vacant for over a decade. Elsewhere, manufacturing continued to move to the suburbs and traditional employers of low-skilled city residents shut down or transferred operations to lower cost areas. Few of the jobs in the new office buildings went to longtime city residents, black or white; most were taken by suburban commuters. Construction jobs were mostly going to white men from outside the city and there was little financial gain to the city from these buildings after White granted them deep reductions in property tax payments. It was almost as if the prosperity of downtown taunted the deepening economic problems in the neighborhoods.

As a result, there continued to be fiscal problems as the city's budget position deteriorated. In 1971 Boston ran a $27 million deficit while annual debt service costs more than doubled to $35 million as White added more than a thousand new positions to his own departments. Though total property tax revenues climbed by 60 percent during the first White term, uncollected property taxes reached $58 million, and the city was forced to borrow $180 million to cover short term shortfalls. State aid, though it had increased, failed to close the deficit, and many city departments were hemorrhaging money including the schools, water and sewer, and health and hospitals. As a result, the city was forced to cut employees and expenditures for most of White's second term. Yet the cuts were insufficient to achieve fiscal health, and as the city closed the books on fiscal year 1975, it was unable to pay back its short term borrowing for the first time since the Depression.[24]

White couldn't solve the city's housing problems either. Even in 1972, 20 percent of the city's housing stock was substandard. Part of the problem was that production didn't keep pace with demolition. Despite the construction of 17,000 new units in the 1960s, the city had a net loss of 6,000. Yet unaffordability problems increased. As a result of inflation and demand pressures, median rents rose from $60 to $99 and median home values went from $13,500 to $19,500 during the decade. Those who had the greatest problem with affordability were the elderly and young families.

Compounding the problem was the lack of effective code enforcement. Between 1960 and 1968, 20 percent of Jamaica Plain's housing stock slid into the deteriorated or dilapidated category. Yet the city did little to enforce its codes, only five cases had been taken to court in the 1960s. Unafraid of city action, landlords let their properties decline and conditions for many residents became unsafe and unhealthy.[25]

One interesting experiment of the White Administration was the establishment of an adult entertainment district, the Combat Zone, to contain the spread of strip clubs and stores selling pornography. The beginnings of the adult entertainment district date to the decline of large 1920s-style movie palaces in Boston and other cities in the 1950s. With the advent of television, these large venues were obsolete and many were converted to other uses or abandoned. The problem was greater here because the city had begun its land takings and demolitions in Scollay Square, Boston's traditional home of seedy bars, brothels, and other adult-related entertainment. The area along Washington Street had already been named the Combat Zone after a series of teenage gang fights on those blocks back in the 1940s. Then in the 1960s, courts ruled that sexually-related films, magazines, and books were protected free speech. Boston could no longer simply shut down any establishmentopenly selling such merchandise.

The Combat Zone in the 1970s. Though it kept adult businesses out of other neighborhoods, it attracted crime.

The city, hoping to keep pornographic businesses from opening in the neighborhoods, created a special zoning district to accommodate them. The era of the notorious Combat Zone began when Mayor White decided it was better to concentrate the open prostitution and dirty book stores there rather than have to deal with them across the city.[26]

There was opposition. The head of the city's vice squad lamented that Boston would soon be a "mecca of pornography" and predicted shows featuring bestiality and all other vices known to humanity. Club owners, however, welcomed the new zoning, even paying a public relations woman to promote the zone at neighborhood meetings and Rotary clubs. The BRA hired an employee to help design signage for the bars.

As feared and predicted, vice flourished as prostitutes and their pimps roamed the streets and the bars. Drink prices skyrocketed to $10 each as nude dancers entertained clients. Men frequented the dirty movie stalls and theaters while crime skyrocketed. Some bars had back rooms for women to turn tricks, others employed young women to hustle customers into buying them $100 bottles of champagne or charging anything else to a willing customer's credit card. Many of the customers were affluent suburban men willing and able to spend $60 to $100 for a few minutes of a woman's time.

Other cities expressed interest in following Boston's lead but none did. Still, the idea worked in that Boston was unique in keeping such establishments out of the neighborhoods. But the experiment did not last. The liberal police chief left for another job and his replacement was not as willing to relax enforcement. Then it turned out that the bars relied heavily on corruption and bribes to keep in business while the public was appalled at the conditions in this small area wedged between downtown and Chinatown. The final blow was a series of highly publicized deaths. One involved a Harvard football player who was knifed and killed after confronting the pimp of a woman who had stolen his wallet. Another was a fatal heart attack of a state trooper out for a good time. The third was a high school student working as a prostitute, murdered by a john. The conservative district attorney, Garret Byrne, used these deaths to order a crackdown on the neighborhood.[27] Yet the porn shops and tawdry bars would blight the area for decades, annoying and hemming in adjacent Chinatown and posing a barrier between downtown and South Cove. The last adult businesses on Washington Street lasted until around 2000 when a new wave of condominium development pushed them out, though there was at least one strip club on a side street in 2015.

Even before the Stonewall riots marked the beginning of the LGBT civil rights movement, conditions in Boston for many gays and lesbians had markedly improved in some ways. The police harassment of bars faded in the mid-1960s. Speculatively, this was most likely not the result of new tolerance but rather the result of what was going on in the streets of Boston: antiwar rallies in the Common, civil rights protests in Roxbury and Beacon Hill, and meltdowns over urban renewal in neighborhoods across the city. The police probably lacked the manpower to raid bars.

As a result, there was a burst of nightlife around Park Square with venues that included Jacques, the Punchbowl, and 9 Carver Street. After the bars closed, many went to the nearby Hayes Bickford restaurant, the Gay Hayes they called it. Some of the bars were upscale and required men to wear coats and ties. Others were more relaxed and became renowned for their backrooms. It was at this time that the iconic Silvia Sydney first took to the stage. One of Boston's most loved and revered drag queens, she became known for her tart mouth, fierce style, and longstanding commitment to advancing civil rights for all LGBT people. For a time, the conformists and the separatists were united.

Many were dissatisfied with the culture that revolved around bars and alcohol, however. One alternative was the Daughters of Bilitis (Bilitis was a fictional poet in Pierre Louys' "The Song of Bilitis"). The organization was founded in San Francisco in 1955 by eight women who wanted to create a club that would provide lesbians an opportunity to socialize outside of bars. The Boston chapter started in 1969 and became independent the next year. The group provided a safe place for women where they did not need to fear hostile bar owners, rogue policemen, or others who treated them as exotic animals in a zoo. The Boston group sponsored educational forums, pot luck dinners, and dances in church halls.

The early 1970s also saw random violence against LGBT people across the city. While most gay men and lesbians could safely go out at any time, no one was ever certain there might not be a sudden attack whether from a bar owner, bouncer, policeman, or random stranger. Fighting back, LGBT people mobilized to pressure Kevin White to rein in the police, and the relationships with bar owners were strained. Women could be attacked inside and out of bars, men were stabbed in the Fenway or on the Esplanade. But as more people came out, the community grew, and at some point, the gay community began to move westward into Back Bay, Bay Village, and the South End. Summer cruising was popular on the Esplanade and the Fens while there were cinemas and bathhouses catering to the adventurous.

In the early 1970s there were no protections for LGBT people from discrimination in mortgage lending, housing, employment or any of the other facets of modern living that straights took as basic rights. Even same sex relations were criminalized. Meanwhile, the remains of Don't Ask Don't Tell still rang strong in some sectors of Boston. The police did not raid bars anymore, but if they showed up to break up a fight, they might easily arrest everyone within sight, not caring who was involved and who might be a bystander. Many men and women were not out to their families, fewer still could risk their employers finding out. There were no legal protections, and the sodomy laws remained on the books. People were disowned, disinherited, fired, or shunned if the word of their sexuality leaked out. Even going to a doctor could be a problem; the medical profession considered homosexuality to be an illness. In April 1972, the Daughters of Bilitis tied to run an ad in the Boston Globe for DOB's Focus magazine. But its check was returned as the paper, "did not care to publish this advertising."[28] Facing pressure, the Globe finally ran the ad in July.

Despite the commonality of interests, the community continued to be split. At the 1977 rally following the pride march, for example, Charley Shively famously burned a bible on the Boston Common to protest religious persecution of LGBTs. Enraged, Brian McNaught and a gay Catholic group called Dignity rushed the stage. Sometimes gay men shunned lesbians while lesbians accused gay men of benefiting from a sexist society. Drag queens taunted closeted men while the latter avoided any contact with the former. Many Boston gay bars notoriously excluded people of color and radicals, and accomodationists accused each other of stalling progress. For the most part, however, the community was still below the radar of most straight Bostonians.

Another traumatic policy of the White administration was the expansion of a revamped Boston Banks Urban Renewal Group (BBURG) program in 1968 into Dorchester and Mattapan. By the late 1960s, Dorchester's Jewish community was in full retreat. Most left voluntarily while many who remained were terrified by the changes in the neighborhood. One particularly horrific incident was the acid in the face attack against Rabbi Gerald Zelermyer of Temple Beth Hillel, who was nearly blinded in one eye. Some residents, particular the elderly, stayed, but many were afraid to leave their houses.[29] The Roxbury-Dorchester Jewish population declined from 77,000 in 1930 to 70,000 in 1950. By 1960 there were 47,000, by 1970 there were 16,000, and but a few hundred by 1980.

The final annihilation of this Jewish neighborhood was caused by Kevin White and a group of Boston banks. As White looked to appease black demands for improved housing in the aftermath of the 1968 riots, he seized upon the small, unused BBURG program as a way to fund black homeownership. Calling together the many small financial institutions that granted mortgages, he convinced them to join a new expanded BBURG program that would make loans to black and Hispanic homebuyers.

There were two critical catches: all minority homebuyers needing a mortgage would have to use the BBURG program, and the program would only be available in a set of neighborhoods from the South End to Mattapan. Bankers, meeting with the city, put a map on a table and drew out a thick red line that purposely excluded many areas with affordable housing: South Boston, East Boston, white parts of Dorchester and Jamaica Plain, Hyde Park, and Roslindale. This meant that minority homebuyers were kept out of most of the city and that the remaining white owners in the few areas now open to blacks and Hispanics would face heavy pressure to sell and leave. Through this one program, White set the boundaries of Boston's ghettos until well after 2000 and destroyed what remained of the Jewish presence in Mattapan and Dorchester. The results could be seen in places such as Washington Street in Codman Square, Dorchester: nearly 100 percent black to the west and nearly 100 percent white to the east. Along Blue Hill

Avenue, whites fought to sell their properties to speculators, not caring how much they lost as they fled. Blacks and Hispanics found they had little bargaining power and overpaid for substandard housing as only speculators profited from this wrenching racial change. Within a few years, the program was abandoned amid charges of racial discrimination in mortgage lending. But the damage was done.[30]

The activism of the era had many positive legacies. One very important initiative took shape in 1969 at a group meeting at a women's liberation conference at Emmanuel College. The twelve women in the gathering ranged in age from 23 to 39, and exchanging information, they realized they had had similar experiences when interacting with doctors. Often their healthcare providers had been brusque, uninformed, or hostile to their health needs.[31] For example, one woman had asked her doctor what was in the birth control pill he had just recommended to her only to be told, "Don't worry your pretty little head." That she was putting powerful drugs into her body was not considered.

Many of these women have been active in social justice efforts and in the antiwar movement. For example, one women first heard about women's rights at a rally opposing Nixon's inauguration in 1969. They were often working class, some were the first in their families to attend college, and some were new to the idea that they could speak up.

The women conducted extensive research. At the time, medical journals were only available in special libraries off-limits to the public. These women took the time to read the literature and then they wrote their analysis of the information they gathered in laypersons terms with the goal of educating themselves on topics that they had not previously been allowed to understand. Seeking to inform other women about what they had learned, the group published a pamphlet in 1971 and a book in 1973. The world famous Our Bodies Our Selves was born and the idea that individuals, women, men, the young, and the old–anyone–should have a say in their healthcare began to propagate across the country.

> We were a group that challenged the role of experts, especially male experts who set themselves up as experts on women. In the medical literature, we were outraged to

read, "women are passive, narcissistic, and masochistic." Our motto, "Women are the best experts on ourselves," was an important theme of the book. That can-do philosophy shaped our approach to the research we did for the course and later, the book. We each chose chapters that particularly interested us and wrote from a laywoman's perspective, turning to our few allies in the medical profession to help us gain access to medical journals, steer us to useful resources, and read drafts of our chapters for medical accuracy. We also collected and shared information on doctors, for women seeking referrals.[32]

From this small beginning, Our Bodies Our Selves would continue for the next forty-five years, empowering women, changing how people interacted with doctors, and redefining the relationship between experts and lay people.

In the context of a city ripping itself apart over race, turf, and busing, White decided to run for reelection for an unprecedented third term in a row. Hicks, exhausted from busing and two unsuccessful races against White, declined to try a third time. The main challenger was Joseph Timilty. In Timilty's eyes, the election of 1975 was about whether Boston would be able to keep its middle class or whether it would be overwhelmed by upper-class new comers. In this view, White was not a son of Irish politicians but a Beacon Hill Brahmin. But Timilty lacked a vision for what he would do for the city, and he failed to reach out to low-income whites or minorities. It was either side with White and look toward the future, or back Timilty and do what, exactly? Another problem was that Timilty was boxed in by the city's racial turmoil. He was personally opposed to busing, three of his children were sent out of his Dorchester neighborhood each morning, but he couldn't speak out against it without being tarred with the sentiments of Hicks and the antibusing protestors. In the twisted logic of the issue created by opponents, to be antibusing was seen as approving the rock throwing and the hatred. If he had been more forceful on the issue, Timilty would have picked up a few more votes in South Boston and Charlestown, but he would have lost just as many elsewhere in the city.

Despite Timilty's clumsiness, White almost lost the election. Between the busing crisis, a series of small but important scandals, and a strange reluctance to campaign – White skipped a Back Bay house party to go to the movies by himself–Timilty slowly edged up in the polls. In the end, White beat Timilty by four percentage points. Gerard O'Neill, author of a book on Boston politics, credits a last-minute slur by Police Commissioner DeGrazia that tied Timilty to unnamed bookies and corrupt cops. Black political analysists suggest it was White's well-oiled machine that pulled in the votes.[33] Longtime journalist Alan Lupo believed it was White's careful piloting of the city during the busing crisis that rewarded him the election. But whatever the cause, White won an unprecedented third term.

1.   Saxenian A. *Regional Advantage.* Cambridge, MA: Harvard University Press, 1994.
2.   O'Neill G. *Rogues and Redeemers: When Politics was King in Irish Boston.* New York: Crown Publishing Group, 2012.
3.   Gillis DA. *The sociology of a city in transition: Boston 1980 – 2000.* Doctoral Thesis, Boston University, 2015.
4.   Lopez R. Boston's *South End: The Clash of Ideas in a Historic Neighborhood.* Boston: Shawmut Peninsula Press, 2015.
5.   South End Project Action Committee. *Special Housing Committee Report.* 1975.
6.   Lukas A. *Common Ground: A Turbulent Decade in the Lives of Three American Families.* New York: Vintage Books, 1986.
7.   Small M. *Villa Victoria: The Transformation of Social Capital in a Boston.* Chicago: University of Chicago Press, 2004.
8.   Vrable J. *People's History of the New Boston.* Amherst, MA: University of Massachusetts Press, 2014.
9.   King M. *Chain of Change: Struggles for Black Community Development.* Boston MA: South End Press, 1981.
10. Tager J. *Boston Riots: Three Centuries of Social Violence.* Boston: Northeastern University Press, 2001.
11. Bouvier L and Krone M. A History of Gay Pride. *Boston Pride Guide 2015.* 2015
12. Uriarte-Gaston M. *Organizing for survival: The emergence of a Puerto Rican community.* Dissertation, Boston University, 1988.
13. Morgan JH. Ethnoconsciousness and political powerlessness: Boston's Irish. *Social Science* 1978; 53: 159-67.
14. Lupo A. *Liberty's Chosen Home: The Politics of Violence in Boston.* Boston: Beacon Press, 1977.
15. Motti TL. *Social conflict and social movements: An explanatory study of the black com-*

munity of Boston attempting to change the Boston public schools. Dissertation, Brandeis University, 1975.

16. Formisano RP. *Boston Against Busing: Race, Class, and Ethnicity in the 1960s and 1970s.* Chapel Hill, NC: University of North Carolina Press, 1991.

17. Jordan R. Hicks pleads for peace on first day of school. *Boston Globe.* September 12, 1974; p. 1.

18. Nutter KB. "Militant Mothers": Boston, Busing, and the Bicentennial of 1976. *Historical Journal of Massachusetts.* 2010; 38: 52-75.

19. Taylor B. White offers $5000 reward in Wagler case. *Boston Globe.* October 5, 1973; p. 1.

20. O'Connor T. *South Boston: My Home Town.* Boston: Quinan Press, 1988.

21. Unseem B. Models of the Boston anti-busing movement: Polity/mobilization and relative deprivation. *The Sociological Quarterly.* 1981; 22: 263-74.

22. Jackson E. Eyes on the Prize II Interviews. *Washington University Digital Gateway Texts.* 1989.

23. Kennedy L. *Planning the City Upon a Hill: Boston Since 1630.* Boston: University of Massachusetts Press, 1994.

24. Slavet JS and Torto RG. *Boston's Recurring Crises: Three Decades of Fiscal Policy.* Boston: John M. McCormack Graduate School of Policy and Global Studies 1985.

25. Shanahan M. *Housing and the urban crisis: Selected community responses in eastern Massachusetts.* Dissertation, Case Western Reserve, 1983.

26. Stithem D. *Zoning pornography: A new solution to an old problem.* Dissertation, University of Wyoming, 1984.

27. Blumenthal S. *Cornering the Combat Zone.* Barrister. 1978; 5: 14-9.

28. Owen MG. Letter to King G. The History Project, 1973.

29. Shapiro L. Street violence seen threatening Jewish communities. *Boston Globe.* May 17, 1970; p. 11.

30. Levine H and Harmon L. *The Death of an American Jewish Community. A Tragedy of Good Intentions.* New York: The Free Press, 1992.

31. Our Bodies Our Selves. *History.* http://www.ourbodiesourselves.org/history/, 2015.

32. Ditzion J, Hawley NM, Doress-Worters P and Sanford W. *Formative Years: The Birth of Our Bodies Ourselves.* Symposium at Boston University, 2014.

33. Jennings J. Urban Machinism and the Black Voter: The Kevin White Years. In: Jennings J and King M, (eds.). *From Access to Power: Black Politics in Boston.* Cambridge, Massachusetts: Schenkman Books, 1986.

Chapter 5

The Rebound Begins: 1976-1983

THE PRECISE YEAR can be debated, but Boston reached its all-time nadir at some point in the late 1970s or early 1980s. To be sure, the seeds of its revival had been planted at least a decade before, but the fruits of new office buildings, medical research expansion, special events, and other contributors to the city's survival were a long way from being harvested in 1976. For most residents, the 1970s were trying times as housing continued to deteriorate, city services were cut to meet budget shortfalls, and political and social turmoil continued to grip the neighborhoods. It was at this point that the Brookings Institute, a private national research organization, conducted a ranking of large United States cities measuring them on population loss, fiscal problems, economics, and social issues. In this study, Boston was rated as one of the most distressed cities in the country, lower than Detroit, St. Louis, and other troubled older cities.[1] Boston continued to stand out as a national problem.

The city's population reached a low point in the 1980 census at 562,994. In the 1970s, Boston's white population fell by almost 140,000, as the total population under 18 dropped by over 50,000. Though whites were still a majority, its non-white population grew by over 40,000. However, indicative of the economic forces beginning to transform the city, the number of people over the age of 24 with 4 or more years of college almost doubled in the 1970s to 67,073 while the number without a high school education fell by 17,000 to 37,824. Underneath the surface, the city was changing.

The mid-1970s saw the beginning of a new fiscal crisis in the city. Mayor White spent heavily to deliver services and jobs in the run up to the 1975 election and, along with costs associated with the busing crisis, fiscal year 1976 saw expenses to be $70 million more than projected. In addition, White had committed $108 million more for building new schools. But in 1975, tight monetary policies prompted a national credit freeze, meaning that the city could not borrow to meet short-term obligations or fund long-term needs, and as Boston's fiscal morass deepened, some businessmen wanted the city to declare bankruptcy. The crisis was solved by a program of budget cuts, increased taxes, and borrowing, but the city had no fiscal reserves should there be a new budget emergency.[2] No one knew it at the time, but a far worse fiscal storm was about to strike.

Meanwhile, busing related violence continued to rock the city, reaching a horrendous peak when Ted Landsmark, then a young lawyer working for a group of minority contractors and who would later become a member of the BRA Board of Directors, was attacked by an angry mob on April 5, 1976; he was nearly speared to death by a youth lunging at him with an American flag. The Pulitzer Prize-winning picture of a well-dressed black man being attacked by a white mob cemented Boston's reputation as a racist city that still harms it to this day. It was the saddest of weeks:

> A tapestry of racial violence became one city's image: a black man assaulted in City Hall Plaza; two black bus drivers assaulted in the predawn hours in South Boston; a 17-year-old white girl stoned by black youths; a 28-year-old black woman and her 5-year-old son attacked by baseball bat-wielding white youths; firemen attacked while answering calls; and numerous other incidents of violence occurring every evening last week.[3]

At the same time, low-income residents across the city were under extreme pressure caused by gentrification, speculation, renewal clearances, arson, and abandonment. Though new development was creating jobs in the city, most of these required high levels of education while workers without a high school diploma, a substantial percentage of the workforce, were being squeezed out of Boston or even out of Massachusetts. And over all these problems governed a mayor, Kevin White, who fancied himself as a "loner in love with his city." Even as he was sworn in for his third term, it was becoming increasingly clear that the love affair was over on both sides. But it was a relationship too complicated to unwind.

Yet Boston did not die, and it did not succumb to the great urban crisis that hollowed out Cleveland, Baltimore, and other once great US cities. In the leafy neighborhoods on the edges of the city, middle-class whites stayed; they did not give up and move to the suburbs. Many poor whites, angered by busing and a new economic and social environment, left the city, but others remained and gave Boston one more chance. Blacks did not leave Boston in disgust, they stayed and continued to make the city their own. Gentrification in the South End and other inner core neighborhoods might be causing great hardship to those who lacked the means to pay higher housing costs, but it also represented a new vitality that energized the city. Gay men, lesbians, entrepreneurs, young people, and older households with wealth wanted to be in the middle of the city, and their affluence attracted others who were less venturesome but equally spirited. Other neighborhoods found new residents as Boston became known as a magnate for immigrants from Latin America, Haiti, and Asia. Boston was becoming more diverse, and less equal. Slowly, without notice, the city pulled itself together.

One factor that contributed to the rebirth of the city was the large-scale increase in employment in the financial services industry that finally began to grow again after decades of quiet decline. Much of this growth was the result of new products targeted to companies and individuals not served by the old trusts. Perhaps the greatest change was in the rise of mutual funds and individual retirement accounts that allowed middle-class households to save and invest. KEOGH plans were first established in 1962, Individual Retirement Accounts were authorized in 1974, and 401(k) plans were created in 1978, so that by 2000 about half the US labor force had some sort of personally-funded retirement account. To service these retirement savings plans, there was a tremendous demand for investment managers, accountants, customer service representatives, advertising and media specialists, and others in companies that took in billions of dollars from millions of investors. Many of these rapidly-growing mutual fund companies were located in Boston, including Fidelity Investments.

Boston still catered to the wealthy, but now they wanted aggressive management of their money. One of the new investment options of the well-to-do, venture capital funds, began quietly in Boston as business and education leaders sought to reverse the region's economic decline. One of the first of these firms was American Research and Development, founded in 1946. It had problems keeping its employees because it didn't compensate them adequately for the deals they were making, so many of its veterans founded their own firms, increasing the range of options available to wealthy investors. One of the most profitable of this early wave of investment was in a small company northwest of Boston: Digital Equipment Corporation (DEC). It received a critical sum of $70,000 from one early venture capital fund, and when DEC went public in 1968, the investment was valued at $355 million, setting off a rush of new money to these funds. Heavily reliant on Harvard and MIT graduates, these early efforts helped create a business model of early stage investment in return for equity.[4] Many of these new investment companies rented space in the office towers popping up in downtown Boston.

In 1974, federal law was changed to allow pension plans to invest in venture capital and limited equity deals. Along with favorable tax law changes in the 1980s, this promoted another explosion of money for private investment. Banks and insurance companies had once provided all the services needed to run pension plans, but changes in technology and lower costs resulted in a whole new infrastructure of independent investing, accounting, actuarial, and other services to assist them. These companies needed office space in central Boston.

Many investment funds used money raised from family trusts, endowments, and pension funds to invest in companies that were in various stages of development prior to going public. Given the changing nature of the national economy, this meant the funds tended to invest in high technology, medical services, or companies that were attempting new market strategies, industries already clustering in the Boston area. In the early years, individual funds were small, but by the mid-1970s, they might approach a billion dollars in total investment capital. Through the 1980s, Boston firms were generally reluctant to fund startup companies, perhaps an additional reason the region lost its high tech leadership to San Jose, but Boston funds were major players in the leveraged buyout and merger trends that began in the 1980s and transformed the national economy.[4]

Cox Building, Roxbury in the 1970s. Connecting the growing prosperity of down-town to the neighborhoods proved difficult.

The prosperity of the new Boston economy did not reach the city's neighborhoods, and many continued to decay, causing abandonment and forcing some long-term Bostonians out of their communities. At the same time, residents in other neighborhoods were displaced by new-comers who could afford much higher housing costs, and developers responded by buying up older buildings and refurbishing them for this new demographic. These twin drivers of change—disinvestment and gentrification—were traumatic for many, and though some moved out of the city voluntarily, other residents were burnt out of their homes. Arson became a national problem with incidents increasing from 5,600 reported in 1951 to 177,000 in 1977. Locally, from 1978 to 1982, Boston reported 3,000 incendiary or suspicious fires. In 1981 and 1982, these resulted in $4.5 million in property losses and 60 deaths. Most of these were in Roxbury, North Dorchester, East Boston, and Jamaica Plain, areas either redlined by banks or undergoing gentrification. This was a problem of the private housing market, not the city's large number of subsidized and publicly-owned units. The fires were most likely to occur in absentee-owned buildings rather than in owner-occupied dwellings, and they almost never happened in public housing. Abandonment was particularly acute in absentee-owned properties in minority neighborhoods. Many burned buildings were empty or were one of many buildings owned by a single owner. This contributed to a housing shortage and affordability problem even as buildings were being abandoned.

There were two kinds of arson fires: escape fires used by property owners to collect insurance and vandal fires in buildings that were abandoned by their owners, often after they had been stripped of value by their owners. The arson problem in Boston in the 1970s and 1980s was not caused by pathological behavior or mental illness. It was the direct result of bank policies, insurance underwriting practices, organized crime, arsonists for hire, bad property owners, and corrupt politicians. Banks lent money to speculators for far more than the value of properties, and as a result, some burned buildings had three or four mortgages on them. These fires were more likely to occur after they were acquired by new owners post foreclosure rather than in what should have been the riskier pre foreclosure period. Similarly, many burned buildings were insured for far more than their purchase price, creating a large financial incentive to burn them. Arson was also used to force out tenants and circumvent anti-eviction laws.

Some of the worst arson fires occurred in the East Fens neighborhood. During its first wave of development beginning in the 1870s, the Fenway represented the height of middle-class stylish urban living. Important institutions including Symphony Hall, the Museum of Fine Arts, Fenway Park and many others moved into the area, and its luxe apartment buildings attracted the well to do. In the middle of it all snaked the Muddy River, conceived by Frederick Law Olmsted to be an essential link in the city's Emerald Necklace. But by the late 1960s, the park needed renovations, the river was polluted and neglected, and the neighborhood had fallen into decay. The Fenway's residents were mostly elderly and poor, many of them would soon be displaced by students flocking to the area's colleges and universities. To take advantage of this new demographic, some building owners torched their properties to evict tenants. Others just burned their buildings for the insurance money.

In 1973-74, the Symphony Road area of the Fenway had over twenty fires that killed five and left hundreds homeless. Eventually thirty-two people were convicted for their role in these fires "including six lawyers, four insurance adjusters, six landlords, two finance company officers, two bookkeepers, two housing contractors, three small businessmen, a city of Boston housing inspector, and two police officers." The anti-arson efforts were led by community representatives. They created the Symphony Tenants Organizing Project, investigated property owners, and held vigils to make city officials step up code enforcement. There were many people who contributed to these valiant efforts, but one of its leaders was David Scondras, a math instructor at Northeastern who would dedicate thousands of hours to working with residents to reclaim their neighborhood.[5]

One factor that helped pull the city through these dark years was a new type of neighborhood-based organization, the Community Development Corporation (CDC). CDCs had two main priorities: building housing and fostering economic development. Overall, they tended to be more successful with housing. The first wave of publicly-funded, low-income housing in the United States consisted of large projects built and managed by local housing authorities set up to comply with federal housing laws. This wave produced the large, often troubled, projects that dot large US cities and in Boston included Orchard Park and Mission Hill Extension. By 1960, due to opposition from neighbors and problems with the often-modernist architecture of many of the developments, there arose a new type of housing production: the federal government provided funds to redevelopment authorities to buy land for housing, often using the urban renewal program, and then provided deep subsidies for mortgage interest to developers to pay for construction. Rents were forecast to be sufficient to cover operating costs, mortgage expenses, and capital improvement while supporting an income stream for pools of private investors who contributed about 10 percent of the total development costs. Examples of housing constructed under this program include Academy Homes in Roxbury and Methunion Manor in the South End. Tragically, the financial forecasts for these developments were overwhelmingly optimistic, and almost every project in the country built using these programs failed and had to be reworked to save their low-income housing. Boston projects shared this fate, and just about every 221(d)3 development in the city would need substantial rebuilding and financial restructuring to survive. One positive result of this failed program was that there were now people who knew how to develop quality affordable housing, and many of these people worked in the city's CDCs.

They took advantage from another dramatic shift in housing policy. Recoiling from the failure of the 221(d)3 program in Boston and elsewhere, in the mid-1970s the federal government began to fund a new housing production mechanism for low-income households and the elderly known as Section 8. In general, this had two programs: subsidies tied to specific units and vouchers given to households that then used them in the private rental market. In Boston, the project-based subsidies were used to rescue failed 223(d)3 projects as well as fund the construction of new housing with most of the new development undertaken by CDCs. Over the following several decades, CDCs built or renovated thousands of units across the city. For the most part well-constructed, managed, and designed, these developments are assets to their neighborhoods. Among the examples of housing built by CDCs in Boston are Nuestra Communidad's Stafford Heights development and Madison Park Village.

CDCs have also developed over 400,000 feet of commercial space in Boston's neighborhoods in projects that have included office space, retail, social service support, and industrial facilities. There have been tensions. To attract financing, many projects needed strong, national tenants, but this conflicted with the goals of promoting local businesses and maximizing community benefits. In other places, new businesses were close to residential areas, and residents opposed the truck traffic and noise they sometimes attract.[6]

CDCs have helped revitalize Boston in several ways. The housing they created directly stabilized troubled areas and helped stop displacement, and in doing so have helped make the city affordable and diverse. They are important job generating institutions as they tend to hire neighborhood residents ranging from low-skilled maintenance jobs, to higher paying construction jobs, to college-educated planners, architects, finance specialists, and community organizers. CDCs are often the training ground for city and state employees.

In the spring of 1975, it looked like the preliminary Stage 2 of busing might blunt some of the most rabid opposition and even mark the beginning of a more moderate faction coming to the fore in the city, but the final plan increased the number of students bused and reinvigorated the militant opposition to any desegregation. Many students faced reassignment for a second time while neighborhoods that had not been part of the first year of busing, including Charlestown, now had their schools integrated with some of their children being assigned to other communities. As a result, violence deepened and spread across the city.

Trying everything it could to create chaos and force confrontations, in the new school year ROAR broadened its protests from the schools to public venues. Members disrupted a ceremony launching the International Women's Year, a reenactment of the Boston Massacre, and an Equal Rights Amendment rally. They held up banners at a Pops Concert in City Hall Plaza and challenged politicians at candidates nights and campaign rallies. At the same time, the violence in and around the schools continued. The first day of school in September 1975 opened peacefully, but attendance dropped to 52 percent. That night, there were sporadic incidents of violence across the city with Charlestown the center of unrest as gangs of young men roamed both that neighborhood and South Boston throwing rocks. Two firebombs were hurled at an elementary school.[7]

Some of the worst violence flared on February 15, 1976, as South Boston protestors battled police for two hours. The streets were eventually cleared with tear gas but not until there had been at least thirteen arrests and ten injuries. Antibusing sympathizers blamed the police, saying that the demonstrators had peacefully assembled at Andrew Square, but others reported that some of the protestors had sawed off hockey sticks and were drinking beer before the march began. Breaking a police line meant to keep the demonstration along its permitted route, "the protestors threw several bottles and rocks. Police scuffled to hold their ground. Then, outnumbered, the police stepped aside while the demonstrators, sensing victory, raced screaming and chanting up Dorchester Street."[8] Again, these scenes were broadcast across the country.

The worst effects of the violence and anger were felt by the students, both black and white. Many, particularly older high school students with fragile academic and attendance records before busing began, simply dropped out, and though most were eventually granted diplomas, their education was over. Others were hardened by the violence, learning hatred from their parents or the society around them, and the number who suffered from what would now be called post-traumatic stress syndrome was undoubtedly large. Forty years later, the bitterness remains.

Yet slowly the protests lost their impact, and the antibusing forces lost energy. One contributing factor to the demise of ROAR was Kevin White's political machine; the mayor did not tolerate any political force in the city that he did not control. Slowly bending ROAR to his will, he made back channel deals with Louise Day Hicks, selectively used patronage to control neighborhood leaders, and played up old rivalries between East and South Boston. Together with the growing realization that busing was here to stay, ROAR withered.

There was progress. Garrity eventually assumed almost total control over the schools and, as a result, he broke the power of the School Committee machine. For the first time, the schools hired teachers and administrators based on experience and education, not their ability to deliver contributions and votes. School employees become more diverse, and the buildings were modernized as they finally attracted federal and state support. Despite the chaos of the 1970s, the percentage of high school graduates seeking higher education increased. In 1960, only 25 percent went on to post-secondary education. In 1970 the percentage was 36 percent, in 1977 it was 44 percent, by 1982 it was 54 percent, reaching 66 percent in 1990.[9] Though many dropped out, those that remained reaped some benefits from the improvements in the schools once their management was wrestled away from the School

Committee.

The lasting effects of the busing crisis have been brutal, and almost every problem in the city since the 1970s has been blamed on it. The physical deterioration and social unraveling of the D Street projects in South Boston, for example, was attributed to busing and forced integration, though it's decline began in the 1960s when busing was still an impossibility.[10] Decades later, many blame busing for the setbacks Boston's lower income whites have suffered.[11] Lost in the many revisionist histories of this era, unfortunately, was that the goal of black parents had not been busing but improved educational opportunities for all students. If anything, the problems in the schools would have been even worse if the court had not intervened. There would have been no attempts to adapt to the changing demands of employers for a better-educated workforce, and the federal and state governments would have stopped all funding (the Boston School Department received about $125 million in state aid in 2015). Busing was a terrible tragedy. The alternatives could have been worse.

The schools were not the only city government function taken over by the courts in the 1970s. The BHA was placed into receivership as well. The impetus was the high numbers of vacant and substandard units in BHA projects. Just as with the schools, the court takeover only happened after years of unresolved conflict.

The BHA is one of the largest landlords in the country, owning over 17,000 units and leasing another 5,600 in 31 family developments, 38 elderly projects, and other scattered sites. Altogether, over 55,000 people lived in BHA housing including a quarter of the city's low-income households and almost 10 percent of the entire population of Boston. Housing authorities were originally authorized and funded based on forecasts that tenant rents would be sufficient to cover administration, maintenance, and capital improvement costs. But soon after the first housing developments were opened, it became clear that deep ongoing subsidies were necessary to keep the housing decent and affordable. Unfortunately, these subsidies were never funded to the extent they were needed.

The BHA had a board appointed by Boston's mayors who for decades used it to reward political supporters. Often, these employees were unqualified and some never showed up to their jobs. By the mid-1970s, nearly a quarter of the BHA's housing stock was vacant and uninhabitable, while many of the remaining occupied units were squalid, overrun by vermin, and falling apart. Tenants were angry. As Boston's economy declined and the private housing stock was squeezed by gentrification and abandonment, the need for its public housing became greater. But the BHA was on the brink of collapse; entire buildings were closed down as they were beyond habitability.

Residents of West Broadway were the first to sue the BHA over housing conditions, but their 1970 lawsuit in state court was dismissed. In 1974, residents filed suit in federal court, but they lost when the judge told the plaintiffs to use the Boston Housing Court, a state-run institution, to seek redress for poor conditions. Complaining that problems were system wide, in 1975 Armando Perez and eight others filed suit in Housing Court.

Judge Paul G. Garrity (no relation to Arthur Garrity, the judge in the busing case) ruled for the tenants in 1975 and issued a consent decree outlining in very detailed instructions what the BHA needed to do in order to improve conditions and have the suit dismissed. But by 1980, it was clear that the Authority was unwilling or unable to comply with the consent decree and the judge placed the Authority into receivership.[12] The judge dismissed the BHA Board of Directors and appointed a receiver to run the Authority. For the first time in decades, tenants in the projects had realistic hopes for the future of their housing.

By the latter half of the 1970s, gentrification and demographic upheaval began to spread outside Boston's core to parts of Jamaica Plain and Dorchester. The change was rapid. When famed journalist Alan Lupo wrote about the anti-highway movement in the 1960s and 1970s, he described Jamaica Plain as a quiet, white, working-class neighborhood where residents were employed in vital but low-paying jobs.[13] A decade later, Jamaica Plain was a neighborhood with well-off families near the pond, low-income Latinos around Centre Street and Egleston Square, and middle-class households sandwiched in between.

In another example of how preservation of the city's housing stock contributed to its revitalization, Jamaica Plain's homes consist of one, two, and three family brick or wood structures on small lots. Though there is little open space in the neighborhood itself, it is bordered by two of the city's most glorious parks: Jamaica Pond and Franklin Park. From its earliest settlement by Europeans, Jamaica Plain had fought to keep itself rural and out of the orbit of Boston. In 1851, it seceded from Roxbury and joined West Roxbury in one final effort to avoid development, but railroads and street cars attracted industry including breweries, tanneries, and manufacturers to the Stony Brook corridor as the area's great estates were subdivided and developed. Jamaica Plain was annexed by Boston in 1873.

Manufacturing declined in the 1950s as small concerns began to be replaced by national, and then multinational, companies. Many businesses shut down or transferred their operations to the suburbs or down south. As they left, so did the neighborhood's working-class families, and what Lupo had described as an oasis of stability began to rapidly change. Beginning in the 1960s, Latino immigrants began to settle in the area along Centre Street known as Hyde Square. Seeking to ease their acceptance into the neighborhood, several churches joined together to organize the Ecumenical Social Action Committee (ESAC). ESAC founded Oficina Hispana in 1973 and then helped launch two CDCs, Urban Edge and the Neighborhood Development Corporation of Jamaica Plain, later that decade. These organizations sought to keep old timers in the neighborhood and help the growing minority population, but the change in the neighborhood was relentless. By the 1980s, Jamaica Plain was rapidly gentrifying as those pushed out of Back Bay or who found the South End unaffordable moved into the neighborhood.[14]

Some owners may have been happy to take the higher offers on their properties, but many owners and renters must have suffered from the displacement as they left neighborhoods that had provided vital services and social connections and moved into other areas that were often more expensive and provided inferior accommodations.[15] By the mid-1980s, the transformation of Jamaica Plain was nearly complete, and its demographics paralleled the rising inequality of the city itself.

The turmoil over urban renewal, civil rights, the Viet Nam war, and busing traumatized many in the city, including Mayor White. His young progressive staff was now long gone and replaced by operatives selected for their ability to get him votes and campaign contributions. After 1975, Kevin White became an isolated man, disconnected from the working-class whites who never liked him and angry with liberals and minorities who he thought were insufficiently loyal to him. Yet he would win still another election in 1979 despite the troubles in Boston as his machine became legendary for its ability to get out the vote and control nearly every community organization. He also used his control over patronage jobs to tame Southie, Charlestown, and other areas plagued by antibusing violence. With working-class whites leaving the city, Joseph Timilty never had a chance in the 1979 rematch and lost by a landslide.

White thrived on meeting dignitaries from outside Boston as he boasted that he had created a "world class city." The trappings of office attracted him more than the minutia of governance, and though he rarely showed up at a community meeting, he spent lavishly on entertaining at the elegant city-owned Parkman House overlooking the Common. One of his most dramatic events in his final term in office was an elaborate dinner in tents in Copley Square where invited guests from around the globe celebrated the city's 350th anniversary in 1980. He also grandly hosted Pope John Paul II on a visit in 1979. On the outside looking in, residents grumbled.

Just as the city seemed to recover from the fiscal crisis of the mid-1970s, two additional budget shots hit Boston, setting the stage for a fiscal collapse. As he announced his budget for fiscal year 1977, White warned that property taxes would have to rise by $56 per thousand, an increase of 28 percent, while the Boston Municipal Research Bureau cautioned that taxes might have to go up another $50 per thousand the following year. Both were underestimates as the tax rate hit an all-time high of $278 per thousand in 1981, and there were fears that the city was facing a New York City-style bankruptcy as it was impossible to raise any more money from the property tax levy. Worse was about to come.

In 1979, the Supreme Judicial Court declared that Boston's old policy of taxing commercial property at a higher rate than residential property was unconstitutional, resulting in a dramatic drop in revenue and a large repayment to commercial property owners. Though voters had passed an initiative to restore these differential rates, the new law would not take effect for several years, choking revenue in the meantime. The city owed commercial property owners $156 million. But its fiscal troubles had not yet peaked.

The next year, voters approved a statewide property tax relief referendum called Proposition Two and a Half. This law limited the total tax levy to 2.5 percent of the total value of real and personal property in the city ($25 per thousand) and allowed the total annual levy to only increase by 2.5 percent plus 2.5 percent of the value of new construction. With its sky high property rate, Boston suffered an enormous cut to its property tax revenues.

The combined impact of lost revenues and the need to pay out millions of dollars to commercial property owners was devastating to the city. White was forced to lay off 3,400 employees including police and firefighters, close schools, and sell off parking garages and municipal buildings in what was one of the bleakest periods in Boston's history as the budget needed to be cut by another $75 million. Residents were furious, occupying fire and police stations scheduled to be shuttered, and there were demonstrations against reduced garbage service, closed parks and recreation centers, and other devastated municipal services. East Boston residents even blockaded the Sumner Tunnel in protest. The state tried to make up some of the losses, but the fiscal distress was statewide as it was coping with lost revenue caused by a recession.

Perhaps the most tragic consequence of the fiscal crisis was that a small group of laid off firefighters and policemen launched a wave of arson to persuade the city to rehire them. There were fires set on Thursday nights in Dorchester, Roxbury, and other poor neighborhoods, and each Friday morning, residents would wake up to the smell of still smoldering buildings in the blocks around them. Fires were set across Eastern Massachusetts, and authorities estimated the arsonists were responsible for 163 fires that injured 282 people and caused $22 million in damages.[16] One particularly serious fire was a blaze at a vacant army building in South Boston. Fourteen firefighters, including one with a pelvic fracture and one with fractured vertebra, were injured when the roof collapsed during the five-alarm fire.[17] Another victim of this arson ring was the office of Boston's *Gay Community News*. Though the Bromfield Street building it occupied was not near the other fires, the arsonists targeted it. Across the city, residents were terrified. As the city burned, schools were shut down and crime skyrocketed; Boston reached its low point.

Eventually, the budget was rescued by a combination of new revenue sources, spending cuts, and, at last, rising property tax revenues from a rejuvenated downtown. The federal government began a program of unrestricted grants to local government known as revenue sharing while the new state lottery also provided revenue to the city. The state continued to take over city functions, and White cut municipal employment. With severe budget cuts, new state aid, and the sale of Hynes Auditorium to the new Massachusetts Convention Center Authority, the city got through the crisis.[18]

Residents were angry with the deteriorating city services caused by the repeated budget crises and were dissatisfied with the nine at-large city council system created by referendum in 1949 at the behest of reformers and downtown business interests. Both minority and white voters felt that their interests were not being adequately represented while developers had too much power. So in 1981, a referendum passed that created a hybrid structure with nine district councilors and four at-large. This set off a scramble on how to draw the district lines and the lobbing was furious.

Given the geography of Boston and legal issues regarding equal district populations and minority voting rights, much of the potential map was set. East Boston and Allston-Brighton would get their own districts, for example, and there would be at least two minority districts created out of Roxbury and Mattapan. Much of the dispute was over how to treat the South End and Dorchester. Some minority advocates hoped to use the South End's precincts in combination with Roxbury and other areas to create a third minority district while South End residents wanted to be in a downtown district with Back Bay and the Fenway. But South Boston politicians saw the South End as an easy way to get up to the required population numbers that would also incorporate the fewest liberal voters into the conservative district.

The Dorchester dispute was the result of it being too large to be in just one district. The choices were to either split the neighborhood along its east-west axis or north-south axis. Both sides suggested that their method would be better at fighting segregation and better represent the neighborhood's interests.

In the end, the South End was attached to South Boston, angering the more progressive South End. Dorchester was split along its north-south axis allowing a strong minority district that encompasses Mattapan. For the most part, these districts have been maintained with only small changes to accommodate population shifts since they were first established. Every ten years, the battle for more minority representation is joined and lost.

The movement of higher income people into the city began in Beacon Hill and Back Bay, and by the 1980s, every core neighborhood potentially faced gentrification. In what would have surprised 1950s sociologists, who called it a slum, one neighborhood that was transformed was the North End. For over one hundred years, it had been one of Boston's poorest neighborhoods as it welcomed immigrants struggling with poverty and the difficulties of adapting to a new land. By the beginning of the twentieth century, it was almost exclusively Italian, and many outsiders were scared to visit the area. Urban planners wanted to demolish the entire neighborhood and replace it, but its density and complexity protected it even as the West End was bulldozed. Residents, seeing their neighbors displaced out of the city, fought city plans for renewal, forcing the BHA and BRA to leave them alone.

In 1950, three-quarters of the North End's housing stock lacked central heat while a similar percentage lacked full plumbing. But a few years later, the North End began to change as its population shifted from foreign-born to native-born Italian. As a result, incomes began to rise, and residents started to improve its housing causing its population density to drop as units were combined and households became smaller. In the 1960s, the North End became nationally famous as a hospitable urban ethnic enclave, treasured by its residents. After Jane Jacobs extensively praised the neighborhood's vitality in her landmark 1962 book, *The Death and Life of Great American Cities*, tourists began to visit and people from around the region shopped in its stores and markets. Jacobs noted how residents could not get bank loans; the rebuilding occurred through savings and a do-it-themselves spirit. Reflecting the change in attitudes toward inner city neighborhoods, in 1969 a famous television commercial featured a mother calling to her son to come home for dinner: Wednesday is Prince Spaghetti day. The era of the neighborhood as a place for families was at its height.

Unfortunately, having preserved the neighborhood from demolition and successfully rebuilt its housing, the North End began to succumb from its own success, and by the late 1970s, it was rapidly gentrifying. Newcomers found it to be safe, close to jobs, and full of activity, and it was cheaper then Back Bay or Beacon Hill. But as the neighborhood gentrified, Italian families left. Those who owned property made lots of money in the process, while renters were forced to find more affordable accommodations with many joining family members and former neighbors in towns to the north. Outwardly, the North End still looks like an Italian neighborhood as its first floor commercial spaces are crowded with Italian restaurants and stores, many run by outsiders. Upstairs, the neighborhood has become a standard upper-class Boston neighborhood.

The 1970s and 1980s may have marked the apogee of Boston's organized LGBT community. There were Dykes on Bikes, Gays for Patsy (a group devoted to country western dance), the Triangle Theater Company, multiple LGBT newspapers, one LGBT political group that focused on Boston issues and another that worked on state issues, and one very important group that focused on the needs of young people.

By the 1970s, inspired by the Stonewall riot and antiwar, feminist, and antiracism activism, the Boston area became a center of gay rights advocacy. One institution with a national reach was *Gay Community News* (GCN), first published in 1973 by a group of activists working out of the Charles Street Meeting House. It soon moved to Bromfield Street with a reputation for aggressive advocacy, strongly placing itself in the camp that held that LGBT people were special and that straight society had to learn how to adapt to their needs. The paper was more than politics as it promoted LGBT services, reviewed plays and concerts, reported gossip, covered day to day life of community members, as well as major national and international issues, and provided a venue for the community to learn about each other and the many activities in and around Boston. Editor Amy Hoffman proudly recalls that "We often claimed that GCN was neutral, and that we were open to all perspectives, including conservative ones, but that was ridiculous. We supported the most radical expressions of the gay liberation movement. We believed in upsetting the social order."[19] GCN had a peak circulation of 5,000 that reached every state and twelve countries. Despite staff turnover, constant financial problems, and the arson fire, it only missed one issue, the one after the blizzard of 1978–the office had lost electricity and phones and staff were stuck at home. The paper ceased weekly publication in 1992 but continued as a quarterly until 1999.

By the 1970s, nearly the entire inner core of Boston was part of the gay world. Men would pick each other up at Downtown Crossing, the Prudential Center, the Esplanade, or the Fenway Victory Gardens. There was a constellation of bars, most serving one group or another but all welcoming everyone, extending from Cambridge and the Fenway to the South End and Bay Village. The more established crowd lived in the Back Bay or Beacon Hill, young professionals claimed South End, and LGBT students settled in Cambridge, the Fenway, and Allston. A few of the more adventurous were moving to Dorchester and Jamaica Plain while in Roxbury, the famous Fort Hill Faggots for Freedom lived together in Highland Park. Women were more dispersed, but they had coffee shops in Cambridge, two bars downtown including the now greatly missed Saints, and were making it known that Jamaica Plain was a welcoming community.

In a first, Kevin White showed up at Buddies when that gay bar opened in 1979 on Boylston Street. He was friends with its manager who he soon appointed to be the city's first liaison to the gay and lesbian community. Later mayors continued to keep the position filled. Ann Maguire, the manager of the lesbian bar Somewhere Else, would be head of Neighborhood Services for Ray Flynn and then the campaign manager for Thomas Menino, and Harry Collings, a well-respected gay businessman, would be a key appointee of Mayor Menino at the BRA.

These were not years of total freedom; repression and anti-gay prejudice could strike at any time. One event that would have repercussions for years was a series of police actions coordinated by Suffolk County District Attorney, Garett Byrne. First he made headlines by announcing the arrest of dozens of men who he declared to be part of a sex ring that preyed on minors in Revere. Then he began to publicly prosecute men arrested at the Copley Library and followed up by establishing a public but anonymous hotline where people could call in to denounce their neighbors as homosexuals. As this was a time when LGBT people could lose their jobs or families, these public actions put them at risk if outed. The community was under siege.

Two groups formed to fight the District Attorney. One was the Boston Boise Committee, named after a similar witch hunt in Idaho. This eventually morphed into the North American Man Boy Love Association (NAMBLA), which would provoke controversy in Boston and across the country for the next several decades. There was support for the Committee, at least at first, mostly among male radicals who saw intergenerational sex as a natural extension of the right to control one's sexuality. Most lesbians, even radicals such as GCN's Amy Hoffman, were much more likely to see NAMBLA's agenda from the prism of exploitation and sexual politics and rejected it from the beginning. Meanwhile, most mainstream gay men were appalled by the suggestion of intergenerational sex and angry that anyone might associate them with its advocacy. NAMBLA quickly became an isolated, tiny fringe group.

More mainstream with deeper roots in the community was GLAD, Gay and Lesbian Advocates and Defenders. Organized in reaction to Byrne's prosecutions, GLAD trained groups of lawyers to inform LGBT of their civil rights, represent defendants in court, draft legislation, and advocate for new laws. They were to become very busy. In addition to defending the basic liberties of LGBT people, they would soon have to defend people coming down with a strange deadly new disease, AIDS.

Another important institution founded in these years was the Fenway Community Health Center. It was organized by community activists who had learned how to be effective by fighting against arson and renewal. Its first decade was dominated by a conflict between those who sought to keep it a volunteer, free clinic and others who saw a need to professionalize the Center and receive payments from insurance providers and government programs. Faced with imminent closure because of tax problems, inadequate infrastructure, and a lack of full-time medical staff, the Fenway rescued itself just in time to be ready for the horrific epidemic that would soon strike gay men in the city.[20]

The LGBT community played an important role in the 1983 mayor's race. Three of the candidates made a serious effort to garner the endorsement of Boston Lesbian and Gay Political Alliance (BLGPA). Though most LGBT voters were with Mel King, a large-scale organizing effort led by several key LGBT aides to Larry DiCara led to DiCara winning the endorsement of the group in the primary. Ray Flynn also sought its endorsement, but the group went with King for the final. No longer forced to be invisible by Don't Ask, Don't Tell, LGBT people were actively courted by politicians.

Dismayed by the loss of population and the realization that many suburbanites viewed the city as a crime ridden wasteland, Mayor White understandably tried to change the way the city was perceived by outsiders. Most importantly, he targeted white middle-class families, the group fleeing or avoiding Boston the most, with programs and projects aimed to bring them back to the city. From this strategic thinking, Boston created a number of institutions that would continue to the present day.

The project that had the greatest physical impact on the city was the redevelopment of Faneuil Hall and Quincy Market. Faneuil Hall had been built to provide space for food vendors on the first floor with an assembly hall upstairs. As the city expanded after Independence, Boston built the adjacent three buildings known as Quincy Market, and for nearly 150 years, vegetable sellers, butchers, and other food providers used the area for wholesale and retail trade. This worked well in the nineteenth century, but by the middle of the twentieth century food production was becoming industrialized and many provisions were trucked into the city from thousands of miles away. The streets around Quincy Market were not able to support this kind of traffic, so most vendors moved north to a new facility in Chelsea that offered room for trucks, access to highways, and better refrigeration while others moved to the Newmarket area in the South End. With its handsome historic buildings and strategic location, the Faneuil Hall/Quincy Market area was ripe for renewal, but the prospects of attracting private investment were grim. White wanted

Faneuil Hall before redevelopment. The area has been transformed, but is mostly visited by tourists rather than Boston residents.

retail and services that would attract the public at a time when cities were in deep decline and unable to compete with enclosed suburban malls.

Mayor White worked hard to find a developer and architect team that would create a major attraction for the city, selecting James Rouse, who had successfully built housing, shopping malls, and a "new town", Columbia, Maryland. Rouse teamed up with local architect Benjamin Thompson who had cofounded the nationally important firm, The Architects Collaborative, with Walter Gropius. Thompson had designed the iconic Design Research building in Harvard Square and was known for his ability to create projects that were both modern and respected history.

No one knew if the project would succeed as Downtown Crossing was rapidly declining and the project lacked an anchor department store; when banks rejected loaning money for the project, the city had to step in and help with the financing. But the new Faneuil Hall/Quincy Market opened in 1976 and was a critical success and was instantly mobbed with shoppers, tourists, and downtown workers on their lunch break. Thompson and Rouse went on to develop similar projects in Baltimore, New York City, and elsewhere and the market remains an important tourist destination.

Another White project that has lasted is the annual Fourth of July Celebration on the Esplanade, begun in 1973. There was a long tradition of pops concerts on the Esplanade led by beloved maestro Arthur Fiedler, but when the city drew national media attention for its busing riots, White and others seized upon the holiday event as a way to showcase the city's history, its skyline, and the lush park along the Charles River. The concerts proved very successful with some crowd estimates approaching a half million each year. Producing the concert and accommodating the hundreds of thousands of people is expensive, and eventually, the well-known philanthropist David Mugar generously stepped in to fund the necessary budget. For many years, the concerts and fireworks were nationally televised, though national media participation eventually waned.

Balancing the summer Esplanade event was a New Year's Eve extravaganza, First Night. It was the product of Clara Wainwright, who was rebelling against the mostly private world of New Year's celebrations that focused on parties, dinners, dancing, and drinking. Many felt excluded by the alcohol consumption, and families in particular were not natural participants in the evening's partying. There was no Boston equivalent of the ball drop in Times Square, so many hailed the New Year by watching televised events going on in other cities. Wainwright consulted another artist, Lowry Bridges, who had organized the city's bicentennial celebration, and the two set out to create First Night. Along with a core group, they established an event that aimed to be culturally diverse, family friendly, city based, and use churches, open spaces, and the streets. Art was at the center of event planning along with music and parades. The *Globe* quickly came on board and the event was well received by the city's philanthropic community. First night 1977 cost $34,700 to produce ($140,000 in 2015 dollars) rising to $1.2 million in 2007, much of it paid for by donations.

At first, many wondered if anyone would show up. "Don't be afraid," led off a *Globe* article on the first event, "Just come in and have a good time." [21] The first celebration was small, just 50,000 to 60,000 attended, but by 1980, attendance was approaching 75,000 or more and buttons were sold to raise money and create priority seating for indoor events. The 1980s saw incredible growth with First Night celebrations spreading to cities around the globe and the management structure of Boston becoming professionalized.

Eventually, however, the suburban nature of its participants hindered its ability to spread across Boston. Participants remained afraid of the city, especially after dark, and balked at attending events outside the Back Bay core. A 1984 controversy developed over shooting fireworks over the Common and Public Gardens with the Fire Marshall prohibited the practice, forcing the fireworks to the harbor. An outgrowth of this dispute was that many realized for the first time how important the event was. It also began to attract tourists from outside the region.

Money was a constant problem. The deficit in 1995 was $80,000 and corporate sponsorships were sought. Income peaked at just over $2 million in 2001 and then began to fall, mostly due to declining corporate support. The problems were not just in Boston; the number of First Night celebrations in other cities dropped from 225 in 1999 to 103 in 2007. In Boston, the evening festivities shrank and most events, except for the kick off parade, were moved indoors. Forced to raise money, buttons were now $20.[22] By 2015, the event was deep in financial distress forcing the city to take over operations and find a new way of funding operations. The continued vitality of the event was at risk.

Though these efforts are rightly seen as positives for the city, their actual impact on Boston are less evident. The summer fireworks, first night celebration, and Faneuil Hall have met their goal of attracting white families from the suburbs to visit the city, but this is the one demographic least likely to move back into Boston. Instead, the city has been revived by nonwhite immigrants, young college graduates, and empty nesters, groups conspicuous by their absence. So these events and Faneuil Hall attract families as visitors, but not as residents. At times, the Independence Day Celebration and First Night seem aggressively pro-family, a great alternative to celebrations involving alcohol but irrelevant to the many fun seeking adults who thrive on city living but don't have children. They also have mostly failed to attract blacks, Latinos, and other minority city residents who find them so white as to be unwelcoming. This partly explains why these events have struggled: they can't attract corporate support because they lack a diversity of participation. Faneuil Hall has a related problem: it is for tourists. But residents rarely, if ever, shop or visit there. The result has been a disappointing mix of retail that has changed over the years from unique Boston boutiques to national chain stores

Some of White's plans were less successful, most notably Downtown Crossing. White and the BRA sought ways to revive the ever increasingly shabby shopping district and, belatedly, tried to prioritize pedestrians. Downtown Crossing was made an automobile restricted zone in 1978 following more than a decade of planning. The goal was to promote the district as the region's premier shopping area and reduce conflicts between pedestrians, cars, and trucks. One major complaint had been that pedestrians kept walking in the street.[23] Unfortunately, the area continued to lose stores. Some suffered from competition with suburban retail, others were lost when national chains closed local outlets. Though the area is adjacent to hundreds of thousands of office workers, year by year it gave up its businesses to the Back Bay, now the hub of Boston retail, or the suburbs. Vacancies increased.

Into black Boston's longstanding mix of Brahmins, Southerners, and Caribbean, a fourth group arrived in the city: Haitians. The first Haitians had moved to Boston at the beginning of the twentieth century, but it was not until the 1970s that they came in numbers so large that Boston began to rival Miami and New York City as a major center of this population. These new immigrants joined a core of older Haitian residents, and together they began to transform Dorchester and Mattapan.

One of the key factors for Haitian settlers were the three Catholic parishes that were very welcoming to the new immigrants: Saint Matthew's, Saint Angela's, and Saint Leo's. These three churches attracted those who wanted to be with other Haitians as well as celebrate mass in their native Haitian Creole. By 2000, there were over 85,000 Haitians in the city with Mattapan having an estimated 40 percent of its population claiming Haitian ancestry. From this center, there were Haitian enclaves that extended west into Hyde Park and northeast as far as Codman

Square. Though many of the earliest migrants were well educated and had held skilled jobs in Haiti, racism, the inability to speak English, and other barriers resulted in their having much more limited employment opportunities and lower relative incomes in Boston.[24]

Some, both inside and outside the Haitian community, at first believed that they were immune from the tremendous black-white racial struggles in the 1970s. Then Yvon Jean-Louis, a ten-year resident of the city, was terribly beaten by a white mob in 1974 when he drove into South Boston to pick up his wife from work. Haitians were also victimized by the notorious BBURG program when many used the program to purchase houses. Thus they were funneled into Mattapan and minority parts of Dorchester where many overpaid for deteriorated housing and subsequently, many lost their homes. Others were met by the same violence that plagued blacks who were trying to move into formerly all-white neighborhoods. Haitians quickly learned that racists did not distinguish between different groups in Boston's black community.

Confronted by televised images of boat people leaving Haiti and reports that the island country was the center for HIV/AIDS, the image of Haitian people in Boston, as well as throughout the United States, shifted in the 1980s. At one time, many thought them to be model immigrants, hard-working and upwardly mobile. But now, many unfairly stereotyped them as illiterate, unemployable, and dangerous carriers of disease. Sadly, these false images shaped how the broader community treated one of Boston's fastest growing groups.

By the 1990s, Haitians were highly concentrated in such jobs as janitors, food-service workers, cabdrivers, and nursing aides. Though many were successful in opening small businesses and earning middle-class incomes, the majority were poor and working class. Yet despite the issues that confronted them, Haitians in Boston continued to feel that they were better off in the local community than were those who lived elsewhere.[25]

After decades of work to revitalize the city's neighborhoods, the people who staffed Boston's network of community-based institutions, many of them veterans of the civil rights and antiwar movements who were also nurtured by growing social movements such as feminism and organized opposition to downtown dominated redevelopment, provided the counterbalance to the Hynes-Collins-White pro-growth machine. As the Kevin White era came to an end, this substantial group of people saw an opportunity to transform the city.

By the final years of the White's fourth term, both the mayor himself and the city as a whole were tired of his administration, and in the early months of 1983, several potential candidates began to make the rounds of wakes, neighborhood meetings, and other gatherings, as residents assessed their strengths and weaknesses. As speculation grew as to whether the mayor would seek a fifth term or retire, an open scramble for the office broke out.

Five men battled for the two spots in the final election. Three of them were traditional politicians: David Finnegan, Larry Di Cara, and Dennis Kearney were all close enough to the pro-growth machine to solicit money from developers. If any of them had become mayor, it would have produced an administration substantially close to how Hynes, Collins, and White had managed development. But two other candidates were substantially different. Ray Flynn and Mel King promised a new way of managing growth in the city, one that would emphasize benefits for the people of the neighborhoods. Neither man was given much of a chance to make the final cut. Ray Flynn was too conservative, when he wasn't promoting liberal ideas such as rent control, and Mel King was too radical, not to mention that no one believed that voters would support a black candidate.

King was born and raised in the New York Streets area; while attending college in the South, he was shocked to hear that his neighborhood was slated for demolition. He became a youth worker for South End House when he returned to Boston and was heartbroken and angry as he saw families displaced by urban renewal. Dedicating his life to service and creating change, King ran unsuccessfully for School Committee several times and became one of the leading activists in the city as he participated in demonstrating at Tent City, the BRA offices, and in 1968 at his then employer, United South End Settlements, which was participating in the renewal program that was displacing so many. Eventually elected State Representative from the South End, King was more imposing because of his deep intellect and strong commitment to social justice than because of his broad six-foot, four-inch frame.

His supporters adored him.

King hoped that the new district election format would mobilize minority voters to come out to the polls. He was partly right, as 20,000 new black voters registered, and many of Boston's minority community saw King as the person who would bring Boston into the new age enjoyed by other large US cities: run my minority mayors with the benefits of development spreading to those who had long been left out. It wasn't just blacks who hoped for this; Latinos also believed he was their candidate, and for the first time, Asian residents, as opposed to just Chinatown business leaders, were involved in politics as they went to the polls to vote for King.

Flynn, born and raised in South Boston, was the son of a longshoreman and a cleaning lady. He was initially a State Representative from that neighborhood and then won a seat on the city council. Outside South Boston, he was first noticed during busing, which he vigorously, but peacefully, opposed. But there were hints that he was not one of the Southie crowd that most associated him with. He had played basketball in college and barely missed out on playing with the Celtics. Out of school, he became a youth worker. He had personal contacts with many blacks through his basketball playing, he was in favor of rent control and special education, and he had voted for a city human rights commission. Yet many liberals were suspicious as his outspoken opposition to busing and his firm support of antiabortion legislation marked him as one more conservative Southie politician.

Among the candidates attracting fewer votes were Larry DiCara and Dennis Kearny. DiCara was a skilled lawyer and former city councilor who was well admired for his uncanny ability to know everyone's name and be able to recall small details to them as he shook their hands at a candidates' night. Yet he never acquired traction in the race. Kearny, who had attracted notice because of his liberal reforms of the sheriff's office, was simply too obscure to have much of a chance.

The frontrunner was David Finnegan, a former School Committee member and talk show host who had grown up in a poor family in Dorchester and then supported himself through college. Slick and connected to the downtown business elite, as well as many politicians, most observers believed he would easily capture one of the two top positions in the primary. But ultimately he was too polished for a city weary of downtown domination of the neighborhoods. After more than thirty years of pro-growth coalitions running city hall, voters were ready for a change. Furthermore, Finnegan was arrogant, he would walk into a candidates' night surrounded by a phalanx of aides in dark blue suits to keep anyone from approaching him.

The election was held during a small window of time when local television stations used new technologies to have cameras on the candidates in order to broadcast snippets from the campaign on the evening news almost every night. When Finnegan provoked Flynn into a meltdown by calling him a chameleon for changing his positions on a number of issues, Finnegan thought he had won the primary. But enough voters reacted to the incident as a negative on Finnegan, and it crystallized the impression he was a connected, cruel elitist and humanized Flynn into a sympathetic character who represented the neighborhoods. By provoking a televised confrontation, Finnegan had fallen into a trap of making the 1983 election one more race between a low-ward (Flynn) and a high-ward (Finnegan) Irish constituency. Only now, for the first time in decades, the low-ward, yet more progressive, Irishman collected more votes. The 1983 election also revealed the split between the more prosperous liberal gentrified gays who supported Di Cara, and the grassroots radicals who were firmly behind King. The power and size of the former surprised the latter, as many had believed they were the majority.

To everyone's surprise, the final was a race between the South End's King and South Boston's Flynn. Race was an undercurrent in the 1983 final, but if Flynn had rerun Louise Day Hick's campaign, he would have also lost. Just as King crossed the old lines to campaign in white neighborhoods, so did Flynn campaign in black areas. He was able to communicate sufficient sensitivity on race so as to attract some white progressives and not scare the large group of white moderates in the city.[26]

The final election was a contest between the multiethnic coalition put together by King and a new alliance between lower-income and higher-income whites created by Flynn. Though Flynn sought to demonstrate that he would be a champion of the poor and unconnected, the two had very different philosophical roots. King wanted to change the fundamental power structure of the city and energize people of color and lower-income residents to control decision making. Flynn was more conventional; his idol was Mayor Curley, and he sought to bend the institutions that shaped the city so that they benefited residents rather than replace them with something new. In the end, Flynn beat King by a large margin.

1. Bradbury KL, Downs A and Small KA. *Urban Decline and the Future of American Cities*. Washington, DC: The Brookings Institution, 1982.
2. Weinberg MW. Boston's Kevin White: A mayor who survives. *Political Science Quarterly*. 1981; 96: 87-106.
3. Barnicle M. A City's Soul Sorely Tried. *Boston Globe*. April 25, 1976; p. 1.
4. Allen DG. *Investment Management in Boston: A History*. Boston: University of Massachusetts Press 2015.
5. Brady J. Arson, urban economy, and organized crime: The case of Boston. *Social Problems*. 1983; 31: 1-27.
6. Hernandez MM. *Impact of commercial development on inner city revitalization: An analysis of projects in Boston*. Masters Thesis, DUSP, MIT, 2001.
7. Ayres J. Schools are Quiet as Phase 2 Begins. *Boston Globe*. September 9, 1975; p. 1.
8. Rogers D and King N. Police, Busing Foes Battle in South Boston. *Boston Globe*. February 16, 1976; p. 1.
9. Boston Redevelopment Authority. *Boston's Economy*. 1994.
10. Vale LJ. Transforming public housing: The social and physical redevelopment of Boston's West Broadway Development *Journal of Architectural and Planning Research*. 1995; 12: 278-305.
11. Stockman F. Donald Trump, Black Lives Matter, and the echoes of busing. *Boston Globe*. December 27, 2015; K1.
12. Lee RAB. *A report on the Boston Housing Authority's management program dripping court receivership 1989-1984*. Masters Thesis, DUSP. MIT, 1984.
13. Lupo A, Colcord F and Fowler E. *Rites of Way: The Politics of Transportation in Boston and the U.S. city*. Boston: Little Brown, 1971.
14. Campos G. *Reinforcing social infrastructure: The role of physical interventions in revitalizing Hyde Square in Jamaica Plain*. Masters Thesis, DUSP. MIT, 1999.
15. Kolodney R. *The effects of displacement on elderly renters in Jamaica Plain*. Masters Thesis, DUSP. MIT, 1981.
16. Bennett P. Confession Put Lid on Arson Probe. *Boston Globe*. July 29, 1984; p. 1.
17. Fire. 14 Firemen Hurt as Roof Collapses. October 3, *Boston Globe*. 1982; p. 1.
18. Slavet JS and Torto RG. *Boston's Recurring Crises: Three Decades of Fiscal Policy*. Boston: John M. McCormack Graduate School of Policy and Global Studies 1985.
19. Hoffman A. *An Army of Ex-Lovers*. Amherst, MA: University of Massachusetts

Press, 2007.

20. Batza CP. *Before AIDS: Gay and lesbian community health activism in the 1970s.* Dissertation, University of Illinois - Chicago, 2011.

21. Menzies I. It's Boston Common for New Year's Eve. *Boston Globe.* December 29, 1976; p. 1.

22. Stone B. *Designing a moment in time: First Night and Boston's public spaces.* Masters Thesis, MIT, 2008.

23. Cutrufo J. *The Downtown Crossing Pedestrian Zone: Should it be Reopened to Vehicular Traffic?* Masters Thesis, Urban and Environmental Policey, Tufts University, 2010.

24. Jackson RO. After the exodus: The new Catholics in Boston's old ethnic neighborhoods. *Religion an American Culture: A Journal of Interpretation.* 2007; 17: 191-212.

25. Ostine R. *After intermarriage: Ethnicity and identity among Haitians in Boston.* Dissertation, University of Michigan, 2001.

26. Gillis DA. *The sociology of a city in transition: Boston 1980 – 2000.* Dissertation, Boston University, 2015.

Chapter 6

Growth and Healing: 1983 - 1993

A FTER NEARLY SEVENTY years of decline, Boston was on the upswing in the 1980s. Beacon Hill, Back Bay, the South End, the Waterfront, and the North End teemed with affluent residents as more middle-class households settled into other neighborhoods. Commuters complained about traffic and finding parking while new residents demanded improved policing, trash pickups, and other services. As soon as they came on the market, condominiums were snatched up by eager buyers, and renters fretted over finding affordable accommodations. Longtime middle-class families in West Roxbury and elsewhere stayed in the city, particularly if they could get their children into Boston Latin or one of the other public exam schools, and a venturous few even tried the public elementary schools as they developed a reputation for providing a good education for students through grade four. There were no longer hushed conversations about leaving the city to escape its chaos; now families were more likely to depart because they couldn't afford ever increasing housing costs.

Yet at the same time, there were large sections of the city waiting for revival. Parts of North Dorchester were pockmarked by abandoned buildings and trash-strewn vacant lots. Teenagers shot each other over the rights to sell drugs in the Bromley Heath projects, and an epidemic of despair fueled suicides and overdoses in Southie. Roslindale Square was deteriorating as stores were shuttered, and across the city, high schools were peaceful yet far from what was needed by their students. In all, Boston was a great place to be rich and a tough place to be poor.

The city's population bottomed out in 1980 and grew by 2 percent in the next ten years, a major accomplishment given that the city had lost population for decades and that most large cities across the United States continued to lose residents. The increase was driven by minorities as the Hispanic and Asian populations grew by more than 50 percent while the black population saw modest growth. The city's non-Hispanic white population continued to fall, dropping by nearly 50,000 in the 1980s, but this was a smaller decrease then the previous decades. The number of adults without a high school degree in the city declined as did the number of residents under eighteen. But the number of adults with a college degree increased by over 60 percent. The city looked very different than it had at the end of World War II.

Though Massachusetts in the early 1980s witnessed phenomenal prosperity, prior to that, a decline in defense spending associated with the end of the Vietnam War in 1975 had pushed the Massachusetts unemployment rate to the highest in the country. But the Reagan-era rearmament coupled with strong private investment via Boston's venture capital community caused a rebound after 1980. Even more important was the invention of the minicomputer, with its center of production outside the city along Routes 128 and 495. These computers were very popular with businesses who preferred them to bulky, expensive mainframe computers. Minicomputers were made by a few, very large Massachusetts firms including Data General, DEC, Wang Laboratories, and others that developed components and software in house.[1] For a few years these were wildly profitable companies, and delegations from other cities and states traveled to the Boston area to learn how to replicate its economy.

Then Apple, IBM, and others developed the personal computer destroying the minicomputer industry and bankrupting the firms that had dominated Boston's suburbs, causing 50,000 jobs to disappear. Creating high technology-based prosperity in Seattle and San Jose, these personal computers used a large number of independent suppliers. The hard drive maker, operating system developer, monitor manufacturer, and so forth were from different companies, and one computer might run software from dozens of suppliers. The minicomputer makers, who produced everything from hardware to software that was incompatible with other systems, could not compete on price or meet the onslaught of innovation sparked by this new business model. Fortunately for Boston, most of the job losses were in the suburbs and the effects on the city were muted even as the effects in the suburbs were severe.

In Boston, the economy improved as financial and business services employment peaked when growing regionalization and nationalization trends promoted consolidation in these well-paying industries. Boston banks created interstate networks as they bought up smaller institutions or expanded beyond their local base. The mutual fund industry gathered customers from around the country and invested both locally and around the globe. The region's higher education institutions grew as students from elsewhere flocked to go to school in Boston. Many stayed once they graduated. All of these created opportunities for investment and an expansion of office space and housing in the city. Boston, the first city in the country to suffer from decline and despair because of the fading of the old economy, was also the first to begin to grow and prosper because of the new. The city, at least its government, benefited from the New Boston, as it was called. Though the budgets were always tight, there were no crises to prompt layoffs or budget cuts during the Flynn years.

Despite its loss of population up to the 1980s, the number of employed city residents was extremely stable between 1960 and 1990, about 288,000 in each year. This masked a low of 256,000 in 1980 and a dramatic change in employment mix. Blue-collar workers fell from 96,500 to 46,500, but white-collar employed residents grew from 126,500 to 191,000. The more highly skilled and compensated professional and technical category rose to 65,000 from 33,500 while managerial workers went from 15,600 to 42,000. Reflecting this change, the number of Boston residents who had college degrees increased from 36,000 to 110,000. This illustrates that it was the elderly and working-class families with children who left the city.

Despite his landslide victory, Ray Flynn had an unsteady grasp on the mayor's office. None of the three main political blocks trusted him. Blacks and other minorities were in mourning over the defeat of Mel King, white conservatives disliked Flynn's friendliness to blacks and progressive neighborhood activists, and white liberals considered him to be an unkempt, unintelligent son of Southie. Flynn's top leadership was convinced that one misstep and the city's electorate would coalesce against him. Flynn was not a cynical politician saying anything to get elected; he truly wanted to solve the puzzle of downtown prosperity versus neighborhood decline, and he continually sought to make the downtown boom translate to better lives for the poor outside its orbit. This effort would dominate his agenda in office.

Flynn campaigning in Roslindale, c. 1985. In contrast to White, Flynn loved to be out in the neighborhoods meeting people.

In seeking to connect to grumbling voters, Flynn was greatly helped by his style of governance. Collins, wheelchair-bound because of polio, was physically unable be an active presence in the neighborhoods while White preferred almost anything to going to a community meeting, and as a result, both relied on subordinates and city employees to meet with residents. So for a generation, the people of Boston had been politically unconnected to city hall as successive mayors sought to disentangle the city's economy from its poor residents. Flynn changed this. He loved talking with people, showing up at neighborhood meetings, and sharing their tragedies and triumphs. Flynn quickly became known for rushing to the scene of a fire to comfort the bewildered newly homeless, he met with mothers traumatized by the deaths of their children due to drug and gang violence, and he became known (and belittled) for riding snow plows during storms.[2] His staffers went to bed at night expecting the Mayor might call at any time to make sure they knew about a broken streetlight or an abandoned car he spotted on one of his many nightly rounds. Even his detractors grew to respect his constant presence in the neighborhoods and the way it connected people to a government they were once so alienated from.

Another asset was that Flynn drew into his administration a mix of longtime neighborhood activists and veterans of community organizations. This was in contrast to White's brilliant, but distant, outsiders who may have had great talent but had little knowledge of the city and, for the most part, no desire to live in it.[3] Many of Flynn's hires were Boston-born who had refused to leave during the declining years. Generally leaning conservative but willing to work across race and class lines, they eyed the young community organizers working alongside them with suspicion. Flynn's progressive appointees might have been newcomers to the city, having moved to Boston for college, but they stayed and put down roots. They were thought to be so liberal, if not radical, that they were collectively called the Sandinistas after the socialist government of Nicaragua that dominated much of the international headlines of that time.[4]

The two wings of Flynn's coalition had to learn to get along both inside city government and in the city as a whole. Working with minority members in his administration, Flynn vastly improved on White's hiring record, and Boston began to heal as its factions cooperated for the greater good. Thus, you could find Billy Doherty, a stalwart son of South Boston, working alongside Yves D'Amberville, one of Boston's Haitian community's most respected activists, Willie Mae Allen, who once ran for State Representative from Mattapan, and Peter Drier, a proud Democratic-Socialist. This set the tone for the city.

Flynn's visibility had to be connected to policies if he were to secure reelection, and he implemented a set of initiatives that had a common desire to use Boston's prosperity to serve those less well off. The most successful of these were related to housing. At the end of the Kevin

White administration, City Councilor Bruce Bolling borrowed a concept called linkage, first used in San Francisco, to create new affordable housing in Boston. The program was simple: commercial or market rate housing projects over a certain size would have to pay a fee of so many dollars per square feet that would be used by the city to subsidize affordable housing. Alternatively, they could include a percentage of affordable units in their development. Predictably, developers and Kevin White hated it. But in the final days of his administration, White agreed to Bolling's legislation in order to stave off stricter regulations later on. Developers, led by Jerome Rappaport, sued, but the state Supreme Court upheld the payments because they were "voluntary"– though it would be highly unlikely that any project would be approved without them. Over the next twenty years, 5,000 housing units would be constructed through the linkage program, many by CDCs. It was not a perfect program. The city has struggled to monitor the program to both ensure that developers are complying with the requirements and that the households that move into these assisted units are eligible for such housing. Yet it created much needed shelter in a city that was becoming unaffordable.

Linkage proved invaluable to programs such as the South End Neighborhood Housing Initiative (SENHI) that marked part of Flynn's efforts to increase the supply of affordable housing. SENHI was based on parcels that the BRA had acquired through urban renewal but had not put out for rebuilding before the program collapsed. Linkage payments were used to help subsidize development costs. Other new housing developments in Dorchester, Roxbury, and Jamaica Plain benefited from linkage payments as well.

Another housing issue that Flynn needed to address was the BHA, now several years in receivership. In 1980, Judge Paul Garrity appointed Harry Spence to oversee the Authority, having dismissed the mayoral appointed board of directors. Most critics were very impressed with Spence's management of the Authority, crediting him with stopping the increase in vacant units, ending corruption in hiring and contracting, and securing state and federal aid to modernize developments. But problems continued: thousands of vacant units and hundreds of millions of dollars in capital improvement needs yet unfunded, developments drowning in crime and hopelessness, and occasional lapses of judgement by Spence that infuriated tenants. For example, after an internal report indicated the BHA was spending millions of dollars on refrigerator purchases and upkeep, Spence proposed to have tenants buy and maintain them. This might have seemed like a logical policy response, but it ignored the very low incomes of most tenants who would not be able to afford refrigerators. After this and other controversies, Spence was ready to move on, and the court gave Ray Flynn the authority to appoint a new administrator.

Flynn selected Doris Bunte, a woman whose past was full of symbolism and talent. An energetic native of New York, after moving to Boston she raised her family in the Orchard Park projects. During her years there she became a tenant activist who fought to keep the development safe, affordable, and in good repair. Impressed by her knowledge of public housing issues, Mayor Kevin White appointed Bunte to the BHA board but then fired her when she refused to comply with his order to hire a patronage employee, setting off a nasty court battle that Bunte lost. After redistricting created new opportunities to elect Blacks in 1972, she was elected State Representative for Lower Roxbury where she proved to be a key voice for people of color. When Flynn appointed Bunte, she was the first former public housing tenant to run a public housing authority in the country.

Even as tenants were frustrated by the dismal conditions in their apartments, Bunte had to find ways to plan renovations and implement improvements without displacing them. She needed to build trust between residents and neighbors of developments, who often disliked each other, and she was forced to battle crime, drug selling, and other problems that afflicted residents. But her greatest challenge was integrating the BHA system of developments across the city. Since it was established in the 1930s, the BHA had assigned tenants based on their race using notations on file cards to ensure that blacks were kept out of all-white projects. This meant that since the 1930s, there had been white-only and black-only projects. Over time, the number of projects open to blacks, Hispanics, and Asians increased, but there were still many that were off limits to nonwhites, a violation of every state and federal fair housing law. When a routine federal audit revealed the two separate waiting lists, people inside city government were horrified, and when the news of this government-created segregation, perhaps the most blatant public discrimination in the country at the time, broke in the press, Flynn was besieged with protests. Facing a lawsuit from HUD over this egregious policy that they knew they could not win, Flynn and Bunte were forced to quickly eliminate the dual waiting lists and begin desegregating all of its developments.

Some of the all-white developments were in Charlestown and South Boston where much of the anti-busing violence had originated barely ten years before, so many feared that the violence that had attended school integration would be repeated. Some white tenants organized protests using the slogan "no forced housing," but the opposition had little support even in South Boston, and the vast majority of Boston residents understood the race-based program was wrong. Furthermore, Flynn and Bunte were very firm that integration was necessary to comply with the law and that they would do everything they could to desegregate the projects and prevent violence. For the most part, integration proceeded smoothly, and the city avoided further conflict and hits to its image. Because the 14,000 households on the BHA waiting list were overwhelmingly nonwhite, BHA owned and operated developments also became mostly minority, even in South Boston.

Another initiative that Flynn took on in the hope of making downtown renewal assist low-income neighborhoods was the Boston jobs policy. The concern had been that few construction jobs had gone to Boston residents. While there was little that the city could do regarding permanent jobs locating in to private development projects, it sought to use its leverage over development approvals to influence who was hired to build them. In the negotiations to get Copley Place built, which included the BRA applying for federal grants and granting tax breaks, Kevin White had reluctantly given in to the demands of Mel King and others to include a guarantee that a certain percentage of the project's construction jobs would go to women, minorities, and Boston residents. Flynn, in the face of strong opposition from the building trade unions, insisted on similar agreements in new projects that needed zoning approval or city assistance. In the decades since this became the standard way of doing business in the city, the number of jobs that resulted from development that have gone to the target populations has increased. Unfortunately, however, these programs have tended to fall short of their goals.

The third major initiative that Flynn put into place was a takeover of the city schools. Boston schools had been run by an independently-elected committee even though city property taxes funded the vast majority of their budget. After the turmoil in busing and the decade afterward in which the schools showed insufficient improvement, Flynn decided to make the schools directly responsible to him. To do this, he filed legislation to abolish the elected school committee and replace it with a five-member committee appointed by the mayor. This was controversial. Many whites were still upset by court mandated busing and resented losing what little input they still had in the schools, while black and Latinos in the city were just beginning to elect minorities to the school committee and they felt their political voice was being silenced. Flynn prevailed, however, and Boston became one of the few school systems in the country that was under the direct administration of the mayor.

In the decades after the end of the Vietnam War, a stream of immigrants came to Boston from Vietnam. Like Cubans, they were legal immigrants fleeing the repression of a communist government, and there were strong differences between older immigrants who were focused on the politics of their former country and their children who tended to be more concerned with issues here. As they adapted to their new country, Boston's Vietnamese community faced cultural issues as they did not have the experience of working with neighborhood and non-profit institutions that were the center of social services and community development in Boston. At the same time, service providers and public agencies lacked staff who could speak Vietnamese and most were ignorant of Vietnamese cultural values, creating a gap with the community. As the population grew, these problems became acute.

In 1980, there were only 3,172 Vietnamese in the state, but a few years later there were over 10,000 in the Fields Corner area of Dorchester alone. Mostly, they had settled on streets that had only recently changed from white to black. Just a handful of Vietnamese were registered to vote in the early nineties, but voter participation increased after that point with most, particularly the older members of the community, registering as Republicans. But as yet their numbers were not large enough to influence election results even in the districts around

Fields Corner.

City Councilor Dapper O'Neill attracted a lot of attention during the Dorchester Day Parade in 1992 when he said "I just passed up there. I thought I was in Saigon for Chrissakes. For Chrissakes, it makes you sick."[5] O'Neill had a long history of insulting minorities, from his race baiting of blacks during busing to his complaining that non-stop airline service between Boston and San Juan made it easier for Puerto Ricans to come to Boston. But his elderly white constituents loved him and kept returning him to office.[6] The major local political fallout from his outburst was that it encouraged many to vote and helped quicken the transition of the Vietnamese to a Democratic voting group.

With its Irish, Vietnamese, African-American, Haitian, Cape Verdean, and other groups, Dorchester was well on its way to becoming the city's most diverse neighborhood. Yet parts of it continued to decline. For example, once situated at the intersection of multiple trolley lines, Uphams Corner had been a thriving commercial district anchoring North Dorchester. In the 1930s, there were 300 businesses in Uphams Corner, but their number fell to 180 by 1970 and to 90 by the 1990s. As the trolleys were discontinued, the neighborhood underwent racial transformation that left it significantly poorer, its population fell as household size decreased, and when residents began shopping elsewhere, the area became increasingly abandoned and the stores that remained were marginal enterprises.[7]

Lying just outside the BBURG line, the area benefited from not being used as a dumping ground for low-income black homebuyers and though there was substantial racial change in the blocks around Uphams Corner, it was gradual and the blacks and others buying houses tended to have higher incomes and more stable families.[8] So in the 1980s it remained to be seen if North Dorchester might revive or fall apart.

Further south in Dorchester, Washington Street had long served as a dividing line in Codman Square with larger, owner-occupied houses to the east. Even as late as 1965, the western side, with its more modest but of similar age housing, was still mostly white, often Irish, but with Jews and Italians as well, and there were only a handful of blacks. The commercial district thrived and there were so many families that one resident joked that there was a need for a traffic cop to deal with the number of baby carriages.

BBURG, along with other forces, changed this creating a stark dividing line along Washington Street with blacks to the west and whites to the east. Whites fled, but the new minority homeowners found they had overpaid for dilapidated housing and defaults were common. The eastern portion was more stable with young middle-income professionals gradually buying houses. The commercial district declined, and there was looting during the Blizzard of 1978 that resulted in a number of stores never reopening. Then the district's only bank closed, further dampening commerce.[9] Though there are many businesses along Washington Street to this day, it is still a struggling commercial district.

Time and again, Boston neighborhoods such as Dorchester have been harmed by speculators. Outside investors looking for quick profits were instrumental in magnifying the BBURG program's problems as they bought up houses from fleeing whites and then quickly resold them at inflated prices to blacks, often with the collusion of corrupt appraisers. Further speculation came in waves. In the 1980s, many bought triple deckers in Dorchester to flip them to others or convert them to condominiums. But too many overpaid, and there was a wave of foreclosure across Massachusetts in the early 1990s as condominium conversions and new construction, along with rising interest rates, severely constricted demand for units. Dorchester was one area hit hard by this boom and bust cycle. There would be more.

In the Codman Square area, speculators looking to quickly flip triple deckers were able to outbid would-be owners and longer term investors. Then when a downturn came, there were more than four hundred foreclosures in a little over two years. Adding to the problem was little oversight by lenders who made profits by writing mortgages and quickly selling them on the secondary market and thus had little incentive to examine the quality of the loans they were making.[10] The foreclosed buildings often deteriorated, creating eyesores, hiding criminal activities, and depressing property values.

The problems of speculation in triple deckers highlight the importance of this housing type in Boston. One of the most distinctive building styles in the city, the triple decker, a wooden building sitting on its own lot with three independent dwelling units accessed by two sets of common stairs, had been the backbone of housing in Boston for over a century. Typically, each unit had its own back balcony and the side yards were very narrow with no off street parking. This resulted in about 28 units per acre with unit sizes ranging from 800 to 1,500 square feet. Though there was much variation, most buildings were 24-28 feet wide and 40-50 feet deep. Each floor was a separate unit, with its own furnace, bathroom, and kitchen.

There were a number of types of triple deckers: a flat roofed, simpler style that originated in South Boston and spread through Dorchester, an often pitched roof style that was more ornamental and originated in Roxbury before spreading to Jamaica Plain and beyond, and the Mansard-roofed three deckers of East Boston. The first triple deckers were built in the 1870s with their development spurred by two reasons: new building codes resulted in triple deckers being about the densest housing that could be built under less restrictive (and less costly) regulations, and the introduction of first horse-drawn (and then later electric) streetcars that opened up large tracts of land on the edge of the city. Most were constructed by small builders. They were affordable: a unit could be rented for about $20-25 a month during years around the First World War.

The heyday of the triple decker was over by World War I, doomed by changing consumer tastes and rising construction costs. A Boston ordinance essentially banned them after 1927, while a state building code change stopped their construction in the suburbs after 1914. But even as late as 2000, they represented about 20 percent of all unis in the city. In some parts of Dorchester and Mattapan, they are 80 percent of housing.

At one time, these buildings provided an important way for people to own their homes; a family would occupy one floor and rent out the other two, sometimes with their children on one floor and their parents on the other. But in the latter half of the twentieth century, this was a less popular form of ownership as many shied away from owning and managing rental units. It was at this point that they became vulnerable to speculators.[11]

After the 1983 mayoral contest, Boston elections became tame affairs as they were rarely close. The reasons for this are as complex as the various factions that had been fighting over control of the mayor's office for the prior forty years, if not longer, as each had their own reason for pulling back from city politics. The business community had secured low property taxes and had the most pro-development environment possible despite the left-wing politics and rhetoric of the Flynn administration. Developers and their allies may not have liked linkage, but Flynn had been careful to keep it from being onerous, and there were still great profits to be made from investing in city real estate. Most saw little reason to speculatively spend money to secure a more sympathetic mayor.

Conservative Irish whites may have simply capitulated after losing the past seven elections. They may have realized they still dominated public sector jobs and the labor unions, so their position was more secure than they had once thought. They may have also finally understood that they could not overturn busing and other decisions they did like and that there were limits to what people of the city could do to keep outside societal forces at bay.

Though many had not supported him, middle-class Irish made their peace with Flynn and simply lost interest in politics in general. However, many were major beneficiaries of the new Boston as their children entered the workforce as highly-educated professionals while they continued to dominate many of the city and state jobs clustered downtown. Secure in their strongholds in West Roxbury and South Dorchester, they had no reason to upset the status quo.

The other potential source for candidates, the city's minority population, was divided. Many Latinos and Asians were not eligible to vote while the black community had ceased to grow, so the chances of seizing political control of the city seemed remote. Yet their share of municipal and state jobs was increasing just as pressure on private sector employers was beginning to have positive effects as well.

Perhaps most important and the overarching factor that reduced the importance of local politics for all groups was that the city had clearly turned a corner. It was not going to collapse, and there was the prospect of increasing prosperity that just might benefit everyone. Now that there were hopes of better times ahead, the stakes were no longer as high as they once were.

This did not mean that Flynn did not face challengers in 1987 and 1991; in both elections there were people who ran against him for mayor. But Flynn won 67 percent of the vote in the final election of 1987 against Joseph Tierney and 75 percent in the 1991 final against Boston Teachers Union President Edward Doherty. There were also several fringe candidates in the primaries who were mostly ignored by everyone else.

Much of the political excitement turned to the city council. Beginning in 1983, there were nine district and four at-large councilors. The at-large councilors reflected the Boston of earlier times as they represented the last hold of conservatives on local politics. In contrast, the districts, though they should have been better drawn to increase diversity, produced a changed council as they included two that securely elected two black councilors and an Italian district centered on East Boston and the North End. South Boston sent James Kelly, a prominent antibusing activist to the council while the progressives had a seat in the district serving Back Bay, Beacon Hill, and the Fenway, held for the first several terms by openly gay activist, David Scondras. The four other districts tended to send moderate white ethnics to the council. The Boston City Council may not have been very powerful, but it did provide a way for residents to have their values and experiences represented in City Hall.

On certain levels, the 1980s and early 1990s were good times for the LGBT community in Boston. Men danced late into the night in crowded bars in the Back Bay, Fenway, and the South End, gay and lesbian arts organizations flourished, and many considered Jamaica Plain to be one of the country's best lesbian communities. A few white gay men reached the pinnacle of the city's legal, government, and medical professions while many of the people involved in Boston area activism moved on to national positions. For example, Urvaishi Vaid ran the National Gay and Lesbian Task Force, Timothy McFeeley became the Executive Director of the Human Rights Campaign Fund, Richard Burns was head of LGBT Community Center of New York, and Eric Rofes steered the Los Angeles Shanti Project.

In 1981, however, the first cases of what had been rare cancers and pneumonia were identified in gay men in Los Angeles and New York. Once reported by the Centers for Disease Control in its weekly surveillance report, the rumors of the disease spread rapidly through

Boston's LGBT community but most were frozen in a mixture of denial and fear. Many hoped Boston, known throughout the gay world as a dull city to live with relatively tame nightlife, might be spared the disease. Fortunately, a few key people began to prepare for what became a tsunami of illness.

Though it took a while to identify the symptoms as the new terrifying disease HIV/AIDS, the Fenway Community Health Center knew early on that it would see cases and began to educate itself on how to care for its victims. For many years, doctors and staff could do little more than offer comfort to those dying, but even the willingness of staff to care for those suffering was a sign of nobility at a time when many refused to even be in the same room as a person with AIDS. GLAD was swamped with discrimination suits as employers, health care providers, and others shunned people with AIDS.

Another important institution was the Massachusetts AIDS Action Committee (AAC), founded by Larry Kessler and others in 1983. A group of concerned men and women had been meeting since the previous year trying to figure out how to address the coming epidemic, struggling to forecast what services might be needed, and looking for ways to raise awareness and change behaviors. As cases began to mount in Boston and elsewhere in the state, AAC had its hands full. It needed to help people with AIDS get access to healthcare (many doctors refused to even let suspected AIDS patients into their clinics), find housing if necessary (it was not uncommon for landlords to evict gay men who were ill), and assist clients to get their affairs in order and deal with family and employment issues. There was a need educate the community about what it could do to protect itself and advocate for increased funding and civil rights laws to address the epidemic. All of these took money and expertise to manage volunteers and paid staff. These were very tough problems as sometimes it seemed like they were fighting people inside the community as well as outside. But as time went on, AAC grew into one of the most effective AIDS service organizations in the country.

Later on a more radical organization appeared as there was a need for direct action against the slow response by government, pharmaceutical companies, and health care providers. The AIDS Coalition to Unleash Power (ACT UP) had begun in New York, but Boston was quick to organize its own chapter. AAC had his hands full trying to educate and provide services, and it grew to depend on cooperation with medical providers and funders, compromising its ability to organize protests. But ACT UP was free to use direct pressure on those who were slow to respond to the epidemic. Over the several years of its existence, the organization most famously held demonstrations outside Mass General Hospital with the goal of convincing doctors to adopt better practices to help their patients. Along with a sister organization, Queer Nation, ACT UP dominated LGBT radicalism during much of the late 1980s.

Over time, Boston's medical community became better at treating patients. Working closely with AAC and the Fenway Health Center, and sometimes cooperating with ACT UP, Boston hospitals and clinics rallied to provide treatment and comfort to the sick. They worked on setting up clinical trials, cosponsored conferences, and conducted important research on HIV.

Yet despite prayers, protests, handholding, and tears, thousands of gay men died horrible deaths in the first fifteen years of the epidemic. Officially, Massachusetts saw over 13,000 deaths from HIV-AIDS, but the number was even higher as many went home to die. Each of these deaths included an individual tragedy: personal suffering, the sadness of a life ended too soon, and the grief of friends and loved ones. Altogether, a significant percentage of an entire generation of gay men perished in this epidemic, which continues to this day.

Race relations improved in the Flynn years, but they continued to be a problem. Fed by a lingering bitterness over busing and disappointment stemming from Mel King's failed bid for mayor, many in Boston's black community supported a proposal to have the city's minority precincts break off from Boston and form their own city, to be named Mandela after the famous South African leader. The new city would have stretched from the South End down to Mattapan, expanding to take in black portions of Mission Hill and Dorchester in what would have been about a third of Boston. It was a controversial idea from the start.

It wasn't a grassroots proposal; it was an idea that arose among a group of four men who lunched at Harvard, only one of whom actually lived within the proposed city limits. Their idea was that by forming a majority minority city, people of color would have control over their destiny, or at least be able to preside over the new city's schools, police, fire, and development departments and shed the powerlessness that stymied black political aspirations and demands for a better future.[12]

At first, many white and downtown interests ignored the proposal, but when proponents succeeded in getting a non-binding referendum on the ballot, they organized to defeat it. The leader of the opposition was Charles Stith, the pastor at Union United Methodist Church and an influential black activist. The proponents of Mandela included Mel King and many members of his Rainbow Coalition.

One key issue in the debate was how much could the city's minority neighborhoods benefit by controlling new development in their independent city. Advocates suggested that there were potentially billions of dollars of new investment that could be harnessed to pay for government services. Opponents argued that there was not as much development potential as promised and that the new city's revenues would be insufficient to cover vital services.

The other major issue was minority control over city government. The 1983 council reforms had produced a council with just two minority members out of thirteen, and the prospects of more were thought to be years away. Farther out was the possibility of a minority mayor, and though Flynn had promised to hire minorities in key positions, the idea of waiting for white largesse at this late date was distasteful to many. In addition, the experience with minority hires in the Kevin White administration had left a lingering bad feeling as many that White hired ended up representing the interests of the mayor to the neighborhoods rather than representing the neighborhoods to city hall.

When the votes were counted, Mandela lost by a two to one margin as voters were not convinced they would be better off in an independent city. Proponents vowed to raise the issue again, but the idea of independence faded and is now forgotten.

Though Boston owes its existence to its port, for most of the city's history the quality of the water in the harbor was a scandal. Replicating the practice of small town England, as Boston developed over its first 250 years, it relied on a hodgepodge of privies, private drainage pipes, and street and backyard dumping to dispose of its waste. Though by law waste was supposed to be transported outside the city, most was dumped untreated into the harbor at the shoreline, through the storm drains, or by unscrupulous contractors.

With the introduction of new water supplies in the mid-nineteenth century, the sewage disposal problem became more difficult as its volume substantially increased. The solution in the 1870s was to create a system that relied on a central sewer that released raw sewage from most of the city into an outfall on the bed of the harbor off Moon Island. The underlying engineering idea was that this remote location with strong tides would dilute the sewage and keep waste from floating back onshore. At first, this was seen to be so successful

Deer Island Pumping Station. Poorly engineered and operated, it never served its function of cleaning waste water.

that the legislature authorized a second large drainage system to serve the areas north of the Charles River with an outflow at Deer Island and a new connection of the Back Bay to the Moon Island system. The same legislation also created the Metropolitan Sewerage Commission to take over the both systems, the first special district in the country devoted to waste water. Finally, a third drainage system for the area south of Boston was built with an outflow at Nut Island. All of these were combined storm and sanitary sewers, and during heavy rains, there were floods and backups, and, what is most important, they all dumped their sewage untreated into the harbor.

In 1901, the sewer and water boards were merged, and in 1919 they were combined with the regional parks agency to create the Metropolitan District Commission (MDC). By now it was clear that the system's disposal method did not work. A greasy film drifted from outfall pipes and tainted water-stained boats, and sewage regularly floated ashore on the beaches. Calm days created extensive areas with oppressive stench, storms resulted in floods of waste. As a result, there were frequent studies and calls for improvements, but beyond some partial separation of storm from sewer drains, little was done. By 1939, 250 million gallons of raw sewage were discharged into the harbor every day.

In response to demands from parents, doctors, businessmen, and others, the MDC built a sewage treatment plant at Nut Island in 1952, and in 1968, a new plant opened at Deer Island that also served sewage rerouted from Moon Island. These facilities only used what is known as primary treatment: settling tanks designed to remove about half of the solids in the sewage and reduce what is called biochemical oxygen demand, the total burden of organic matter, by about a third. The sludge from the settling tanks was then put in large tanks where microorganisms digested some of it to render it partly inert. But in a strange decision, the MDC then dumped this partially treated sludge directly into the harbor, negating most of the potential benefits of treatment and not surprisingly, these plants had little positive impact on water quality. Yet neither the city nor the state felt any urgency to remedy the situation. As with so many problems that affected the city, change would only come from outside forces.

Pressured by the growing environmental movement, Congress passed the Clean Water Act in 1965 mandating that states establish minimum water quality standards for rivers, lakes, and harbors, and Massachusetts passed its own law a year later. Yet these laws had minimal impact, and despite problems, the state certified that the treatment plants along the harbor met the new standards. In 1968, on the eve of the opening of the new Deer Island plant, over 460 million gallons of raw or partially treated sewage and 60 tons of sludge were being dumped each day into the harbor. The water stank and all but the very poorest avoided the harbor.

Secondary treatment that relied on bacteria dramatically reduced pollution, so the EPA required all public authorities receiving federal dollars to use it. But the Agency could grant waivers in certain cases, and, despite the mess in the harbor, Boston was one of the few cities that received one. The new Deer Island plant never worked properly because the MDC had purchased pumps that could not handle variable flows of sewage–a critical mistake. Furthermore, the plant was understaffed with poorly trained operators who found it easier to ignore problems than try to fix them. To make matters worse, the Nut Island facility, now twenty-years old, was slowly breaking down, and any time either plant was taken off line meant raw untreated sewage went directly into the harbor without even primary treatment.

In 1972, Congress passed a set of amendments to the Clean Water Act that prohibited the discharging of sewage into navigable waters and set a standard that surface waters should be drinkable, swimmable, and fishable. These guidelines required secondary treatment and authorized $18 billion to assist cities and states to meet the new standards with the federal government paying up to 75 percent of capital costs. Sludge could not be dumped into waterways, and storm water systems had to be separated from waste water. Both the EPA and private citizens were permitted to sue to force compliance with the law. But despite being in violation of the law, Boston, the MDC, and the state did nothing.

The EPA was unable to enforce its regulations as the MDC constantly asked for waivers, pleaded for time to voluntarily comply, or used the excuse that it was planning to fix conditions as ways to stave off actions and citations. Fed up, on December 17, 1982, the city of Quincy filed suit against the MDC. The next year the Conservation Law Foundation, a major regional environmental advocacy organization, sued the EPA as well. Paul Garrity, a self-described "Irish Street kid" and the man who had appointed a receiver for the Boston Housing Authority, was assigned to be the judge for the state case. Finding the MDC had shirked its responsibilities, on July 8, 1983, Garrity appointed Charles Haar as special master to get the cleanup started. He reported to the judge that the MDC lacked the staff and legal authority to comply with the law, so a new agency, one with the ability to float bonds and collect fees, was needed.

At first the state resisted this step, but when the legislature failed to act, Garrity imposed a moratorium on new sewer connections forcing a crisis in November 1984. The moratorium was overturned on appeal, but then the EPA threatened to sue and warned it also would impose a moratorium. Still the legislature stalled and Garrity threatened to place the MDC into receivership. Finally, pressured by lawsuits and the judge, the state admitted that the MDC was unable to clean up the harbor and created a new independent agency, the Massachusetts Water Resources Authority (MWRA), to take over responsibility for both water and sewer services in the greater Boston region.[13]

Despite the establishment of the MWRA, the EPA was dissatisfied with the progress of the cleanup and filed a federal lawsuit on January 31, 1985. The various lawsuits were consolidated by Judge A. David Mazzone who ruled on September 5, 1985, that the region was in violation of the Clean Water Acts and called for the parties in the case to submit remedies. The Dukakis Administration, sympathetic to the lawsuits, declined to appeal, and the judge's findings remained in effect.

Finally, the MWRA developed a serious plan for cleaning up the harbor including consolidating all sewage operations in a new plant at a Deer Island (with secondary treatment), building a pipe to transmit sewage from Nut Island to Deer Island, and constructing an outfall pipe miles out beyond the harbor deep in Massachusetts Bay. Groundbreaking for the project took place on August 10, 1988, with construction completed on September 6, 2000. The project cost $3.8 billion, only a portion of which came from anyone other than the rate payers. One persistent myth is that if the project had not been delayed, it would have been funded by the federal government. In reality, Massachusetts had always received its fair share of federal antipollution grants and had used them for other projects across the state. It was Massachusetts that had used Boston's money elsewhere.

The cleanup cost the ratepayers dearly. The MWRA estimated that the average combined water and sewer bill was $113 in 1986; by 2002 it was $511 and bills were projected to rise to $792 in 2010.[14] The average bill in 2013 was $1,389, but some communities had rates twice as high as others.[15]

As a result of this expensive project, the water quality of Boston Harbor dramatically improved. Beaches opened for swimming during the summer, and seals and other wildlife reappeared after centuries-long absences. Families could take advantage of the new federal park created on the harbor islands, and ferries and water taxis proliferated. The revitalized harbor is now a resource, not an embarrassment.

Flynn tried to repair the city's troubled race relations by settling a longstanding legal case over an unlawful shooting by a policeman, appointing black department heads, and carefully using conciliatory language in his public speeches. But he could not control racial incidents in the city, and his instinct to back close associates who permitted racist actions overwhelmed his good intentions. The worst of these failings came in the aftermath of the notorious murder of Carol DiMaiti Stuart on October 23, 1989.

Carol and her husband, Charles Stuart, were driving home to the suburbs after attending a childbirth class at Brigham and Women's Hospital. Stuart reported that after he took a wrong turn, a black man jumped into the car while they were waiting at a stoplight and forced the couple at gunpoint to drive to a street behind the Mission Hill Projects. There, the assailant started firing his gun at point blank range, killing Carol and her unborn son and shooting Charles Stuart in the stomach. Fighting to maintain consciousness, he called emergency dispatchers, who directed ambulances and policemen to his car by noting if sirens sounded louder or fainter.

Filled with grief for the horrific death of the young mother and unborn child, the public demanded that the police arrest the murderer. Flynn and other politicians went on record promising that every measure possible would be used to find the perpetrator, and the police locked down Mission Hill, randomly stopping and frisking young (and many not so young) black men and threatening residents with retribution if they did not help identify the murderer. Residents complained but were told that the imperative of hunting down the murderer was so great that civil rights did not matter. The press screamed for action and the murders were used to demonize Boston's black community, particularly its young. Finally, the police found their suspect, Willie Bennett.

Stuart identified him in a police lineup, and the public relaxed as Flynn and others heaped praise on the talents of the Boston Police Department for solving the atrocious crime.

Charles Stuart had lied. His brother, conscious stricken that he was helping to send an innocent man to jail for life for a murder he did not commit, confessed to the police that he had assisted his brother in murdering Carol Stuart, disposing of the gun and other evidence north of the city. Charles Stuart, knowing that the police were about to arrest him, jumped off the Tobin Bridge on January 4, 1990.

From the very beginning of his plotting his wife's murder, Charles Stuart was counting on the racism of the police to get away with the crime. The sad reality is that in the majority of cases when women are murdered, it is their husband or boyfriend who is the guilty person. But Stuart played off the fear of black on white violence and the biased perceptions of black neighborhoods when he shot his wife to deflect suspicion. The white police force, led by Francis "Mickey" Roache, was duped by Stuart because of their racist assumptions regarding young black men. It was easier for many to believe a poor black youth would kill a pregnant woman rather than a white middle-class man.

Roache, despite his incompetence in the case, escaped any punishment and kept his job because he was a childhood friend of Flynn. Despite several damning investigations of the Boston Police Department, no one was reprimanded for how they behaved in the case. Roache even went on to serve on the Boston City Council and as Suffolk County Register of Deeds, elected by conservative white voters. The black community seethed about the injustice for years but was ignored. Only the city's reputation was harmed.

Many of the major projects constructed in the 1950s had to be rebuilt as they proved to be harmful to the city. The largest of these do-overs was the Central Artery/Third Harbor Tunnel project, known as the Big Dig. By the 1980s, the Central Artery was a nightmare: clogged with traffic, blighting potentially valuable land, and rusting away to the point where engineers feared it would collapse. Realizing that it needed to be completely rebuilt, state planners decided to demolish the un-loved Artery and replace it with an underground road. In addition, they proposed to build a new tunnel to East Boston and reconfigure the approach roads. It would be the single most expensive highway project ever built in the United States.

The man who was to have the greatest influence on the city's transportation in the final decades of the twentieth century was Frederick Salvucci. He had been heavily influenced by the negative impacts of post-war transportation planning: his mother had lost her home to the Turnpike Extension, and he had been director of the Little City Hall in East Boston when Massport destroyed the area along Neptune Road to make way for its expansion. First appointed to be head of transportation by Governor Dukakis in 1975, he sought to consider the needs of those in the path of so-called improvements. Dukakis was another transit advocate; he famously rode the Green Line to work at the Statehouse from his home in Brookline. Back in office in 1983 after Dukakis defeated Edward King, these two anti-highway advocates conceived this multi-billion-dollar road project.

The Central Artery's congestion rippled out through all the region inside Route 128. The tunnels to Logan airport were also well beyond capacity, providing just two lanes in each direction and clogging for hours, particularly at times when businessmen wanted to get to flights. This put pressure on Massport for another tunnel that they might have rammed it through East Boston, destroying even more of that neighborhood. Solving these problems would be expensive and complicated but Salvucci had a plan: build the tunnel so it emerged on Massport property, sparing East Boston more disruption, and tying its funding and construction to the replacement of the hated Central Artery. To further appease skeptics, he vowed that the Central Artery and approach roads would be kept open during the construction of the new underground highway and tunnel.

Almost everyone had a reason to oppose the project: East Boston advocates feared another tunnel approach smashing through their neighborhood; environmentalists objected to a large new highway project; and big downtown interests feared the disruption of replacing the artery believing the high cost of rebuilding it would bankrupt the state or force an increase in taxes. But Salvucci and Dukakis persevered.

A vital ally was Speaker of the House Tip O'Neill who represented East Boston, Charlestown, and other parts of the city in Congress. Without his support, the project would never be able to secure enough federal funding, so Salvucci used all his powers of persuasion on him, going over the plans personally with the Speaker, demonstrating the new proposed route and guaranteeing that neighborhood opposition had been addressed. At one key meeting, the colorful O'Neill carefully studied Salvucci's construction plans, terrifying aides as he dropped hot cigar ash on the chemically-infused blue prints. Fortunately, O'Neill liked what he saw and dedicated his final years in office to shepherding it through the federal funding process.

Securing Republican support was more difficult. Senate Finance Committee Chair Robert Dole and his wife, Transportation Secretary Elizabeth Dole both opposed the project while Southern Republicans, consolidating their power under Ronald Reagan, had no love of liberal Massachusetts. Salvucci had to enlist business leaders with Republican credentials, and thus Bechtel, a San Francisco engineering firm led by President Richard Nixon associates, was awarded the design contract. This satisfied two of Salvucci's other needs: the State Highway Department lacked the staff to manage the rest of the state's construction projects, and he doubted they could design and build the project under any circumstances.

The chief target of lobbying was the head of the Federal Highway Administration, Ray Barnhart, who liked the tunnel but was skeptical about the artery. Eventually, he said he would give his approval to the combined project if the cost/benefits of the artery portion equaled those of the tunnel. He needed to see legal justification for the federal takeover of this state roadway as well. After long lobbying and multiple requests for information, Barnhart announced in 1985 that though he was not in favor of the full project neither would he oppose it. Congressman O'Neill had retired by this time, but his successors in the House kept on pushing for the combined project in recognition of his mentorship. The Democratic recapture of the Senate in the 1986 elections was a boost for approval as well.

The final obstacle to federal funding was President Ronald Reagan. He was opposed to federal transportation spending in general, and the Massachusetts project was so large it was particularly controversial. Despite efforts to sway him, on March 27, 1987, Reagan vetoed the federal transportation bill, citing its high cost and large number of pork barrel projects including the Big Dig. The veto was easily overridden in the

House, but the effort failed by one vote in the Senate. Though thirteen Republican senators voted to override, one Democrat, Terry Sanford of North Carolina, voted to sustain the veto because of a commitment to help the governor of his state who faced a tough reelection fight. Senate Democrats, led by Ted Kennedy, unleashed brutal pressure on Sanford, threatening to exile him from the leadership, suggesting they would cut off tobacco subsidies to farmers, and using every other possible promise and argument on him. Sanford crumbled, and though Reagan tried to sustain the veto, he lost. Even so, Sanford had to be personally escorted by Kennedy and Senate Majority Leader Robert Byrd to vote for the override. The project now had a federal funding commitment.

Yet the funding was not the blank check it seemed to be because the entire interstate highway program was coming to an end. Only one more transportation bill would be available to provide funding, and as the Big Dig was still in the planning and design phase, the total cost of the project and its funding needs were as yet unknown. As costs climbed in 1991, the era of 90 percent highway support by the federal government was over and the replacement for the Interstate program was funded at only a fraction of the previous law. Though federal dollars would be essential, they would not be sufficient.

Massachusetts politicians grumbled that the state had never received its fair share of Interstate money and that Route 128, the Tobin Bridge, Callahan and Sumner Tunnels and many other local projects had been built with state funding only. But in reality, though Interstate Highway moneys were distributed using a formula that favored rural states (and thus the state had been underfunded to a certain extent), Massachusetts had decided to use its federal dollars on other projects including building the outer ring highway, Interstate 495, and extensive highways in other parts of the state. The lack of federal dollars for the Big Dig was partly a Massachusetts decision-making problem. But in any case, the state had to find the money to pay for its share of the Big Dig.

Even at this point, however, not everyone in the state was sold on the virtues of the project. Many were veterans of the highway and urban renewal battles of the 1960s and 1970s, and they were skeptical of Salvucci's promise not to condemn houses or businesses in downtown

Boston and to minimize takings elsewhere. People and organizations had to be talked into supporting the project one by one. Salvucci secured support by modifying the design and promising to accommodate site specific issues all along the project. Thus, he allowed Donald Chiofaro, the developer of International Place, to have a ramp relocated for his buildings and promised Gillette that he would use a specially constructed dry dock to spare its South Boston manufacturing plant any disruption.

Not surprisingly, the biggest opponents were members of the State's environmental organizations. But they acquiesced to the project after they were promised extensive new parks and major expansions of the regional transit network, much of these accessories secured by negotiations led by the Conservation Law Foundation. The parks included a revitalized Spectacle Island (including covering trash dumped there with dirt from excavations), an expanded Harbor Walk, new open spaces along the Charles, and the Rose Kennedy Greenway along the old route of the Central Artery. Transit improvements included the extension of the Green Line to Somerville, the construction of the Greenbush Commuter Rail, and the building of the Silver Line, an underground bus system in South Boston and a bus rapid transit line in the South End and Roxbury.

Delivering on these promises was difficult. The Rose Kennedy Greenway has suffered from a lack of infrastructure support and has long been the subject of controversy over who was going to pay for maintenance, the city or the state. Building the transit extensions has been extremely problematic. The Greenbush line was completed in 2007, but it was very expensive and ridership has been modest. The Silver Line in South Boston opened as promised, but it has proved to be inadequate for the needs of the new Seaport area while its South End/ Roxbury segment is so poorly implemented that it is hardly an adequate bus line, much less anything that remotely resembles rapid transit. The Green Line extension may still be built (large cost overruns threatened its planning), but it is decades behind schedule. Even the contribution of the road to solving Boston's transportation problems has been questioned as it primarily serves suburban commuters, not city residents who are more likely to walk or take public transit than drive.

When Dukakis left office in 1991, Salvucci stepped down as head of the Department of Transportation. As of this point, construction had yet to begin, and the project was deep into the design and planning phase. Republican Governor William Weld picked Richard Taylor to be the new Secretary of Transportation, but the real driving force of state transportation policy was James Kerasiotis, an acolyte of tough talking Governor King and a staunch supporter of highways. Believing that the most effective management strategy was fear – he was said to keep a hatchet on display in his office – Kerasiotis publicly threatened and ridiculed his employees, but he was committed to making the project happen. Appointed Highway Commissioner, the lure of being the master builder helped him focus on the Big Dig.

A major issue evolved over who would be responsible for the construction and maintenance of the project. Salvucci considered and rejected the idea of having Massport be the prime agency because Massport's priorities were aviation, shipping, and economic development, and it did not want to be involved in highway construction. So instead, he proposed having the Massachusetts Turnpike Authority be the lead local agency. But the now sleepy Turnpike had not built anything in thirty years. However, it had vast bonding power and a steady income stream of tolls and fees that could be used to support the project.

Complicating the management decision, the Turnpike's assets were in great need of improvement, having suffered years of deferred maintenance so that tolls could be kept low and by the 1990s, the entire 135-mile turnpike needed repairs. Tolls were rising even before MassPike revenues could be used for the Big Dig, and Governor William Weld, faced with a $500 million budget deficit, wanted MassPike's revenues to help balance his budget. In another challenge, Senate President William Bulger used Weld's pursuit of the Turnpike revenues as a bargaining chip for him to seize control of the Massachusetts Convention Center Board, which was looking to build a new facility in South Boston. Despite these sideshows, slowly the consensus emerged that MassPike should be the lead player in the Central Artery. In 1995, the legislature passed a law transferring the responsibility for the third harbor tunnel over to the MassPike. In return, the MassPike was to eventually contribute $2 billion to the project.

Constructing the Big Dig required propping up the Central Artery and keeping its traffic flowing while excavating muck, mud, and fill underneath to construct a modern road. As such, the project was one of the most complex engineering plans ever proposed. To cross the harbor, also a working entity that could not be closed, the tunnel was constructed using prebuilt segments that were floated into place and then lowered into a trench that was partly dredged silt, partly blasted bedrock. One highway segment near South Station required superchilled liquid pumped into mud to freeze it before excavation and foundations were constructed. The main central artery was built using slurry wall construction and special girders to keep a functioning highway from collapsing while the dirt underneath it was removed and the new tunnel built.[16]

Preliminary engineering work had begun in 1982 with the bulk of construction between 1991 and 2002 with the final project completed in 2007. The statistics on the size of the project are difficult to comprehend: 16 million cubic yards of soil excavated (890,000 from the bottom of the harbor), 3.8 million cubic yards of concrete poured, nearly 5,000 trees and 30,000 shrubs planted, the widest cable stayed bridge ever constructed, and 26,000 linear feet of slurry wall,[17] The project was 7.5 miles long containing 107 lane miles. And through it all, the traffic never stopped flowing on the elevated highway until it was time to shut it down.

The costs were also massive. As Salvucci left office in 1991, the budget was thought to be $6 billion. Then five years later, as the full engineering and construction issues began to emerge, the cost was estimated to be $11 billion. Costs continued to balloon, but staff were scared to inform Kerasiotis. There were political concerns as well. Keeping the rising price tab secret avoided a scandal, and it enabled a string of Republican governors to boast they were fiscally conservative. But Democratic State Treasurer Shannon O'Brien, the person who had to float the bonds for the project, forced a crisis in 1999 by demanding a full financial accounting. Kerasiotis chose this moment to give an interview to a reporter that belittled his new boss, Governor Paul Celluci. By this time, Kerasiotis had alienated almost everyone from the Federal Highway Administration (FHWA) to the state legislature. Adding to the pressure, the FHWA had put a cap of $10.8 billion on the project, but there was a new working cost estimate of $12.2 with many internal estimates substantially higher. In any case, there would be no additional federal dollars for the project and it would be up to the state to pay for it. When the new numbers were made public, the state and federal government were stunned by the overruns. Kerasiotis was forced to resign in April 2000, but the finances of the project were in shambles. His successor, Andrew Natsios, was a political appointee who further plunged the MassPike into chaos. He was forced out too, and as leadership changed and construction commenced, the budget kept increasing. The final cost was about $14.6 billion, but with interest on the bonds used to pay for the project, it will ultimately cost $22 billion. By the end of the project, the federal share of funding was down to 48 percent.

James Aloisi, onetime Assistant Secretary of Transportation and general counsel of MassPike, boasted that the state never raised its gas tax to pay for the Big Dig, which was true.[16] But funding this project bankrupted almost every other transportation agency in the state leading to Congressman Barney Frank famously suggesting that it would be cheaper to raise the city than lower the Artery. Given the threat of rising ocean levels caused by global warming, this might have been a prescient idea. One of the most problematic solutions to the highway funding crisis was the decision to transfer billions of dollars of debt to the MBTA. In addition to this being a politically expedient way to hide the full cost of the project, it made some sense because the MBTA would be the ultimate owner and operator of the many transit improvements that were required as environmental mitigation in the state's settlement with the Conservation Law Foundation. But the MBTA itself had tremendous capital needs and large annual deficits.

So the result was that the MBTA is billions of dollars in debt and shifting costs to it was one factor that contributed to the collapse of the transit system in the winter of 2015. In this perverse decision, transit riders in Boston have subsidized suburban car owners. On the highway side, the fiscal results of the project were almost as bad as the state floated billions of dollars in bonds to pay for its share of the project. Mass Highways can't meet its debt obligation and pay for its maintenance costs so it rolled over its operating budget into new bonds, a tremendously fiscally irresponsible act. The state highway system also veered close to a fiscal collapse – for years it had to borrow money just to meet its operating expenses, but the state's gas tax was never increased.

After all the many billions spent on the Big Dig, the natural question is, was it worth the expense? Proponents say that it vastly improved the performance of the entire highway system, created a new linear park, and contributed to billions of dollars of new investment. But others maintain that highways are inherently bad and the system's overall congestion failed to improve; the park is nice but hardly a major asset to anyone but a few tourists and that new investment would have occurred anyways.[18] Many of the benefits would have happened if the state had simply torn down the artery and never replaced it. Such bold thinking was never seriously considered, however. The only thing that both sides of this argument agree on is that the demolition of the elevated highway removed a vast blighting structure that had torn apart downtown.

Flynn easily won election to a third term in 1991 and there was no reason to think he would not try to match Kevin White's four terms as there was no one in the city who could have beat him in the next election. Yet Flynn was tiring. The pace of his constant travels around the city, and the late-night meetings followed by early morning runs with old buddies, were taking a toll on his health. In addition, though the press kept it quiet until he ran into problems as Ambassador to the Vatican, Flynn had an alcohol abuse problem and was notorious for his ability to outdrink reporters and political associates.[19] The pace was becoming too much, and by 1992, his interest in being mayor seemed to wane and the city was in a holding pattern. However, because the economy continued to grow, there were few rumbles of discontent.

1. Saxenian A. *Regional Advantage*. Cambridge, MA: Harvard University Press, 1994.
2. Merry GB. Running a city: 100 days with Ray Flynn. *Christian Science Monitor*. 1984.
3. Lukas A. *Common Ground: A Turbulent Decade in the Lives of Three American Families*. New York: Vintage Books, 1986.
4. Canellos PS. The legacy of Boston's Sandinistas. *Boston Globe*. November 2, 2010; p. A11.

5. Editorial. A new depth for Dapper. *Boston Globe*. June 12, 1992; p. 18.

6. Le U. *Strategies for multicultural cities: Overcoming barriers to effective planning and community development in three Vietnamese American communities*. Masters Thesis, DUSP. MIT, 2009.

7. Waxman A. *Utilizing economic theories of retail to revitalize inner-city neighborhood business districts: The case of Uphams Corner Main Street*. Masters Thesis, DUSP. MIT, 1999.

8. Sternlieb JD. *Why low-income communities need their own development financial institutions: A case study of Upham's Corner, Dorchester, Massachusetts*. Masters Thesis, DUSP. MIT, 1993.

9. Kendall GL. *Community development corporations as an instrument of economic power and change: The Codman Square Experience. Masters Thesis*, DUSP. MIT, 1979.

10. Barcan SE. *One-to-four family foreclosures in South Dorchester: The role of the secondary mortgage market*. Masters Thesis, DUSP. MIT, 1994.

11. Wegmann J. *What happened to the three-decker?* Masters Thesis, DUSP. MIT, 2006.

12. Kenney C. The Aftershock Of A Radical Notion The Mandela Debate Is Still Very Much Alive - In The Painful Issues It Raised And The Enemies It Created. *Boston Globe*. April, 12, 1987; p. 14.

13. Haar CM. *Mastering Boston Harbor: Courts, Dolphins, and Imperiled Waters*. Cambridge, MA: Harvard University Press, 2005.

14. Dolin EJ. *Political Waters*. Amherst, MA: University of Massachusetts Press, 2004.

15. MWRA Advisory Board. *Annual Water and Sewer Retail Rate Survey*. 2013.

16. Aloisi JA. *The Big Dig*. Carlisle, MA: Commonwealth Editions, 2004.

17. Brown-West O. *In Defense of the Big Dig*. Marshfield, MA: Diabono Inc., 2007.

18. Flint A. 10 years later, did the Big Dig deliver? *Boston Globe*. January 3, 2016; p. R26.

19. Robinson W. Flynn at the Vatican: His mayoral style didn't cut it. *Boston Globe*. October 3, 1997; p. A1.

Chapter 7

The City Reborn: 1993-2004

A S 1993 BEGAN, there were hints of change flying around city hall, a building whose harsh concrete walls caused even the faintest rumor to echo and reverberate. Almost completely ignored in these hushed, but constant, discussions, Thomas Menino had been elected president of the city council. This was a routine vote for the modest man who had taken his seat in the council when the city had moved to its hybrid system of at-large and district councilors in 1983. In keeping with his low-key profile, no one considered that the president of the city council would become acting mayor if Flynn left office. Though Mayor Flynn had been a major supporter of in-coming US President Bill Clinton, and was known to be lobbying the President's transition team for an important position in the new administration, political observers were mixed on his chances of an appointment. Only a high visibility job would appeal to Flynn, but his South Boston reputation mitigated against that. In addition, though Flynn and Senator John Kerry were close – they had worked hard for each other in their campaigns over the years – Flynn's relations with Senator Edward Kennedy were more distant, and no one was sure if Kennedy might veto a Flynn appointment just as he had blocked Kevin White's ambitions decades before.

Then, on March 17, 1993, Raymond Flynn stood on the steps of a South Boston to church to announce he was being appointed Ambassador to the Vatican by President Clinton. When Flynn formally resigned on July 12, 1993, Menino became Acting Mayor with a primary election to fill the Mayor's office scheduled barely two months away. A mad rush for the office, one not seen since 1983, hit the streets of the city.

From the moment rumors began to circulate that Flynn might resign, potential candidates began to consider running for mayor. This required tricky maneuvering as Flynn was still a formidable power and would not tolerate any potential rivals locking up commitments of support from his loyalists. Flynn's control over his political machine was not as ruthless as White's had been, but his supporters were emotionally drawn to him and no one wanted to insult them. So after Flynn's announcement, the race rapidly took off as the support of nearly every constituency and voter was suddenly in play.

Menino, who liked his new job, faced seven challengers, most of them serious threats. City Councilors Rosario Salerno, a liberal favorite, and Bruce Bolling, a member of a prominent Roxbury family and the city's first black city council president, were well known and had been elected several times to the council. Yet both failed to win a place in the final as the city was not yet ready to give the Mayor's office to a black man or a former nun rumored to be a lesbian. Similar serious threats that faded were Suffolk County Sheriff Robert Rufo, who finished in third place by barely 2,500 votes, and Christopher Lydon, the sophisticated anchor of the region's public television newscast. Neither was able to translate high name recognition into votes perhaps because in the case of the former, no one quite knew what that the sheriff did and in the latter, most of his viewers lived outside of the city. Even more quixotic was the candidacy of disgraced police commissioner Francis Roache, who came in seventh with barely 3 percent of the vote, perhaps his only real punishment for his handling of the Charles Stuart murder case.

The final was a match between Menino and the popular Savin Hill State Representative James Brett, a protégé of Senate President William Bulger. Despite the fact it was a contest that featured Menino's Italian ancestry and problematic speaking style up against the slick and polished Brett, this was another race between the inner awards and the liberal/minority/outer wards. Demonstrating what little influence these dense inner Irish wards now held over elections, Menino easily won the final with 64 percent of the vote. The political coalition that once rammed Curley into office was now isolated and powerless.

Menino's personal style was closer to that of Flynn than White, Collins, or Hynes and he played up his working-class roots. He was born in the Readville section of Hyde Park, the son of a factory fore-man, and he never did well in school, dropping out before going back to get a college degree while serving on the city council. Menino had been a long-time aid to Joe Timilty and proudly represented the south-ern corner of the city as it began to see portions of the area become home to minority families moving in from neighboring Mattapan.

The press openly mocked Menino and his slow-tangled speaking style, calling him 'Mumbles.' Menino's accent was strong, and he had an amusing habit of using wrong words in his speeches, but over time, the public came to love his honesty and genuineness. He was a mayor without pretense, and voters reelected him four times; in 1997 he was unopposed, the only uncontested mayor's race in the second half of the twentieth century. Even when opposition surfaced, Menino never received less than 57 percent of the vote.

Menino's unsophisticated demeanor helped insulate him from suspicions he was too close to business interests on development is-sues. But he shared Kevin White's pro-development agenda, and like White, he actively inserted himself into design and land use decisions. Menino did not repeal any of Flynn's linkage or job ordinances, but neither did he attempt to expand them even though there would have been little opposition to his doing so. Nor did he press too hard to enforce existing laws, and though the BRA received negative publicity for its lackadaisical monitoring of assisted housing, linkage payments, and jobs requirements, these mini-scandals never sparked any reform. Menino was also famously against new technologies: city hall became known for its lack of voice mail, its reliance on secretaries to take mes-sages on pink memo pads, and its hesitance in using email and the internet.

Menino's appointments tended to draw on city residents, old and new. In contrast to White's glittering national superstars and Flynn's mix of over-achievers, Menino's aides tended to be bland and never threatened to outshine the humble mayor. Calling himself the urban

Mayor Menino. The longest serving and perhaps most loved of all Boston mayors.

mechanic, Menino and his administration never bothered to articulate broad goals and strategies. They even failed to create a comprehensive plan for the city.

Though the United States suffered from three severe recessions during the years that Menino was in office, Boston was relatively less affected than the country as a whole, a dramatic turnaround from earlier decades which saw Boston disproportionately impacted by economic downturns. By the 1990s, Boston had a very diversified economy that rested on a number of industries very different than what had been the main sources of income and jobs during its last period of economic prosperity in the early decades of the twentieth century. One of the strongest pillars of the New Boston economy was medicine and medical research. The 1990s saw a tremendous increase in spending on medical services, and the costs of doctors, drugs, hospitals, and every other type of medical spending dramatically out-increased inflation. In 1980, the United States spent 9 percent of its Gross Domestic Product on healthcare, for example, but by 2013 the healthcare percentage was over 17 percent. Boston benefited from this increase in several ways. Its eight major hospitals and numerous smaller clinics and specialized providers collectively employed over 100,000 people, most in well paying, recession proof jobs. The city's three medical schools anchored the country's most important center for medical research, and Boston received more money from the National Institutes of Health than any other city in the United States. Between 1993 and 2003, institutions and private companies in the city were granted a total of over $30 billion, and since 2000, about $1.6 billion of federal medical research grants were awarded in the city each year. In addition, the world's pharmaceutical companies built new facilities in the Boston area to facilitate the development of new drugs and treatments for diseases. For many years, much of this investment was across the river in Cambridge, but as time went on, many companies chose to open up research facilities in Boston particularly in the booming Seaport area. In addition, many of their employees wanted to live in Boston itself, and they were a strong driver a population growth and housing investment in the city.

Another very important factor underlying the New Boston was higher education. Schools such as Harvard and MIT had long had a national and global draw. Then other Boston colleges and universities beget to upgrade themselves and seek students, first from across the country and then from countries around the world. Perhaps the most successful of these remade institutions were Boston University and Northeastern University. Boston University began its upgrade in the 1970s under the very controversial leadership of John Silber. He battled faculty, students, and the press and was a notorious misogynous, once calling the English Department a "damn matriarchy" because it had too many tenured women.[1] Because, or despite, his propensity for insulting nearly everyone, by the time he left office, Boston University had a national reputation and was a leader in attracting top faculty and large research grants.

Northeastern University had been founded by the Boston YMCA to help educate the children of immigrants and working-class families that either couldn't afford traditional colleges or did not have the time to attend class during the day. In the 1960s, it began to transition to a full-time university, yet it still drew students primarily from families of modest means in the Boston region. Then in the 1990s, Northeastern become a major higher education player with a national reputation for excellence. Part of its appeal was its popular and well respected co-op program in which students took a year off to work at jobs related to their majors. Coming at a time when education costs were becoming a major drain on family finances, this emphasis on employment drew students from around the world.

At the same time these institutions were upgrading themselves, other colleges in the city – such as Boston College and Emerson College – also began to draw from outside New England. Altogether, the colleges and universities in Boston and the region had budgets that totaled in the billions, bringing in large amounts of donations, grants, and people into the area. The growth in students, faculty, and staff at higher education institutions both in the city and in the surrounding suburbs also had a tremendous impact on the city. Many of the people employed by these colleges and universities chose to live in the city, and Boston was enlivened by the hundreds of thousands of students. Many stayed on after graduation.

The third great pillar of the local economy was business services even though there was a tremendous churning in its employment mix. During the early 1990s, many of the best paying of these jobs were in banking and legal services. But then consolidation resulted in Boston offices becoming outposts of banks and law firms headquartered elsewhere, and by the year 2000, there were no large Boston-based banks and very few Boston-headquartered law firms. Fortunately, outsiders were willing to pay a premium to buy Boston talent, and business services remained as important as ever with the overall employment in these industries stable. In addition, the city increasingly became a preferred location of venture capitalists, hedge fund leaders, money managers, and many other providers of non-banking financial services that worked with clients from around the world. Thus, the city was one of the major beneficiaries of globalization and integration of world markets. At the same time, Boston continued to have offices for architects, specialized legal services, technology providers, and others who were highly compensated. Again, many of these very wealthy people chose to live in the city, not just the suburbs.

Finally, the Boston area continued to be a center for high technology companies. Though Mark Zuckerberg famously left Harvard to move to Silicon Valley to establish Facebook, graduates of local universities founded and grew many companies that contributed to the great explosion of internet-related businesses at the beginning of the twenty-first century. For the most part, these were still outside of the city, more likely to locate in Kendall Square than they were in Boston itself. However, they added to the general prosperity of the region even if their employees tended to live in Cambridge and Somerville.

As a result of these forces, Menino oversaw one of the largest booms the city ever experienced as tens of millions of square feet of office space were built. Relatively little of this construction was in the financial district, however; most was in Back Bay, the Longwood Medical Area, and other areas of the city. One of the most important projects was the redevelopment of the Prudential Center. Planning began during the Flynn years, but in Menino's term it was transformed into a true asset of the city as its owners built new housing and office buildings on the ring road and reconfigured its dreaded outdoor arcades into enclosed amenities. In what was one of Menino's most publicized intrusions into the process of development approval, the top of 101 Huntington Avenue was redesigned to comply with Menino's preference that no flat-topped skyscrapers be approved by BRA's design review process.

Menino's housing record was mixed. In the 1990s, the city added only 1,072 new units, but almost 10,000 other units went from vacant to occupied as many of the city's remaining substandard, vacant, and abandoned units were renovated and reoccupied. Then in the 2000s, 20,546 units were constructed, the most of any decade since at least the 1920s. Many of these units were built in high-rise buildings that swept across the inner core of the city. Unfortunately, there was an ominous new trend that emerged in the first decade of the new millennium: the number of vacant units increased by over 7,100.[2] These new vacancies were not the result of decay or abandonment, often the cause of vacancies in other older cities; in Boston they were caused by speculators and part-time residents buying the units. Many vacant condominiums were purchased by individuals or families who meant to hold on to the properties for several years, unused, and then resell them for a profit. Others were bought by people who lived elsewhere and only visited Boston for a few weeks or months out of the year. These units are counted as vacant by the U.S. Census and city planners. The result, however, is that these units are effectively not part of the city's available housing stock, and they constrict the amount of housing available to low and moderate income households.

One result of prosperity was that the city enjoyed stable finances. State law caps property taxes at 2.5 percent of assessed valuation, and the total annual city levy cannot increase by more than 2.5 percent plus the amount of new construction. In both the 1990s and 2000s, total property valuations rose faster than this amount meaning that Boston's total allowable property tax levy dropped to less than 2.5 percent. With classification, Kevin White's initiative that shifted taxes from residential to commercial properties, and a generous home owners' exemption, the levy on owner occupants in the city dropped. As a result, home-owners had smaller tax bills in Boston than they faced in most of the city's wealthy suburbs where high taxes to fund school budgets were paid for by residential owners. In what was a stunning reversal from previous decades in Boston—and the situation that prevailed in almost every other major city in the country—property owners could save as much as 30 percent on their taxes by moving into the city. For those homeowners who didn't have school-aged children, this proved to be particularly enticing, and in Boston's wealthy suburbs, parents actively planned to move into the city once their youngest child graduated from high school.

Another major factor in easing Boston's fiscal problems was the privatization of Boston City Hospital (BCH). For nearly 150 years, BCH had provided health care to the poor of the region, whether they could pay or not. Successive mayors expanded its facilities in the corner of the South End, adding wards and clinics in an effort to curry favor with the voters. Curley boasted of his expansion effort as proof of his support for the poor, and Flynn pointed out his mother had cleaned floors at BCH as he pushed the City Council to approve his plans to upgrade its physical plant. But by the Menino years, the ever rising cost of delivering health care (which benefited employment in the city) was making the Department of Health and Hospitals a major drain on the city budget.[3] This was not just a Boston problem; across the country, public hospitals were under pressure and either closing, merging, or being privatized as local budgets could not meet their deficits. Menino staked a great deal of personal political capital on selling BCH to Boston University, which operated its own money-losing hospital next door. Labor unions were very opposed to the sale, and many of the regulators and office holders who had to approve the sale were reluctant to take them on. But the crush of rising costs and stricter reimbursements for care for the uninsured and poor made the sale imperative. Boston University purchased BCH and merged into what is now Boston Medical Center, still one of the largest hospitals and the largest provider of care to the poor in the state. The non-medical providing programs were assembled into a new city agency, the Boston Public Health Commission, marking the reinvigoration of the country's oldest municipal health department, started by Paul Revere and others back in the eighteenth century. These moves also stopped a tremendous drain on the city's budget.

Despite the prosperity of many Boston neighborhoods, there were two important limits to the community-based economic development model developed by Flynn and continued by Menino: market constraints and funding limitations. The Menino years demonstrated the difficulty of translating a booming economy downtown to help promote job development in minority neighborhoods. The experience of community-led economic development in Roxbury and other minority neighborhoods was disappointing as attracting private investment and job-creating development proved elusive. Communities created detailed master plans that strongly articulated neighborhood values and objectives, but attracting developers who had the experience and access to capital to turn plans into reality mostly failed. Perhaps the strongest barrier to success was racism. Developers mostly decided to invest outside the minority community in projects that ignored people of color. For example, thousands of person hours were donated to create the Roxbury Strategic Master Plan, a document that could serve as a national model for articulating the needs and local expertise of a poor to middle-income black community. But despite great ideas for parcels, such as those near Ruggles Station, little new private job creation resulted and few buildings were constructed by for-profit developers.

There have been exceptions. Hyde Square in Jamaica Plain has been a showcase of Latino-owned businesses that attract people from around the region, while nearby Egleston Square has few empty storefronts. Grove Hall has a small bustling neighborhood business district anchored by a supermarket, but far too many of Boston's minority residential neighborhoods have struggling retail districts pockmarked by vacancies or marginal enterprises.

A similar problem affected housing development. Developers displayed an ever-accelerating interest in building housing for the wealthy, but only CDCs and a few for-profit developers specializing in subsidized housing were willing to build for poor or middle-income households. So as the century ended, there was a crisis in affordability, not just for low-income residents but also even for middle-class residents.[4] Households had to pay high percentages of their incomes on rent or mortgages; families with children who needed larger units were forced to move to the suburbs. As with his predecessors, Menino was not able to connect the prosperity of the central part of the city to the neighborhoods that needed it the most.

As the new century began, one of the most important changes in the city was the dramatic fall of the Catholic Archdiocese of Boston. For most of the twentieth century, politicians had been afraid to cross the church hierarchy, wondering "how would Lake Street (the location of the Cardinal's residence) react," and some credit Cardinal William O'Connell's support for Maurice Tobin for the defeat of James Curley back in 1937.[5] But in December 2002, a scandal broke, and by the end of it the Church's reputation was in tatters and its ability to influence either elections or public opinion was ended. The cause was the shocking revelation that the hierarchy had protected priests who had abused children. For years, Cardinal Bernard Law had ignored the magnitude of the problem and instead tried to remedy abuse by transferring priests between parishes or attempted to address their predations via ineffective therapy or empty threats. Instead of turning them over to the police or defrocking them, "Law, his bishops, and their predecessors had moved abusive priests around like pawns on a chessboard."[6] By the time the scandal fully emerged, thousands of children had been abused, hundreds of thousands had their faith shattered, and many left the church or stopped attending services. Cardinal Law, one of the most influential prelates in the country, had been secreted away into the Vatican bureaucracy, and the political power of the church in the city was shattered and destroyed.

For decades, there had been evidence that there were problems, but the public did not know the magnitude of the abuse and the church did not change its ways. In other parts of the country, the first public sex scandals occurred in the mid-1980s but were often viewed as isolated incidents. In Massachusetts, the crisis began in 1992 when James Porter, a retired priest, went on trial in Fall River. The public was aghast, but no one outside the church knew about accusations against other priests.

Predatory priests took advantage of the social and economic declines that afflicted many communities during the late decades of the twentieth century. Social disintegration was catching up with Boston's poor large Catholic families, and many women found themselves abandoned and forced to raise multiple children alone with particular problems parenting their sons. For example, one family of victims was a single woman with four boys, another consisted of a lone woman raising her four children as well as four nieces and nephews. When a local parish priest took an interest in a boy, their mothers, in their innocence, were often relieved that a male authority figure was there to help. These families, desperate to cope with poverty, substance abuse, and domestic violence, needed the stability that a wise priest might provide. So the predators purposely sought out children from these families because they were most vulnerable and most likely to welcome them into their houses. Intact middle-class families rarely felt a need to open their doors to these priests, and their children were much less likely to be victimized. Providing respite to overworked parents, abusers took children out for ice cream or camping trips or had the children visit them in their offices and private quarters.

Priests abused boys everywhere: rectories, confessionals, bedrooms, summer homes, motel rooms, and the bleachers at Fenway Park. Betrayed by the church's esteem, time and again, children would bravely report the abuse they suffered and their parents would complain to church officials. But the response was almost always to counsel the victims and their families to keep quiet and to assure them these were isolated incidents. At most, a priest would be temporarily sent away to be treated or reassigned to another parish because the hierarchy was more intent on secrecy and protecting priests than they were on serving abused children and their families. Often the supervising priests in the new parish were aware of a priest's past and rumors about individual priests were widespread inside the archdiocese. Only parishioners were kept uninformed.

At the center of the scandal was Law, a robust, white haired, Harvard graduate whose energy, faith, and charisma led to comparisons with the Kennedys and Cardinal Richard Cushing. Bostonians had never warmed to his predecessor, Cardinal Medeiros, whose Portuguese background, quiet faith, and pro-integration policies had distanced him from the lay people of the archdiocese. Law, on the other hand, was one of their own, an Irishman in charge of one of the most heavily Irish dioceses in the country.

Within six months of arriving in Boston in 1984, Law received his first written complaint from a parent regarding sexual abuse, and year by year more reports about predations were sent to him. The first public incident in Boston was a 1996 lawsuit against Father John Geoghan filed by a mother on behalf of her three sons. The head of St. Andrews parish in Jamaica Plain, Geoghan looked like a kindly uncle or a meek corner store owner, perhaps like a little imp, but he was a monster, molesting as many as 800 boys over his career. Not caring about his impact on these vulnerable children, sometimes he would lead his victims in saying a Hail Mary while pulling down their pants. Geoghan was convicted of child abuse in 2002 and was murdered in prison less than a year later.

As more stories about abuse slowly became public, additional victims came forward and Law was repeatedly advised, begged, and threatened to take action by victims and their families. But each time

Cardinal Law. Supporters could never reconcile the Cardinal's compassion for those needing assistance with his ignoring the victims of the church abuse scandal.

he demurred, and instead, the church focused on two questions: should priests be returned to parishes after treatment where they would still have access to children? Should crimes be reported to legal authorities? The Boston Archdiocese, like others across the country, decided yes and no. After brief time outs for treatment, and following a policy not to notify the police, these priests were returned to schools and parishes. Free of restraint, the abuse continued.

Though he avoided publicity for a time, the Cardinal couldn't control the damage as new victims kept coming forward. During the period 1992 to 2002, the archdiocese settled many lawsuits, in almost every case requiring victims to sign agreements to keep quiet in return for receiving compensation. Under Massachusetts law, a charitable institution such as the Catholic Church could only be held liable for $20,000. So the lawyers for the abused sued Law and other members of the hierarchy personally, and the archdiocese paid out tens of millions of dollars in settlements to victims. The Archdiocese was facing bankruptcy. At one point, the Archdiocese made a deal to settle about 80 of the suits by creating a compensation pool but then revelations about Father Geoghan sparked over 500 more abuse claims. The church reneged on the deal because it could not afford it, and eventually, over seventy Boston priests had suits brought against them.

Even as the lawsuits increased, the church kept the knowledge that the hierarchy had ignored the problem out of the press, and its reputation was still intact. Law was content to mislead the public that the problem concerned only a few rogue priests. Then, in September 2001, the *Boston Globe* filed suit to have records regarding priests abusing boys made public, and in November a judge ruled for the paper. The archdiocese appealed, but in January 2002 ten thousand pages of records were released. When the *Globe* published a series of articles based on the records shortly thereafter, the full horror of the problem was at last made public. The Archdiocese was humiliated, and the public was outraged.

The revelations that Law had done little to protect children were devastating. It had taken over a dozen years to defrock Geoghan, for example, despite hundreds of complaints. Isolated and cold hearted, Law seemed incapable of understanding the depth of the public's demand for change. Belatedly responding to the *Globe* articles, he declared that all current priests with credible charges against them had been removed from parish positions but then had to reassign eight more priests. As lay people demanded he be made accountable for his actions, Cardinal Law became a recluse, unable to interact with the public without being harassed by protestors and reporters. Even the Cathedral of the Holy Cross in the South End was off limits to him as it was surrounded on Sunday mornings by victims and their advocates calling for justice. He was ridiculed by comics and commentators, and most parishioners wanted him out.

By April 2002, Law was almost a ghost, abandoned by his once enthusiastic inner circle of wealthy and influential businessmen and politicians, hounded by the press, and even shunned by his fellow American cardinals. He took to flying out of Newark Airport, driving for hours rather than risking being seen at Logan Airport. Many who knew Law, both priests and others, were most surprised by his lack of empathy with the abused. Here was a man known for his prayerful compassion for grieving families at funerals and other tragedies yet unable to understand the catastrophe for children and their families that he had done nothing to stop. He had to leave. Offered a post in the Vatican, Law resigned his position in Boston on December 13, 2002.[6]

Many of the victimized children were scarred for life. Some turned to drugs and alcohol, others never learned how to trust or love anyone. The effects went beyond depression: "souls darkened, hearts broken, lives shattered, families disillusioned, faith abandoned."[7] After the scandal, the church was an empty shell. In the words of conservative advocate Philip Lawler, "In the space of a generation, the Catholic Church in Boston had dropped from a position of unquestioned dominance to one of public obloquy: from bully to whipping-boy."

Boston grew in the 1990s. The city's white population continued to decline, and though for the first time ever Boston had a majority minority population, the drop was much smaller than in any other decade. Boston's black population was stable, but this masked continuing change within that community as Haitians were joined by another immigrant group, Cape Verdeans. The first Cape Verdeans had settled in New Bedford during the whaling era in the nineteenth century; the island's residents had a strong maritime tradition, and their numbers grew slowly until after 1970 when new immigration laws and unrest in Cape Verde prompted thousands to move to Boston. Most settled in North Dorchester.

Similarly, there was a changing mix of Latino residents in the city as new groups crowded in to the city, fleeing unrest in Central America, much of it fostered by military dictatorships backed by the United States government. Though they shared a common language with

Puerto Ricans, Dominicans, and others, there were substantial cultural differences, even if white native-born Americans often lumped them all together. Yet they were welcomed into the community.

Even greater differences marked Boston's growing Asian population as it now included engineers and scientists as well as farm workers fleeing political turmoil and communist governments. Boston's Asian community included Indians, Pakistanis, and Filipinos in addition to longer established Chinese and Vietnamese enclaves.

There were winners and losers in the new Boston. In some respects, changes in the city reflect changes in the national economy with a hollowing out of the middle class, but in Boston, these were more pronounced. Overall, well-paying jobs that did not require a college degree disappeared while most new jobs either required high levels of education and paid very well or were very low paying and relied on immigrants, blacks, and other low-wage workers. Meanwhile, the white working class contracted. There were additional implications from this bifurcation. Those with high incomes could purchase quality housing anywhere in the city while those without were increasingly squeezed into a few high poverty neighborhoods or were forced to leave Boston altogether. The city now had a ring of low-income suburbs including Chelsea, Brockton, Lawrence, and Lowell.

Despite the city now being majority non-white, people of color had only minimal participation in such major initiatives such as the Big Dig and the development of the Seaport District.[8] The lack of minority participation extended across the social, economic, and political landscape of the city. Rarely did (or do) major boards of directors of businesses in the city include more than one or two minority persons (and few have more than a small percentage of female members), and beyond a few sports figures and politicians, most are absent from any sort of public endeavor. The city's non-profit institutions fare no better, and it is still rare to find a board member of color among the many key organizations in the arts, education, health care, and other important drivers of progress in the community.

The New Boston had a serious impact on one of its most traditional neighborhoods, Chinatown. For generations, city and state policies had put Boston's Chinatown at risk as public agencies took land for the Masspike and Central Artery, allowed the expansion of Tufts New England Medical Center (NEMC), and created the Combat Zone. The two highways alone destroyed half of the land in the neighborhood and one third of its housing. The 1965 South Cove Urban Renewal Plan enabled the medical center to use federal, state, and city money to take properties and triple its size. By the 1990s, Chinatown had been reduced to 46 acres housing 5,000 people and hundreds of restaurants and businesses.

The first large-scale Chinese movement to Boston began in the 1870s. Some came after being used to break a strike in North Adams, others moved to the city to work in construction, and still others were fleeing racist persecution on the West Coast. For many years, the area's Asian population remained small as racist immigration laws prevented new arrivals from China and Japan. These laws began to be relaxed during World War II and then were eliminated altogether when immigration laws were reformed in 1964. Along with turmoil in China, this resulted in a new wave of immigrants moving into Chinatown in the 1970s.

There was no room to expand housing in Chinatown, and the neighborhood spilled over into adjacent areas of the South End. Some moved to other neighborhoods or suburban towns, but the demand for housing in and around Chinatown remained extreme, even though the low incomes of many immigrants made it difficult to afford the rents there or elsewhere. It was in this context that a proposal to use Parcel C, a 25,000-square-foot lot zoned for housing, as a site for an 850-space parking garage for NEMC ignited large-scale opposition. Bowing to the needs of Chinatown, the BRA turned down this 1986 proposal and initiated a process to turn the parcel over to the community for assisted housing. In 1990, NEMC acquiesced to the idea, abandoning a lawsuit and excluding the parcel in its Master Plan submitted to the city that year. Seeking peace, the BRA reaffirmed the parcel's residential zoning and specifically prohibited institutional uses. But in 1993, NEMC again wanted Parcel C, this time for a 455-space garage and ancillary space. In return for the BRA selling it the lot, NEMC promised $2 million to the BRA and $1.8 million in community benefits. The BRA endorsed NEMC's proposal and, despite protests, so did the Chinatown Neighborhood Council, a supposedly representative group that had been appointed by Mayor Flynn. Rushing to make the deal happen, the BRA designated NEMC to be the developer even though 250 people showed up to protest and 2,500 signed a petition opposing the plan. The BRA also gave NEMC a lease for $1 a year. Angry protestors formed the Coalition to Protect Parcel C for Chinatown, an organization with the immediate goal of stopping the garage and a long range plan to overturn the influence of the neighborhood council by empowering residents, most of whom were low-income immigrants who lacked access to the BRA's development decision making process. In many ways, this dispute was a reiteration of the battles over urban renewal in the South End in the 1970s, and organizers of the Coalition consulted with Mel King and other veterans of those efforts.

The neighborhood council was the latest version of a small, connected group of Chinatown businessmen used by the city to give a veneer of community approval to predetermined plans. The first group to be the public face of the community had been the Six Companies, a mutual aid group headed by a few businessmen. Over the decades, this was replaced by the Chinese Consolidated Benevolent Society, another business dominated group, and finally, the neighborhood council. By the 1990s, this succession of mostly similar groups had become very disconnected from the mass of low-income, non-English speaking immigrants and the employees of the social service organizations that worked with them.

The first battle was convincing the state to require a full environmental review. Once this process began, the Coalition used an extensive network of lawyers and consultants to help keep neighborhood concerns included in the process. The Coalition also organized young people from Chinatown to manually count traffic around the parcel, and they found that NEMC had underestimated the current traffic burden by a third to a half. Very significantly, the Coalition held a referendum on the proposal, attracting 1,700 voters including 664 Chinatown residents with 1692 voting no and 42 voting yes, demonstrating that the community was overwhelmingly against the garage. Unfortunately, the Coalition was unable to use this momentum to elect its own slate to the neighborhood council in the next election.

By now Flynn had been replaced by Menino, but the city continued to support NEMC and refused to meet with the Coalition. Frustrated, the Coalition considered a demonstration but decided on a community fair instead because it feared that any arrests resulting from a civil action might harm the immigration status of some of its members. The Coalition also filed a civil rights complaint, charging this was one more in a series of discriminatory actions against the community. Finally, on October 5, 1994, the city caved and terminated the garage plan. The Chinese Consolidated Benevolent Society was designated developer.[9]

The efforts to preserve Chinatown included a new wave of activists such as Lydia Lowe. She had been born and raised in California, the daughter of a college professor, and completed her education at UMass Boston after moving to the city in 1981. First active in education issues in Pasadena and then working to prevent the evictions of elderly San Franciscan Asians, Lowe brought her passion to a new organization, the Chinese Progressive Association.[10] Boston's reputation as an activist city helped it grow, and in turn these newcomers helped make the city a better place for all.

By the end of the White administration and continuing through the Flynn and Menino administrations, many people were dissatisfied by the city's efforts to preserve, protect, and promote Boston's built and social infrastructure. In response, they organized numerous advocacy groups that helped shape the city and greatly contributed to its quality of life. One of the oldest of these organizations was the Beacon Hill Civic Association. Organized in the 1920s to protect the area's historic fabric, it was kept invigorated by subsequent threats to the area that ranged from Mayor Curley's attempt to replace the Hill's brick sidewalks with concrete to Mass General Hospital's proposed expansion across Cambridge Street.[11]

In 1970, the Beacon Hill Civic Association, the Neighborhood Association of Back Bay, and others helped organize the Friends of the Public Garden whose agenda also included protection of the Commonwealth Avenue Mall and the Common. Led for forty-one years by the indefatigable Henry Lee, the Friends group was the inspiration for similar groups across the city. Lee was a Boston Brahmin from one of Massachusetts' oldest families, born in Beverly Farms and a graduate of Harvard and Stanford. He represented the best of a generation committed to making the city a better place, and he raised millions for the Public Garden and Common, fought Kevin White when the Mayor proposed office projects that might cast shade on the parks, and worked to nurture public spaces that welcomed everyone, young and old, rich and poor.

Lee and the Friends of the Public Garden were not the only group working to make the city better. By the 1980s, there were other important organizations: the Boston Harbor Association who, with others, secured the city's commitment to create the Harbor Walk, a thirty-nine-mile of pedestrian ways and open spaces along the waterfront, and the Boston Greenspace Alliance helped rejuvenate the city's many neighborhood parks and school yards. The success of these organizations was founded on the willingness of individuals, foundations, and businesses to donate time, money, and resources to their causes as well as the tremendous energy and talent of their leadership. The Boston Harbor Association, for example, was steered by the visionary Vivien Li for almost a quarter center. She not only was a vital part of the Boston waterfront dramatic transformation, she was also an effective lobbyist for cleaning up the harbor and preserving public access to areas along the shoreline. "Her blessing was highly sought by the developers building a skyline along the city's waterfront."[12] The daughter of immigrants, Li began her environmental activism in high school in New Jersey. She first came to Boston on a fellowship to MIT, then moved here permanently to work on environmental health issues for the state. By the time Li left for Pittsburgh to work on waterfront issues there, she was one of the most prominent environmentalists in the region.

The success of South End tenant groups to acquire housing and control development along with the trauma of displacement in that neighborhood helped jumpstart the organization of the Dudley Street Neighborhood Initiative (DSNI), a nationally-recognized community organization that works to revitalize the area around the intersection of Dudley Street and Blue Hill Avenue. Founded in 1984, it successfully empowered its diverse population—meetings are translated into English, Spanish, and Cape Verdean—to turn around what was once the city's most troubled area into a model of resident-owned housing and economic development. Though Boston never had the vast tracts of abandoned housing and vacant buildings that plagued most older United States cities, the Dudley triangle area was rapidly on its way to being the exception. Lots were piled high with trash and construction debris, dumped by unscrupulous contractors from around the region; the piles sometimes reached eight feet high. There was high crime and every sort of twentieth century urban problem in this small area. Alarmed, a consortium of non-profit organizations and funders came together to create a new organization to work on the area's problems. When they presented their plan to the public, residents reacted angrily and demanded the right to set agendas, create plans, and manage programs. Stung by the rebuff, the outside institutions agreed to fund a resident driven process.[13]

It took years for residents to educate themselves, assess problems, and develop a strategy to promote change, but funders grew to appreciate the tremendous energy and depth of commitment that residents brought to the meetings. Slowly they began to create a vision for the area: through community land trusts and by working with CDCs and others, they would build housing for residents and implement a coordinated set of social service programs aimed at involving all portions of the community. One of DSNI's successes was convincing the Flynn Administration to grant DSNI the right to use eminent domain to acquire vacant tax delinquent properties in its core area. Eminent domain is a powerful tool, forcing owners to sell their land (at fair market value) and allowing new development to happen on parcels with clear title. The BRA and other city agencies were initially very skeptical; no community-based organization in the country had ever been granted this power, but DSNI won over skeptics through political gamesmanship, the quality of its proposed plans, and humor: they famously first presented Flynn department head Lisa Chapnick with a map of the world, then produced a neighborhood map prompting Chapnick to say that their proposal looked reasonable when contrasted with the size of the globe.[14]

DSNI's work began to produce tremendous results in the 1990s as new housing was opened, noxious land uses were cleaned up, and programs assisting residents began to show results. One very interesting strength of DSNI's work was the lower rate of defaults among homeowners on land trust developments in the 2008 recession. The area was largely spared the large numbers of foreclosures that swept over other low-income areas of Boston.[15] Always mindful that they were working for the community, DSNI attracted several talented executive directors including Gus Newport, former mayor of Berkeley, California; Gregory Watson, who went on to become a major advocate for community-based agriculture in the state; and John Barros, who began his involvement with DSNI as a teenager and ran for mayor in 2014.

Throughout the 1990s, the city's LGBT community slowly gained important freedoms as social mores changed and their legal status improved. Though there were still too many exceptions, gay men and lesbians found that no one at their worksites cared about their sexuality, family members kept on loving them after they came out, and the police were now generally sympathetic. The Supreme Judicial Court had invalidated one statute against sexual relations between consenting adults of the same sex in 1974, and when GLAD sued to have the other law overturned in 2001, the case was tossed out when the plaintiffs could not cite a single instance of it having been enforced in the past several decades. In 1989, the state passed a comprehensive law prohibiting discrimination against LGBT people in employment, credit, housing, and public accommodation, and after his election in 1992, Governor William Weld implemented a number of LGBT friendly policies while Boston was similarly supportive of LGBT people.

This did not mean that LGBT people were now free of all discrimination, but it meant that most overt repression had ended. Upper-class white men experienced the greatest freedom and security while LGBT people of color continued to face higher levels of adversity. Transsexuals and people who didn't conform to conventional gender norms were confronted by the greatest threats. Yet with two openly gay Congressmen and many state and local elected LGBT officials, the age of 'Don't Ask, Don't Tell' was in the past.

There was a price paid for increased integration with mainstream society: important institutions withered during the decade. Though the local LGBT community maintained close connections with elected officials, its two major political organizations slowly lost membership as politicians learned how to make direct appeals to LGBT voters. Many politically active LGBT people drifted towards supporting the Human Rights Campaign, but most of that organization's attention was at the national level or in other states. It had little influence inside Massachusetts.

Acceptance was accompanied by assimilation, at least for some, and this caused a change in the geographic distribution of LGBT people. Troubling for many people was demographic change in the South End. For more than two decades, it had been the center of the city's gay community. But continued gentrification priced many gay men out of the neighborhood with those who remained tending to be older, less visible, and more in the moderate assimilationist camp rather than radicals.[16] This change in what were once gay urban neighborhoods was taking place across the country, but the loss in Boston seemed particularly severe. Though as late as 2010 the South End's adult population was still 20 percent gay male, it felt much less gay and no other neighborhood stepped up to be a new center of the community. There was no other cluster of bars or businesses deliberately serving the LGBT community, and for many it reinforced the idea that Boston was a dull place to live.

Boston still had a central role to play in one of the greatest LGBT civil rights victories in U.S. history through its role in legalizing same sex marriage. Massachusetts was the first state to allow men to marry men and women to marry women, the result of a Supreme Judicial Court ruling in 2003 that held that prohibiting it violated the state constitution. The first legal same sex marriages were performed here in May 2004. Nine years later, the federal Supreme Court extended the right to all fifty states. That the center of this advancement was located in Boston needs greater analysis, but it was most likely related to the level of LGBT political organizing in the city, its liberal political establishment, and the lack of a strong religious-based opposition.[17] The region's Catholic Church had collapsed as a political and moral force after the abuse scandal, and the area lacked a significant evangelical movement since the nineteenth century.

Marriage was the solution to a large set of issues that affected many in the LGBT community. One very important problem for many LGBT people was the lack of legal standing in family, taxes, and other areas of the law. Unless same sex couples completed an elaborate set of legal documents, they could find themselves powerless during crises such as hospitalizations, inheritances, separations, or even when it came to pick up a child at school. And even if a couple completed all the necessary paperwork to establish their relationship in Massachusetts, they could still run into trouble out of state as these documents had no interstate validity nor were they recognized by the federal government. Two people might be a committed couple, but they could not inherit each other's estates without paying taxes nor could they ask their employer to provide health insurance to a loved one without having to pay taxes on the benefits.

The first effort to recognize gay and lesbian families involved convincing employers to offer health and other employer provided benefits to partners of gay and lesbian employees and their children. Given that health care costs were rapidly rising in the 1990s and that most people relied on their employers or spouses for coverage, this was a critical right for many people. The first local major employer to offer these benefits was Cambridge-based Lotus Software (the American Friends Service Committee, Screen Actors Guild, and the Village Voice were the first organizations to do so nationally). After Lotus implemented their benefits with the assistance of a Boston-based consultant, domestic partner benefits, as they came to be called, spread throughout much of corporate America. By the end of the 1990s, many states had also adopted a legal category usually called civil unions. These tended to create, more or less, a special entity giving two people many of the rights and responsibilities of marriage without using that word. However, neither domestic partner benefits nor civil unions had any federal recognition nor did most other states accept them as legal. Health insurance for a gay partner was taxed as income.

Massachusetts did not create civil unions, not because there was no demand for them, but because of a strategic decision to press for full recognition of same sex marriage. If they had passed a civil union law, the fear went, the courts might be less likely to overturn the strictures against marriage. Central to this developing strategy was Boston's large, experienced legal rights organization, GLAD. By this time, GLAD had grown into a multistate organization, litigating and negotiating on behalf of LGBT clients across New England.

Studying how black advocates had advanced civil rights through the courts in the 1950s and 1960s, advocates for same-sex marriage began to plan a legal strategy that would help move it forward. Though the federal government establishes many of the legal rights of marriage, the regulation and definition of marriage itself is a state responsibility. Furthermore, under the U.S. Constitution's full faith provisions, each state is required to recognize legal marriages in all other states. So once one state legalized same sex marriage, the legal fight could be taken nationally. At this intersection of legal and social-political context, Massachusetts was the perfect state to begin the fight given its history, demographics, and status of LGBT people.

Finding the right plaintiffs for a lawsuit was critical. Not only did they need to have to provide a strong legal argument, they would also need to be sympathetic so that there would be a public and judicial willingness to consider the merits of the case. The plaintiffs also needed to be physically strong; they would undergo intense media scrutiny and there was no predicting if there might be a backlash against them, even physical violence was possible. So GLAD spent months screening potential plaintiffs and eventually found seven couples they thought illustrated the breadth of need for fully recognized marriage. The lead plaintiffs were Hillary and Julie Goodridge, a couple who had met eighteen years previously at a Harvard seminar on disinvestment in then apartheid South Africa. The couple had a daughter and one owned an investment management firm while the other worked in the grants-making arm of the Universalist Church.[18]

The woman leading GLAD's legal challenge to prohibition against marriage was Mary Bonato. A graduate of Northeastern Law School, Bonato had traits that lent themselves to the suit: she was brilliant, tireless, media savvy, and personable. A lesbian in a long-era relationship, she knew firsthand how important this case was, and after a career in providing legal services to LGBT people, she had skills and experience almost no one else in the country could match. In her work, she was supported by the ongoing expertise of GLAD, which had grown into an extremely capable public service law firm, winning cases on the state and federal level (including at the U.S. Supreme Court) and could call on the services of some of the best legal scholars in the country. Bonato had lost a previous LGBT rights case at the Supreme Court when the organizers for the South Boston Saint Patrick's Day parade successfully argued they had the right to exclude gay people. She was determined not to lose this case as it was based on the Massachusetts, not the United States, constitution.

In Massachusetts, marriage licenses are issued by city and town clerks in each of its 351 cities and towns but are overseen by the state Department of Public Health. It is the state that establishes rules for issuing licenses and ultimately is responsible for denying marriage to same sex couples. Thus the case, filed on April 11, 2001, was known as Goodridge versus the Department of Public Health.

From the beginning, people on both sides of the issue knew it would be decided by the Massachusetts Supreme Judicial Court, presided over by Chief Justice Margaret Marshall, the wife of Pulitzer Prize-winning *New York Times* columnist Anthony Lewis. She was a native of South Africa, raised by a family that had opposed its racist apartheid policies. Marshall had been appointed Chief Justice by Republican Governor Paul Cellucci over the opposition of some conservatives.

The court handed down its historic Goodridge decision on November 18, 2003, declaring that the Massachusetts constitution affirmed the dignity of all people and that marriage was a fundamental human right. It was a total win for the plaintiffs. The state was given six months to implement the decision meaning that unless something drastic could be done to stop it, same sex marriage would become legal for the first time in the United States on May 18, 2004. The legal case decided, the political battle began.

It was at this point that the unique political and social environment of Boston shaped the strategies of both same-sex marriage opponents and advocates. Because the right to marry was found by the court to be rooted in the state constitution, opponents needed an amendment to overturn the ruling. Massachusetts has two ways to adopt an amendment, and opponents pursued both options. One was to have the legislature, sitting jointly in a constitutional convention, ratify an amendment creating civil unions by majority vote in two consecutive legislative sessions. The second method relied on a petition signed by voters. This would have required approval by 25 percent of the legislators in two sessions. Under either method, the amendment would then go to the voters.

LGBT lobbyists had spent years developing a strong network of allies from labor unions to prominent Jewish and liberal Protestant clergy. Most media outlets were in favor of same-sex marriage as were the majority of business leaders. Very significantly, the leadership of the overwhelmingly Democratic legislature was sympathetic to LGBT rights, and it did everything possible to defeat the amendments. This reflected the political reality that most of the public supported it as well. Massachusetts lacked an effective opposition as it had few evangelical churches, often a center of anti-gay rhetoric in many other states, and the Boston Archdiocese was battered by the priest abuse scandal. Yet, the battle was close at first.

As the date for first marriages approached, there was tremendous anxiety whether it would actually happen. Governor Mitt Romney, who had been elected on the promise of moderation but was moving sharply to the right in order to recruit conservative support for a run for President, introduced several measures to stop same-sex marriage. But an advisory ruling in February 2004 by the Supreme Judicial Court specifically excluded civil unions or domestic partnership legislation as viable alternatives, blocking Romney's efforts. President George Bush declared his support for an amendment to the United States constitution to prohibit same-sex marriage, but that effort went nowhere and would not have come soon enough to stop Massachusetts marriages. Still, advocates were worried that there would be a last-minute action by Romney or other opponents to stop the marriages.

As the date of legalization approached, there was excitement across the LGBT community, and couples began planning their weddings. On Sunday night, May 17, Cambridge city hall opened its doors at midnight for the first legal same-sex marriages in the United States as a crowd of several thousand joyously celebrated outside in the middle of a closed-to-traffic Massachusetts Avenue. The next morning, city and town halls were flooded with happy couples applying for licenses. In Boston, Lexington, and elsewhere, supporters met the newlyweds with balloons and cheers. One couple joyously told a reporter, "This is amazing. You never thought this would ever happen, not in any amount of lifetimes you could think about."[19] The fight was not over, however, as the battle in the legislature to approve the two amendments grew heated.

Both amendments were approved on their first consideration, but both failed to get a second approval as advocates used their lobbying power, honed through decades of advocacy on various legislative initiatives, to convince the rank and file members of the Great and General Court to defeat them. As the reality of same-sex marriage sunk in, the ability of opponents to stop it faded. Over time, additional states permitted same-sex marriage and eventually, the U.S. Supreme Court upheld the right to same sex marriage as well. By then some Massachusetts same sex couples had been married for almost a decade.

Though Boston was now a majority minority city, white politicians continued to dominate city hall. However, their hold began to weaken, and new faces began to participate in running government. There was a major shift in the balance of power on the city council after 2000 when minority candidates began to capture at-large seats. For decades, citywide councilors had included notorious race baiters such as Albert "Dapper" O'Neill who used antagonism towards minorities to win votes and Mickey Roache, a politician who completely ignored minority voters. Now at-large councilors tended to be people of color or white progressives. While the numbers of minority councilors did not match their proportion in the city, politically it seemed that there was much better representation of Boston. It was a slow process. The first sign of the change to come was when Michael Flaherty knocked Dapper O'Neill out of the council in 1999. Less abrasive conservatives, Mickey Roache, Peggy Davis-Mullen, and Steven Murphy, still kept their at-large seats, but minority voters could at least see that they might aspire to have their voices heard.

In 2001 Davis-Mullen gave up her at large council seat to run for mayor, creating an opening. Menino backed Robert Consalvo but he came in fifth behind Maura Hennigan. Felix Arroyo came in sixth as progressives and people of color were began to show their numbers at the ballot box. Then in 2003, Arroyo gained a seat along with Hennigan, Flaherty, and Murphy. Patricia White, Kevin's daughter, failed to win an at-large seat and blamed a "liberal explosion."

The transition was nearly complete in 2005 when Flaherty, Arroyo, and Sam Yoon were the top three finishers in the at-large council race; the only remaining conservative at-large counselor was Murphy. Even relatively moderate John Connelly came in fifth with conservatives Patricia White and Edward Flynn (the former mayor's son) finished out of the running. The only liberal to lose was Matt O'Malley.

The year 2007 saw very light turnout, allowing Connelly to defeat Arroyo, but in 2009, his son, Felix G. Arroyo, and Anaya Pressley were elected along with Murphy and Connolly. The strong liberal and progressive presence on the council continued. In 2011, Presley topped the ticket, followed by Connolly and Arroyo. Murphy held on to the top spot by barely 1,000 votes over Flaherty. In the next election, 2013, Presley and Michelle Wu topped the ticket followed by Flaherty and Murphy, and in 2015, Presley topped the vote, followed by Wu. Flaherty was third, the only white at-large councilor as Annissa Easaibi George knocked Murphy out of the council. The council was substantially different than it had been in the urban renewal era of the 1950s.

One of the most joyful moments in Boston history was the night in October 2004 when the Red Sox won their first World Series since 1918. The popular myth, made vivid by *Boston Globe* reporter Dan Shaughnessy's book *The Curse of the Bambino*, was that the Red Sox's decades of misery were the result of owner Henry Frazee selling Babe Ruth to the Yankees in 1920. In fact, the source of the Red Sox's despair was much more likely the racist mismanagement of owner Tom Yawkey and his successors. Though he repeatedly announced his desire to win a World Series, for decades Yawkey hired managers and coaches who were so drunk they passed out during games, mistreated players, and most reprehensibly, operated the most racist team in a league of renowned racist owners.[20] The Red Sox passed on Black Hall of Fame players Jackie Robinson and Willie Mays, were the last team to integrate (for many years the team notoriously abused its Irish Catholic players), allowed a segregated social club to entertain white players and exclude blacks well into the 1980s, and were cited for discrimination against black personnel by the Massachusetts Commission Against Discrimination in the 1990s.[21] Though they had three appearances in the World Series during these decades, inept policies and racist atmosphere did not end until the Yawkey Trust sold its ownership in 2002. Given the openly racist management, it is no wonder that black players had clauses in their contracts prohibiting them from being traded to the Red Sox and that many Boston blacks would root for teams other than the Sox.

The team slowly declined in the decade after Jean Yawkey died in 1992. Now owned by the Yawkey Trust and controlled by long-time baseball administrator John Harrington, the team made it to the playoffs but was never able to get to the World Series as they lost in morale breaking fashion to better teams. There were personnel issues as well. The team gave up on its star pitcher Roger Clemons, calling him too old. So Clemons jumped to the hated rivals, the Yankees, where he won three Cy Young awards and earned the lasting enmity of Boston fans. In another terrible public relations blunder, team personnel showed up in court to provide support to a player who was accused of domestic abuse, and the Red Sox's tawdry history on race was once again on display when management was involved in a series of unrelated, but very public, racial incidents. The fans continued to love the team but contempt for the management was growing. Then in a final act guaranteeing he would be hated, Harrington declared that Fenway Park, the oldest and most loved sports stadium in the country, was beyond saving and needed to be demolished.

The great novelist, John Updike, famously described Fenway as a "lyric little bandbox of a ballpark. Everything is painted green and seems in curiously sharp focus, like the inside of an old-fashioned peeping-type Easter egg. It was built in 1912 and rebuilt in 1934, and offers, as do most Boston artifacts, a compromise between Man's Euclidean determinations and Nature's beguiling irregularities."[22] Harrington wanted to replace Fenway with a bland state of the art facility such as had been built in Baltimore, Denver, or a dozen other lesser cities. Perhaps it would be placed on the waterfront amidst its parking lots, or the Sox would get the BRA to use its powers of eminent domain to take the land next door to the existing stadium. In any case, he told the world that Fenway Park's days were numbered. Confronted by the potential loss of the most loved building in the city, some Sox fans cried, others were speechless, and many vowed to throw themselves in front of the bulldozers.

Fenway Park, and the hearts of Red Sox fans, were spared when Major League Baseball stepped in and declared that the franchise could no longer be controlled by the Trust and would have to be sold. The purchaser was a consortium led by John Henry, a businessman who had made his money by using mathematical models to place bets on stocks and commodities. A longtime baseball owner, he came to Boston vowing to bring the city a World Series championship.

By now, the rivalry with the New York Yankees crackled with hatred. Season after season, the Red Sox's road to the World Series was blocked by the Yankees as they added to their collection of thirty-six titles. Henry and associates began to use quantitative methods to create a championship team, playing the part of Boston academics versus the New York glitz used by the Yankees. Technically called sabermetrics but more popularly known as moneyball, Henry used modern statistical analysis to dictate everything from who to sign to a contract to whether a batter should swing at a first pitch. First used by the Oakland Athletics, these rational-based methods would soon sweep baseball, replacing decades of accumulated superstition and management by instinct. They appealed to Henry because of his business background and were also in sync with Boston fandom, which increasingly paralleled the shift in the region towards a scientific and technology-based workforce.

Red Sox supporters are different from other sports fans. They are most nervous and distressed when their team is successful because they know that heartbreak is about to strike. For them, bad years are easier to bear because fans can be secure that they will not be wrenchingly disappointed one more time. On the road to the World Series in 2003, Henry's team made a large-scale contribution to the nervous hysteria of what was now called Red Sox Nation.

Having taken control of the Sox a year earlier, it was the first season the new management shaped the team using the services of Theo Epstein, the youngest general manager in baseball history, and Grady Little, a respected veteran. Late in the season, the Sox came alive and secured a wild card spot in the playoffs by having the best record behind the three division leaders. In the best of five first round of games, they quickly fell behind the Oakland Athletics two games to none. But then they rallied in an effort that included heroic pitching by ace Derek Lowe who came in as a reliever in game five to win the Sox the series.

This set up the Sox for a best of seven games series against the Yankees, causing long nights of nervous insomnia for the fans. Tensions were high: during a bench clearing brawl between the two teams, for example, Pedro Martinez threw Yankees bench coach, Don Zimmer, to the ground when the seventy-two-year-old rushed at the skinny Sox star. In another sign of the intense dislike between the two teams, a scuffle broke out in the Yankees bull pen when a pitcher took a dislike to a Fenway groundskeeper.

The seventh game was a rematch between Yankees star pitcher

Roger Clemons and Pedro Martinez. After the fourth inning, when Sox batters forced Clemons out of the game, Sox fans hopes, and fears, were very high. When Clemons was relieved, the score was four to nothing in the Sox's favor, and though the Yankees posted two runs, the Sox had added another run of their own. Not a fan could relax, however. The Sox were either at the brink of ecstatic victory or horrific defeat. Born in the Dominican Republic, Martinez was a hothead, prone to outlandish antics and statements off the field. But he was a great pitcher who would eventually be elected to the Baseball Hall of Fame. At this point in his career, he was known for his ability to throw a variety of pitches with amazing accuracy rather than the speed of his fastball, and now, all the hopes of Boston of erasing the decades without a championship rested on his shoulders. But as the Yankees came to bat in the eighth inning, Sox fans wailed in horror when they saw Martinez return to pitch another inning. All season long, when Martinez threw more than one hundred pitches, opposing batters hit off him. It was by now accepted as part of how the fans and nearly everyone else thought of his skills as a pitcher: use his talents, but pull him when his pitch count grew too high. But the only man whose opinion on keeping him in the game mattered inexplicably forgot this rule, Manager Grady Little. Across Boston, desperate fans screamed at their televisions, cursed the sale of Babe Ruth, threatened Little with physical violence, and begged any and all deities for a relief pitcher as Little left Martinez in long enough to allow the Yankees to tie the game. Stretching the agony out, the Yankees won the game three innings later as grownups openly wept and many swore to give up on the team forever. It was the worst defeat since the disaster of 1986 when the Red Sox lost to the New York Mets when they were one out away from winning the World Series. Even cold blooded rationalists thought the Sox were cursed by supernatural forces beyond their control.

It was a bitter winter with fans finding no solace when the Sox fired Little, replacing him with Terry Francona and making a number of other changes. The first half of the season saw the Sox doing poorly, which at least promised the fans they would not be heartbroken that year. Then in August, everything jelled and the team won the wild card spot again; the Yankees were too good of a team for the Sox to win their division. Though the players were upbeat, the fans prepared for another soul crushing loss. Then to everyone's surprise, the Sox beat the Anaheim Angels in three games, though Curt Schilling, the best starting pitcher at the time, tore a tendon, effectively ending his season. Once again, the Sox were up against the Yankees, or as Sox fans called the team, the Evil Empire.

The Yankees won the first three games, shredding all hope out of the fans with a 19-8 victory in game three. A professional baseball game can be played in two and a half hours. But with pitching changes and commercial breaks, these games were exhaustingly longer. Game three, with its numerous hits, took four hours and twenty minutes, with each minute a mixture of tension and dread that made it difficult to breathe. As a result, fans, and there were millions of them across the region and elsewhere, felt they had barely gotten to bed when they again took to the stands at Fenway or switched their televisions to game four. Work and school became filled with sleep-deprived, hopeless fans who could not avoid watching their team painfully lose once more. After the third loss, despair was complete, no baseball team had ever recovered from a 3-0 deficit in the playoffs.

In game four, the Yankees took an early two run lead but then the Sox scored three runs in the fifth inning. Then hopes of a rally faded when the Yankees scored two more runs. All the Yankees had to do was get the next twelve batters out and the Sox would have another tearful winter. But then the usually unbeatable Yankees closer Mariano Rivera gave up a lead walk and the Sox had Dave Roberts pinch run. Roberts stole second base and then scored on a single. Just like that the game was tied, setting up the Sox to lose in still another agonizing way. But this time, the Sox won in extra innings. And then they won game five. Hopes grew, but with them also came the agonizing suspicion there was going to be another horrific loss in game six or seven.

Game six was back in Yankee stadium. Curt Schilling, his ankle sutured together, gave a stellar performance even as his sock grew increasing bloody as his stitches ripped open. By this time, the games were taking their physical toll on fans and players. Game five had taken almost six hours to complete, brutally long whether a fan watched the game while standing at Fenway park or sitting on a couch at the edge of their seat. Miraculously, the Sox won game six in a relatively short three hours, and fans prepared themselves to endure another game.

Game seven began ominously; the Yankees had Bucky Dent, the man who had destroyed Boston's hopes in 1978, throw out the ceremonial first pitch. But to everyone's surprise, it was the Red Sox who triumphed as they beat the Yankees 10-3 in an easy romp, and for the first time since 1986, the Red Sox were in the World Series. The jubilation of the fans was enormous as crowds poured into the streets from Kenmore Square to Government Center to celebrate. As several thousand jumping and drinking young people flooded onto Lansdown Street, the police fired a pepper spray projectile into the crowd, tragically killing a young woman. The Sox went into the World Series against the St. Louis Cardinals on a somber note.

At first the World Series seemed anticlimactic as the Sox easily defeated the Cardinals in four games. But as Sox fans savored their first baseball title in nearly ninety years, the outpouring of emotion was extreme. As one sportswriter put it, "New England danced under an eclipse-reddened moon early today, toasting a baseball championship whose elusiveness since World War I had become a regional badge of futility, worn by four generations."[23] Perhaps most heart rending were the shirts and hats placed on graves in cemeteries across the region as the children and grandchildren of departed Sox fans tried to touch the souls of those who had not lived long enough to see a World Series victory in Boston. There would be other Sox triumphs in 2007 and 2014, and the Celtics, Patriots, and Bruins would win their league titles as well. But the glory of the 2004 Red Sox will last for decades.

The Red Sox victory capped a several-decade run of prosperity as Boston grew into one of the most desirable places to work, study, or live in the country. Not everyone equally shared the good times, but even many of the city's disadvantaged believed it was better to live in a growing city than a declining one. The despair of 1945 was forgotten.

1. Loth R and Lehigh S. Weld says Silber Holds "Sexist Attitudes". *Boston Globe.* October 11, 1990; p. 1.
2. Boston Redevelopment Authority. *Boston by the Numbers.* 2013.
3. Boston Municipal Research Bureau. *The Future of Boston City Hospital: Analysis of Proposal to Merge BCH and University Hospital.* 1996.
4. Costa PM. From plan to reality: Implementing a community vision in Jackson

Square, Boston. *Planning Theory and Practice*. 2014; 15: 293-310.

5. Beatty J. *The Rascal King: The LIfe and Times of James Michael Curley (1874-1958)*. Reading, MA: Addison-Wesley Publishing, 1992.

6. The Investigative Staff of the Boston Globe. *Betrayal*. New York: Little, Brown and Company, 2003.

7. Lawler P. *The Faithful Departed*. New York: Perseus, 2010.

8. Jennings J. Urban planning, community participation and the Roxbury Master Plan in Boston. *Annals of the American Academy of Political and Social Science*. 2004; 594: 12-33.

9. Lai Z, Leong A and Wu CC. The lessons of the Parcel C struggle: Reflections on community lawyering. *UCLA Asian Pac Am I J* 2000; 6: 1-42.

10. Cheung A. *Lydia Lowe: Chinatown Activist*. Bostonchinatownblog.org/2015/11/lydia-lowe. 2015.

11. Beacon Hill Civic Association. *Beacon Hill Civic Association*. www.bncivic.org. 2016.

12. Adams D. Boston Harbor leader Vivien Li takes Pittsburgh position. *Boston Globe*. July 21, 2015; p. 1.

13. Medoff P and Sklar H. *Streets of Hope*. Boston MA: South End Press, 1994.

14. Lipman M and Mahan L. *Holding Ground: The Rebirth of Dudley Street*. 1996.

15. Dwyer LA. *Mapping Impact: An Analysis of the Dudley Street Neighborhood Initiative Land Trust*. Masters Thesis, DUSP. MIT, 2015.

16. Lopez R. *Boston's South End: The Clash of Ideas in a Historic Neighborhood*. Boston: Shawmut Peninsula Press, 2015.

17. McCauley J. On the right side of history: How lesbian and gay activists galvanized culture and politics to make Massachusetts the first state with legal same-sex marriage. *Sociology and Anthropology*. University of Windsor, 2012.

18. Weddings/Celebrations. Hilliary Goodridge, Julie Goodridge. *New York Times*. May 23, 2004; p. Style 23.

19. Abraham Y and Klein R. Free to marry historic date arrives for same-sex couples in Massachusetts. *Boston Globe*. May 17, 2004; p. 1.

20. Gutlon J. *It was never about the Babe: The Red Sox, race, mismanagement, and the curse of the Bambino*. New York: Skyhorse Publishing, 2015.

21. Bryant H. *Shut out: A story of race and baseball in Boston*. Boston: Beacon Press, 2003.

22. Updike J. Hub Fans Bid Kid Adieu. *The New Yorker*. October 22, 1960.

23. Farragher T. Victory transforms a regions's identity. *Boston Globe*. October 28, 2004; p. A1.

Chapter 8

Affluence and Change: 2005 - 2015

THE BOSTON BOOM continued after 2004. Along with the rest of the country, the city experienced a sharp downturn after the 2007 financial meltdown, but the recession was relatively mild in Boston as strong investment in education and medical research cushioned the impact of the bust. In addition, these industries used the downturn as an opportunity to build new facilities, and Boston benefited from the construction jobs. As a result, Boston recovered from the recession sooner than most other areas of the country.

There were problems associated from this prosperity. Those who did not benefit from the types of jobs created by the New Boston–the poor, the elderly, those who lacked higher education–found themselves crowded into smaller parts of the city or pushed out to distant suburbs. Inside these areas, poverty rates are high, school quality is low, and there is too great a risk of violence. These neighborhoods seem far away from the booming central core. Unlike the well-to-do inner districts, these parts of the city continued to severely suffer from economic downturns. The number of foreclosures in the 2008 recession was much smaller in Boston than in other cities, but the rate was several times higher in Roxbury, Dorchester, and other minority neighborhoods than the citywide average.

As the recession ended, it was clear that prosperity caused staggeringly high housing prices. With a small city hemmed in by water and containing many buildings of great architectural and historical significance requiring preservation, there is little room for construction, and any new development proposal has the potential to severely impact close by neighbors. It is difficult to build in the city. As a result, Boston has some of the highest housing prices in the country. In 2015, the median housing price in the city was $475,000, meaning that a household needed an income of well over $100,000 to afford it. Rents are similarly high with a two-bedroom apartment going for $2,800 a month. Over 50 percent of all families in the city are paying more than 30 percent of their incomes on rent.

Real estate interests succeeded in eliminating rent control in Boston through a statewide referendum in the 1980s, promising a boom in new construction that the city is still waiting for. Some pro-growth activists have proposed that relaxing zoning and building codes would create more affordable housing, but though these have powerful theoretical arguments in their favor, there is no reason to believe they would work in Boston without destroying the historical integrity of the city. Nor is there much state or federal money available to build more affordable housing. As of 2015, there was no solution to the city's high prices.

A very sad part of South Boston history began its final chapter on June 22, 2011 when James "Whitey" Bulger was arrested in Santa Monica, California. From the 1970s to the 1990s, Bulger had dominated organized crime in South Boston, becoming a legend noted for both his charitable acts and his extreme ruthlessness to anyone who crossed him. Whitey's criminal exploits had at one time epitomized what many thought was best about the neighborhood: devotion to friends and family, opposition to drugs and disorder, and fierce love for South Boston. In reality, Whitey Bulger exploited the good will of Southie residents for his own purposes, twisting loyalty in a code of silence that protected his murderous crimes and manipulating a cherished hope that the community was free of drugs to hide his control of its narcotics trade.

James and William Bulger were two of six surviving siblings. One of the first families to move into the Old Colony projects when they opened in 1938, the Bulgers' apartment had three bedrooms: one for the parents, one for the boys, and one for the girls. Bulgers' father had been maimed in an industrial accident, and the family was very poor, limiting the options for their children.

Whitey rose to power through his membership in the Irish-dominated Winter Hill gang that was battling the Providence-based Italian mob that had a local outpost in the North End. As the two groups fought for control over the region's drug sales and rackets in the 1970s, bodies began to pile up. Bulger survived because of his intelligence and ruthlessness, killing his enemies before they could kill him. The FBI took notice of this because of a national initiative to destroy the mafia, and they hoped to use the Winter Hill gang to collect evidence on the Italians. Exploiting this, Whitey began to give reports to John Connelly, a childhood friend of the Bulgers who was an up and coming FBI agent. Connelly protected Bulger in return for information used to arrest mob members.

Meanwhile, his brother was a rising politician. William Bulger was first elected as a state representative in 1960 and held his seat for ten years. When a state senate seat opened up in 1970, Bulger easily won and quickly became part of the legislative leadership. Bulger's path to the Senate presidency was cleared in 1976 when Senate Majority Leader Joe DiCarlo was indicted for taking bribes from a contractor–the agent on the case was John Connelly. The next year, the scandal engulfed Senate President Kevin Harrington, enabling Bulger to replace him in 1979 and to hold that position for eighteen years, the longest in state history. Through his control over legislation and the budget, and his extreme popularity in his district, Bulger was the most powerful politician in the state. To oppose him or even his most personal and petty requests, was dangerous. Yet he also helped cement Massachusetts' reputation as one of the most liberal states in the country even as much of the nation's politics were moving to the right during the Reagan years.

The high point of the brothers' power was in the 1980s. Whitey had wiped out all rivals for the control of crime in South Boston, helped by his ruthlessness and FBI contacts. With everyone who opposed him dead or silenced, he was free to run his rackets, control the sale of drugs, and destroy anyone he disliked. Along with violence, Bulger secured his position by paying bribes to Connelly, and in return, Connelly thwarted investigations and fed information to Bulger that was used to eliminate informants. "Something always seemed to happen when the law got too close to Whitey–wiretaps would be compromised, bugs discovered. Cops hot on his trail would find themselves demoted or transferred. Witnesses would disappear, or recant, or forget."[1]

Feeling invincible, Whitey became even more brazen and ruthless.

Southie residents credited Bulger with keeping the neighborhood safe from drugs and crime, but in reality, South Boston was sinking into the hold of a strong and profitable criminal enterprise that ensnared many in its violence and heartbreak. Cocaine and methamphetamines were openly sold in bars and in the projects; heroin was off limits, but was easily purchased in the South End just blocks away around East Berkeley Street and City Hospital, areas controlled by Whitey's close business partner, Steven Flemmi. The drugs flooded Southie at a vulnerable moment. For years its economy had been sinking as its relatively less-educated work force was unable to access jobs in the new economy of the city. At the same time, isolated by the blatant racism of the antibusing protests and its aftermath, social service organizations were reluctant to assist the neighborhood, and others didn't want to hire its residents. Southie was alone and in trouble.

The people of South Boston paid the price. Young men began to die of overdoses, people went missing or died in a bursts of gunfire. The teenage pregnancy rate skyrocketed along with reports of child neglect and abandonment. Suicides stalked the projects and the Lower End, and families were left alone in their grief.[2] Still, no one could dare challenge Whitey or his henchmen. No one would admit there were problems in the neighborhood.

Meanwhile, Senate President William Bulger was not shy about advancing his brother's interests. At one point, William tried to get Mayor Flynn to appoint Connelly chief of police, but Flynn, whose intelligence Bulger publicly mocked, was too smart for that. Even so, the toxic combination of the two brothers reached deep into local politics. After William Bulger had the Massachusetts Convention Center Authority name his former aide Francis X. Joyce its chief, several employees related to Whitey's associates were hired by Joyce. Another time, Bulger submitted an amendment to the State budget that would have forced the resignation of the state police investigating his brother. Much of the homage paid to William was humiliating, but no matter how much they disliked him, politicians showed up to be ridiculed from the stage at Bulger's St. Patrick's day breakfast, found jobs for those Bulger needed to reward, and never publicly said a word against the man.

Whitey's murders were gruesome. He shot victims at point blank range and strangled two of Steven Flemmi's girlfriends with his bare hands. Some of the bodies were disposed of in muddy graves or under basement floors, others were dropped off in public places to make a statement. Some victims had their teeth pulled out to hinder identification, some were dismembered and left in trash bags to serve as warnings to others. One of the most prominent murders resulted from his control over World Jai Alai. When Roger Wheeler bought the company and threatened Bulger's skimming of its cash, Bulger ordered him murdered. Wheeler was shot in the middle of the afternoon in the parking lot of his country club in Oklahoma in 1981. Then to cover up that murder, another was committed in Florida.

The beginning of the end of William's political reign began in 1988 when accounts of a shakedown surrounding a complicated real estate deal for a State Street office building surfaced. Bulger succeeded in preventing any real investigation of how he ended up with hundreds of thousands of dollars from a sale he had no part of, but after that point, he lost control of the press as reporters relentlessly investigated him. Slowly, Whitey's power began to erode under the pressure of federal Drug Enforcement Agency investigations. By now, other law enforcement agencies had learned of the need to keep their investigations hidden from the FBI, and through a series of wire taps and raids, they were slowly getting closer to Whitey. Then in the 1990 Republican sweep of state offices, Bulger lost much of his control over state jobs.

Under pressure from new investigations, first the bookies and then the drug dealers working for Whitey flipped. When none of them mysteriously disappeared, more talked; the investigations were slow, but thorough and getting closer to their target. William easily survived a 1993 insurrection against his senate presidency, but he was smart enough to know it was time to get out, and in 1995 he was appointed president of the University of Massachusetts. Bulger tried to get his son to succeed him but his influence in Southie was waning. Steven Lynch won the special election.

Whitey was also preparing his end game. Tipped off by John Connelly that he was about to be arrested, Whitey disappeared on December 23, 1994. He had been preparing to vanish for almost two decades, stashing cash in safe deposit boxes, collecting false identifications, and carefully rehearsing escape routes. Putting his plan into action, he fled with girlfriend Catherine Greig, eventually settling in Santa Monica in a bland apartment building not far from the beach.

In the wake of Bulger's disappearance and confessions by some of his former associates, the FBI began to investigate Connelly and other corrupt agents in the Boston office. Enraged by one of the worst breaches of ethics in FBI history, the new leadership cleaned house. Several agents made plea bargains, and Connelly was indicted in December 1999. He was convicted in 2001 and found guilty of second degree murder in Florida in 2008.

For a while it seemed that William might survive his brother's fall, secure in his job running the University of Massachusetts. But then his past caught up with him. The event that brought down William Bulger was a phone call he received from his brother in January, 1995, a month after Whitey had disappeared. For years, William had denied having any contact with his brother and only admitted to the call when questioned before a grand jury in 2000. His belated confession under oath spared him an indictment, but the resulting firestorm cost him his job.[1]

For years there were reported Whitey sightings around the globe, but none panned out. He was finally captured when a woman in Iceland watching a television show on the fugitive recalled seeing Bulger in Santa Monica and called the police. Bulger and Grieg were soon back in Boston, and he went on trial in June 2013 on thirty-one counts of murder and racketeering. He was convicted and sentenced to two life terms in jail; Greig received eight years for harboring a fugitive.

It took decades for South Boston to recover. Families needed to heal from suicides, murders, and drug abuse. Victims were slow to come to terms with the trauma of assault. But South Boston could draw on its strengths: family ties, neighborhood loyalty, and the commitment of thousands to one of the city's most desirable places to live.

Perhaps one the best symbols of the current economic vitality of the city is the transformation of the area along the South Boston waterfront from windswept parking lots to a new neighborhood of office buildings and housing. Now called the Seaport District, it covers 1,000 acres, an area almost larger than Back Bay and South End combined, and as of 2014 over 10 million square feet of office space had been approved with another 20 million possible. The neighborhood is popular, and during the weekday there are thousands of employees in new offices, some with spectacular views of the harbor, as many important biotechnology companies, law firms, and other high profile companies moved to the area. On weekend nights, the area along the harbor is alive with people at its restaurants and night clubs. But in some respects, the area is a disappointment. Its streetscape is unfriendly and pedestrians cross traffic at risk to their lives. Transportation, whether by car or by transit, is overwhelmed, and there is a growing sense that Boston missed an opportunity to create a district that would have rivaled Back Bay.

With the decay of Boston's manufacturing and shipping industries, the South Boston waterfront was mostly empty or underutilized buildings and parking lots by the 1960s. Massport took over the old South Boston Navy Yard and created a thriving marine industrial district; there were a handful of restaurants along the waterfront, but for the most part, the area was deserted. Artists began to move into the area in the 1970s, soon to be followed by small businesses, but it was the construction of the federal courthouse in 1999 followed by the completion of the Big Dig (2003), Silver Line (2004), Massachusetts Convention Center (2004), and Institute of Contemporary Art (2006) that launched the area as ripe for development.[3]

Planning for a new community adjacent to the downtown financial district began in the late 1980s under the Flynn administration. At the time, the BRA proposed that the land be used for manufacturing, just as how the planners in the Hynes era had hoped to convert the New York Streets area to factories and warehouses. Similarly, the promotional materials for the waterfront cited the area's access to highways, the airport, and rail. If the plan had worked, there would have been thousands of low-skilled, high-paying jobs for Boston residents. But the city had ignored the lesson of the New York Streets, and their plans were crushed by the same reality: there was no demand for new manufacturing space, and the vast parking lots remained vacant.

To make the area work for factories, the plan laid out broad avenues to accommodate large tractor trailer trucks and created big blocks to enable the construction of massive horizontal buildings for assembly, manufacturing, and storage. This set the stage for the Seaport's cur-

Seaport District, 2015. Though it has attracted billions of dollars of investments, its physical design has disappointed the city.

rent design problems. It was never intended to be a pedestrian-friendly community.

By 2000, it was clear that Flynn's plan had failed, and the BRA, realizing that there was an opportunity to create a new destination that could rival Kendall Square, the Longwood Medical Area, or the Back Bay, decided to rezone the area for offices along with some limited residential and associated commercial uses. Unfortunately, they did not revisit the street plan. As a result, the Seaport is an office/residential district built on top of an industrial park, and its streetscape shows it. There are vastly too-wide streets, big intersections, and super-block-sized parcels. As a pedestrian travels from the older Fort Point Channel area to the Marine Industrial Park, the area becomes increasingly unwalkable and pedestrian unfriendly.

The area has been a success in other ways, and eventually the Seaport District will be the home of over 25,000 residents and 70,000 jobs. Several major law firms have moved to the area and the Seaport has attracted offices and investments from pharmaceutical companies and others who contribute to the new Boston economy. As a whole, the city has been greatly enriched by the development of the Seaport and it has helped reconnect Boston to the harbor.

Unfortunately, poorly served by an extensive underground bus network called the Silver Line and constricted by its problematic street grid, the Seaport is choking on traffic and has failed to attract retail or the vibrant street life of Back Bay or other parts of the city. Furthermore, because the Seaport is near the approaches to Logan Airport, the federal government has imposed strict height limits on its buildings. This produces flat topped buildings that lack much personality and are far too broad to be inviting. It is no wonder that Robert Campbell, architecture critic for the *Boston Globe*, said that the Seaport District "has all the charm of an office park in a suburb of Dallas."[4]

Another major problem with development in the Seaport is that most of its jobs are beyond the reach of city residents. Most require a college degree or high English language skills, but many residents tend to lack these skills and the relatively smaller number of jobs that are open to low-skilled workers are in the restaurant or hotel industry and pay much less. Job training will not address this mismatch.[5] The area is crowded but is a missed opportunity, at least for now.

The first decade of the new century saw the opening of an important new park in the city, the Rose Kennedy Greenway. One of the major selling points to generate public support for the Big Dig was the promise of a large linear park through downtown replacing the hated elevated highway. But with the vast cost overrun of the Big Dig and the lack of any perceived benefit to residents in the neighborhoods, there was only a minimal constituency to come up with the additional financial resources necessary to pay for the Greenway.[6]

To push for the Greenway, the Artery Business Committee (ABC) was formed in 1989. Containing over eighty members, it was closely affiliated with the Boston Chamber of Commerce. One of its founders was Norman Leventhal who along with his brother developed some of Boston's most elegant buildings including Rowes Wharf and 75 State Street. He and others were concerned that the demolition of the artery and construction of its underground replacement would snarl traffic, rendering downtown inaccessible for years and dampening support for the project. So they sought to create something that would spark the imagination of Boston residents and help make up for the inconvenience.

There were three ideas proposed for the land uncovered by the demolition of the artery. One called for a series of monumental public spaces and buildings. Another envisioned large-scale buildings along with a series of small open spaces and separate north-south arterials. City traffic engineers wanted a new arterial, which would have defeated one of the goals of taking down the artery in the first place. The adopted plan envisioned a ribbon of open space that would rival Olmsted's Emerald Necklace and preserve much of the older urban fabric along the new parkland with new construction limited to a few key parcels. It was partly the result of the work of Ken Kruckmeyer, a South End resident, pedestrian advocate, and veteran of the battle against the inner belt, who co-chaired an effort to make the greenway pedestrian friendly.

The final result, much compromised, has problems that need to be addressed. Of the twenty-seven acres created by the demolition of the artery, twenty were to be open space and seven were to be used for streets or development. The first stage of the planning process culminated in a master plan and a special zoning overlay district for the new corridor in 1991. Together these allocated land for development or open space and set height limits, maximum floor area ratios, setbacks, and other requirements.[7] Unfortunately, the logistics of building on the new parcels, most of which are over the highway, have been so daunting that none have been developed.

Another issue centered on which organization would fundraise and oversee the management of the Greenway. The ABC favored a plan that would have maximized private control; the city ultimately decided on a structure that allowed it more oversight but with significant representation of ABC members.[8] As a result, the park is administered by the Rose Kennedy Greenway Conservancy which leases the land from the Massachusetts Turnpike Authority. Charged with overseeing programming and development, the state matches funds raised from private sources.

In some respects, the Greenway has been a disappointment. Proposed facilities, including a museum and a new YMCA, have been abandoned. Some parts of the Greenway are only moderately visited at best. But other sections have become very popular and in the summer are crowded with lunchtime visitors and tourists. Slowly, buildings have been constructed or repositioned to take advantage of the open space, and it has been enlivened by fountains, a merry-go-round, and thought-provoking art. The Greenway may not have captured the public's love like the Public Garden or Common, but the park has made good on their promise of reconnecting the city to the waterfront. The visionaries who created it have succeeded in bringing thousands to an area that was mostly empty outside of working hours.

Boston, along with the rest of the country, mourned the loss of life from the terrorist attacks on September 11, 2001. Two of the airplanes that crashed that day had taken off from Logan Airport, and many of the passengers on the planes were residents of the region. Then twelve years later, another terrorist attack shook the city, striking at the heart of Boston when two brothers set off bombs near the Boston Marathon finish line.

Perhaps nothing symbolizes the union of history and the present in Boston like the Boston Marathon. First run in 1897 in honor of the modern Olympic Games, the late nineteenth century was a time when Boston's Yankee elite was infatuated with the culture of ancient Greece, and the marathon reminds the world that Boston considers itself the Athens of America. Organized by the Boston Athletic Association, the race is on Patriots Day, the anniversary of the battles of Lexington and Concord that started the American Revolution. A marathon is a grueling race that celebrates the triumph of mind over physical limits, and though there are many reasons racers might drop out, no one completes a marathon without overruling a tired body begging to stop. It captures the spirit of the city.

The Boston marathon has not been static over its history. Its length has been changed to conform to international standards, the start was moved from Ashland to Hopkington, and women were allowed to run in 1967 (after several years in which they participated surreptitiously). The finish line in Boston has been moved several times and prize money added to attract international competition.

Other changes were made to address specific issues. After Rosie

Ruiz cheated to win the women's marathon in 1980, new measures were implemented to guard against mischief. The race also has become a celebration of Boston's contribution to the world of medicine. With over thirty thousand runners, the Marathon became a world training ground for doctors on how to respond to medical emergencies during large events. Each year, teams of medical professionals staff triage tents and screen runners for problems. With close ties to the city's emergency rooms, doctors learned how to respond to dehydration, overheating, muscle spasms, and heart attacks. The marathon became a model of cooperation, service, and learning.

In the 1990s, Patriots Day had been marked by serious violent events. In 1993, federal agents stormed a compound run by the Branch Davidian sect outside of Waco, Texas, resulting in the deaths of seventy-six men, women, and children. Two years later, a van filled with explosives was set off in Oklahoma City killing 168 in what was the worst act of domestic terrorism in the United States. As a result, security at the marathon gradually increased, but it was never oppressive. Along the race, fans cheered on runners, gave them water and oranges, and many used the day to gather with friends and family to party. Even at the finish line, security was vigilant but porous.

Dzhokhar and Tamerlan Tsarnaev presumably knew nothing of the history of the marathon when they set off two bombs on Boylston Street at the 2013 Marathon. Immigrants from Russia, the brothers' family had been displaced from Chechnya by Russian authorities suppressing a succession movement there. Their parents had been granted asylum in the United States in 2002 with the children arriving two years later. The elder brother, Tamerlan, had aspirations of becoming a boxer but mostly held small jobs, and though he had been accused of several domestic violence incidents, he was never prosecuted. Tamerlan became radicalized, severely criticizing western customs and strangely blaming the United States for Russian aggression against Chechnya. The younger brother, Dzhokhar, seemed to fit in better in his new country, graduating from Cambridge Rindge and Latin High School and attending the University of Massachusetts at Dartmouth.

Tamerlan recruited Dzhokhar to carry out a plan to kill people and sow panic at the Marathon. The brothers learned how to make the bombs on the Internet and designed them to maximize their ability to maim, packing two small pressure cookers with nails, ball bearings, other small pieces of metal, and powder procured from fireworks purchased in New Hampshire. The two bombs were set off about thirty seconds apart at 2:49 in the afternoon as thousands of spectators and runners were strung along Boylston Street.

One nearby witness reported that he "heard boom, boom, then people screaming," Suddenly, "There was blood all over the place. I saw a leg, people with bones sticking out of their skin." There was sudden chaos with "scores of bloodied victims lying in the street, the marathon route stained with blood and strewn with shards of glass. Witnesses to the explosions described a heart-rending scene–limbs torn by shrapnel, cries of pain and disbelief, runners tearing off their shirts to stanch the bleeding, medics whispering to the wounded that they would be OK."[9] Three people died–Krystie Campbell, Lu Lingzi, and Martin Richard–and more than a dozen lost limbs with total casualties numbering over 150.

The bombs tore at the heart of the city. It was not just the horrendous carnage caused by the explosions, it was that almost everyone in Boston has a reason to visit the area of the bombings on a regular basis. Whether it is a trip to the Copley Library's majestic McKim Building that the city so treasures as a democratic service open to all, a shopping visit to a nearby store or the farmers market in Copley Square, or simply a brisk walk down Boylston Street on the way to a doctor's appointment, Bostonians routinely spend time there. It is the vibrant heart of the city, and on top of grief for the victims, there was the sense that anyone could have been killed or injured by the brothers.

Though the bombing represented the darkest abilities of humanity, it also demonstrated people at their best. Even before the shock of the first blast wore off, police, emergency responders, and medical personnel rushed in to help the wounded, oblivious of their own potential danger. People flooded emergency rooms to donate blood, neighbors checked in on neighbors, and for at least a few weeks, everyone was welcomed as a Bostonian regardless of their place of birth or ancestry. It was a shared tragedy. David Ortiz, the Red Sox slugger who in the twilight of his career had touched so many fans, cemented his love affair with Boston when he was caught on video using an expletive to defend the city. He was merely saying out loud what many felt and was all the more loved for it.

Mayor Menino also contributed to his legacy of warm regards by residents via his response to the ordeal. Mayor for twenty years as the city rose to prominence and prosperity, he was in failing health and had been hospitalized to have his knee operated on. Yet he pulled himself out of his sickbed to attend a news conference on the crisis. It was the finest hour of his time as mayor as he brought the shattered city together.

Rumors swirled as law enforcement personnel from all levels of government sought answers as to who was responsible for the bombings. There were reports of other bombs; one paper published the name of a man who turned out not to be a suspect, nearly destroying his life, and people's nerves were on edge as the week took on a surreal aspect. Many had Patriots Day off, and as news of the bombing spread, others left work to join friends and loved ones at home. Much of the area around Copley Square remained cordoned off, and then other parts of the city were sealed when President Barack Obama came to participate in a healing service at the Cathedral of the Holy Cross in the South End two days later. The weather turned unseasonably warm for April, yet many were forced to stay indoors.

On Thursday afternoon, authorities released security camera footage of two men they believed to be the bombers. Tips poured in, but they remained unidentified. Then that night, the brothers attempted to grab the gun of MIT policeman Sean Colliers, fatally shooting him. The Tsarnaevs fled and then carjacked a man in Allston, forcing him to drive them around as they plotted to go to New York City to bomb Times Square. The victim fled while they were fueling his car at a gas station, convincing a store clerk to call the police and reporting he had left his cell phone in his car. Meanwhile, police had finally identified the Tsarnaevs through the license plate of their abandoned vehicle, and with the help of the victim's cell phone in the hijacked car, police had suspects and could track their movements.

The police followed the car to Watertown where in the chaos of a shootout, Dzhokhar fatally ran over Tamerlan. Dzhokhar managed to escape but was believed to be somewhere in the area. In a controversial move, Governor Duval Patrick ordered the residents of Boston, Cambridge, Watertown, Brookline, and other surrounding communities to shelter in place on Friday morning. From dawn until nearly 7:30 in the evening over 800,000 people sat in their homes wondering if and when the perpetrators would be caught. The city held its breath.

From a command post in a nearby shopping plaza, authorities crept door-to-door searching for Dzhokhar. As dusk approached it appeared that he may have eluded authorities and could have been almost anywhere. Then a homeowner noticed that the cover of his boat in his backyard had been disturbed and on closer inspection saw blood. The police were called and a task force of specially trained agents talked Dzhokhar into surrendering.

Many of the survivors faced difficult struggles to recover from the bombing. Some had multiple operations and needed to learn how to walk using artificial limbs; others had long-term hearing loss and post-traumatic stress problems. The people of Boston responded to the tragedy by creating an organization called Boston Strong. It raised millions of dollars to provide care for victims and survivors, and its charitable works and special events helped heal the city by giving people an opportunity to grieve and provide service to the community. Though the charity disbanded once its work was complete, the shout of Boston Strong! remained a communal cry from the heart.

Countless people left mementos of their grief and compassion at spontaneous memorials in and around the bombing sites. Many of these were carefully collected and conserved by the City of Boston Archives Department and will be permanently kept in the collections for generations to come. Longer-term, there will be a memorial to that tragic day either in Copley Square or nearby and a park named in honor of Martin Richard is proposed for the Fort Point Channel area.

The trial of Dzhokhar Tsarnaev took months to prepare. The issue was not his guilt, the evidence was overwhelming, but whether or not he would be sentenced to death. His defense team tried to use Dzhokhar's young age and the greater villainy of his brother to save him. Massachusetts does not have a death penalty, so federal prosecutors stepped in to try Tsarnaev on national charges that could be used to impose capital punishment. Empaneling a jury willing to condemn Tsarnaev to death was not easy as polls indicated a majority of Bostonians did not want to see him die but using a very long questionnaire and strategic analysis of potential jury members, the federal government successfully convicted Tsarnaev and convinced the jury to sentence him to death. The appeals process is expected to take years.

In 2015, the memory of the bombing was still too close to provide perspective. At this time, the last words on this tragedy should go to Martin Richard. A photograph of the eight-year-old victim showed the wise-eyed lad holding a sign saying, "No more hurting people. Peace."

The post 2000 prosperity reached out to include more distant parts of the city, not minority neighborhoods but pockets just outside the core that had been neglected for decades. One area that had one of the most dramatic changes was the West Fens. As late as the end of the twentieth century, much of the Fenway was a student ghetto with young adults packed into overcrowded apartments with beer and loud music flavoring weekend nights. Though the Fenway CDC built some family and elderly housing developments, little had changed over the past several decades with outer Boylston Street lined by parking lots, fast food joints, and serving as little more than a conduit to Fenway Park. The Red Sox were looking to move, perhaps next door, perhaps to the waterfront, and the area looked abandoned.

The city, seeing an opportunity to knit together the Back Bay and the Medical Area, rezoned Boylston Street while working to preserve the old, if student crowded, apartment buildings elsewhere in the neighborhood. The beginnings of change were rooted in a planning process that called for the rebuilding of Boylston Street into high rise apartments with 20 percent being affordable, though many in the neighborhood had hoped for more home ownership in the mix to tone down the number of students in the area.[10]

The first major project was the redevelopment of the old Sears warehouse into offices, big box retail, and movie theaters. It was successful in attracting tenants squeezed out of the Medical Area and encouraged more development. The rezoning began to affect the street after 2005 as developers rushed in to build high-rise units as the area was dramatically transformed.

The end result was a row of sleek high-rise apartment buildings along upper Boylston Street between the Back Bay fens and the Medical Area. The Fenway Health Center moved into new offices, and most of the first floors of the new buildings were filled with restaurants catering to Red Sox fans and others in search of barbeque, sushi, and gourmet hamburgers. The apartments have high rents, the amount of affordable housing is not generous, and on-street parking, never easy, is now impossible. Yet the area has a liveliness not seen in generations.

A similar remake occurred in the New York Streets area. Fifty years after its bulldozing for a failed urban renewal project, the city initiated a new planning process that resulted in its rezoning for high density residential. Along with redevelopment further west in the Albany/Harrison corridor, the area is being rebuilt with thousands of residential units in what is the largest expansion of the South End's housing stock since urban renewal. The difference is that most of the new units planned for the area are very high cost rentals.

So many new units have been proposed in what was once a two to three-story area, that at the end of this redevelopment boom, there may be more people living in the New York Streets area than it had on the eve of its destruction. Strangely though, the redevelopment has focused its homage to the past on the former Herald newspaper plant rather than the rich multiethnic community that was lost. One of the first developments to open was called the Ink Block and its grocery store contains mementos from the newspaper. Former residents are still waiting for some commemoration of what they lost.

The rebirth of the city has occurred despite the neglect of critical infrastructure. In the winter of 2015, the MBTA, the vital transportation lifeline of Boston and the region, collapsed under the pressure of a combination of disinvestment and terrible weather. The implications for the health of the city's economy, its ability to serve current and future residents, and the resiliency of Boston in the face of global climate change, were questions on everyone's mind.

Ever since it expanded beyond its colonial era core, Boston has been highly dependent on its public transportation system. Unfortunately, the successive agencies that have run the region's transit services have suffered from nearly one hundred years of financial and management problems. Like most older U.S. cities, Boston's transit system began as a privately financed and owned set of companies operating under special franchises granted by the state. Most of the companies serving the city were consolidated into a single entity by Wall Street financiers soon after 1900.

As multiple street car lines connected far flung neighborhoods to the financial district, the congestion became intolerable, and the legislature implemented a master plan that included the consolidation of rail road lines into terminals at North and South Stations, the construction of the Tremont Street subway, and the building of elevated lines to the north, south, and along Atlantic Avenue. In addition, the legislature set fares and regulated profits and dividends of this private company.

Over time, subway and trolley lines were extended to Cambridge, East Boston, Dorchester, and Jamaica Plain. In the 1920s, the company began to replace the city's extensive trolley system with buses, pulling up tracks, and in the process, contributing to the demise of several once important shopping districts such as Uphams Corner. Despite these efforts at modernization, however, the company could not compete with automobiles, and in 1947 financial problems resulted in a newly charted government entity, the Metropolitan Transit Authority (MTA) taking over ownership of the subway and trolley lines. Its service area covered fourteen cities and towns in the heart of the metropolitan area. Boston, which paid for the bulk of the shortfall between fares and expenses, constantly sought to convince the state to pick up the tab but the legislature balked.

By the 1960s, continued financial losses at the MTA combined with crises at the companies operating commuter rail as the Pennsylvania Railroad and other providers stumbled into bankruptcy. In response, the state stepped in again to create the Massachusetts Bay Transportation Authority (MBTA) in 1964 to run transit operations in 74 cities and towns in the greater Boston area. The state and member cities continued to provide deep subsidies, yet even in the 1960s, the monthly deficit of operating expenses over income (including subsidies) was $2.5 million a month, and the expanded agency was never fiscally solid. Revenues were always well below expenses.

Buoyed by pro-transit policies implemented by Governors Sargent and Dukakis, the MBTA took over most of the commuter rail lines as well as many suburban bus systems. In one of its most popular moves, the MBTA created its famous color name structure for the subway/ trolley service calling its line to Harvard the Red Line (after Harvard's crimson), the East Boston line the Blue Line (for the harbor), the Roxbury Line the Orange Line (Washington Street's original name was Orange Street), and the trolley system the Green Line (in honor of Frederick Law Olmsted's Emerald Necklace). It expanded its rapid transit service to its present extent, extending the Red Line to Braintree and Alewife and replacing the Orange Line elevated routes with at or below grade lines in Charlestown, Roxbury, and Jamaica Plain. Still the MBTA never could generate a profit and was highly dependent on subsidies from member communities and appropriations from the state. Each year, the deficit was partially covered after the books were closed, making it impossible for the state or communities to budget for transit and leaving the MBTA chronically underfunded.

Over time, the deficit grew and cities and towns as well as the state found it difficult to pay for the constant deficits. Struggling to pay its bills, the MBTA postponed maintenance and vital capital improvements. Then in what would be a critical mistake in the 1990s, the state used the MBTA's bonding capacity to help cover cost overruns on the Big Dig. This caused the MBTA's total debt to balloon to over $8 billion which necessitated annual debt service payments in the hundreds of million dollars. The MBTA was bankrupt. To add further strains to the budget, the State imposed a new funding formula that had the admirable goal of enabling communities and the state to be able to accurately forecast their annual subsidies to the MBTA, but also further limited the public dollars flowing to the agency. In the final blow to the Authority's stability, the many capital improvements that were built in the 1970s and 1980s reached the end of their useful life and needed to be replaced. The MBTA entered the new century in a very precarious position: underfunded, massively in debt, and with a decaying physical plant.

The MBTA was extremely vital to the city's economy. One of the largest transportation agencies in the country, a half million people used the system each workday. Suburbs on commuter rail lines had more expensive housing than those without as people wanted to live in places they did not have to drive to get in and out of the city. As economic activity was increasingly focused in the core of the metropolitan area, the costs of commuting by car rose, and people crowded into central neighborhoods where they did not have cars, so the MBTA was more important than ever. But as ridership surged, its equipment began to fail.

One of the many serious impacts of global warming is that extreme weather events are becoming more common, and most of the city's largest individual snow falls have occurred in the past fifteen years as intense blizzards increasingly strike the region. The winter of 2015 set an all-time record of total snow with over ten feet falling, almost all of it in the six weeks beginning at the end of January. As the snow piled up and intervals of frigid weather snapped switches and stalled rolling stock, the MBTA couldn't keep its rail lines operational, and it shut down buses, subways, and commuter rail lines. At one point, the MBTA suggested that people make alternative transportation arrangements, a comical idea because for most people, public transportation is the alternative. As a result, commutes took hours with people waiting in the cold or giving up on getting to work as it was impossible to walk, drive, or take public transit. Businesses and workers lost millions of dollars in revenues and wages, and schools were closed for days.

As the public demanded fixes, the MBTA's general manager quit and charges flew over who was responsible for the years of neglect in the system. It took weeks for the MBTA to recover, and there is no guarantee that system won't collapse again. The snow began to fall less than a month after governor Charles Baker was sworn into office. Conveniently ignoring the fact that he was the one who had saddled the MBTA with its crushing debt during the Big Dig–he had been Secretary of Administration and Finance and finalized the transfer of debt to the MBTA–Baker swore that the MBTA would have to right itself before the state would commit any further funds to solve its physical problems. He appointed a fiscal monitoring board that promptly initiated a fare hike that would burden users without doing much to solve the MBTA's fiscal problems. The result of this new austerity on a system that has no money was unknown. Despite promises, another round of bad weather or another unknown factor could shut down the transit system for days or weeks.

The role of sports in Boston public life has been central to the city's identity. After years of mourning, the city has had the ecstasy of World Series victories. Many older Bostonians relish the glory years of the Boston Celtics when they were arguably the greatest sports franchise of all time, and the Boston Bruins were one of hockey's most popular franchises. And the New England Patriots are now the city's most favored team. So perhaps it was inevitable that some people thought that Boston would be the perfect city to host the summer Olympic Games. Unfortunately, rather than rallying the city towards a shared goal, their idea ended in blame, defeat, and recrimination. The controversy lasted for only a few months, barely a blip in the city's history, but it illustrated how much Boston had changed.

Bostonians had come together to prepare a bid for the games in the 1990s, but that proposal quickly died before it garnered serious consideration. Then in 2014, a small group of businessmen led by construction company owner Ed Fish decided that Boston should submit a bid for the 2024 games. They had reasons to be optimistic: many observers believed that the Olympics were ready to return to the United States, Boston's large number of colleges and universities suggested that many venues either already existed or would be welcome additions to their infrastructure after the games were over, and from the Marathon to political conventions, Boston had proved itself capable of hosting large events.

Though the initial announcement of the bid attracted some attention by sports enthusiasts, the general public paid little attention. This reflects a fatal flaw at the center of Boston's Olympic process: the businessmen (they were all white men) who put forward the bid made no effort to sell others on the games, made no attempt to engage residents in their proposal, and never tried to line up support from key opinion leaders, the press, or politicians. Ignoring the past fifty years of Boston's experience with renewal, gentrification, and development, they assumed that they could impose their will and ideas on a city that demanded long-term negotiation and consultation on any proposal, large or small, that might impact the city and its neighborhoods. They ignored how involved residents were in civic life and how much Bostonians loved their city.

Despite these flaws, Boston's bid gained traction with the United States Olympic Committee (USOC) who would decide which of a handful of competing cities would be the country's nominee to the International Olympic Committee (IOC). After tremendous expenditures on producing other Olympics that resulted in either funds supplied by dictators or the bankrupting of local governments, the IOC had moved to openly favor bids from cities that promised to limit budgets and reduce the scale of the games in order to contain costs. Boston, proposing to use existing facilities inside the tight geography of its central core, took advantage of these new requirements and in late 2014, beat out other cities to become the USOC's nominee to host the Olympics. Suddenly, this remote, abstract idea was at the center of everyone's radar. Yet neither the public nor Boston's elected officials had seen the bid, and instead of details there were rumors and vague promises. The Boston Committee wanted to keep its bid secret and resisted making anything public while the press, state and local officials, and Boston residents demanded full disclosure of every condition and detail. Perhaps if Fish and the others who had prepared the bid had known about the scars of urban renewal from the West End to Roxbury or had stopped to understand the lack of trust in public institutions from the FBI to the Catholic Church, they might have gone about the bid differently. At the very least, they should have involved the mayor and the governor as they were relying on the city and state for billions of dollars of financial support.

As the effort floundered, the Boston Committee was forced to reveal the bid's details. Parts of the proposal were very alluring as it showcased refurbished and modernized transit, a new office and residential district at South Bay once the Olympic Stadium was demolished, new dormitories for UMass Boston in what would have once been the Olympic Village, and improvements to facilities around the region. Most events would be accessible by transit and there would be a new grand boulevard between the Broadway MBTA station and the Olympic Stadium. Water taxis would grace Fort Point Channel.

Despite its gloss, however, the plan alarmed the public, elected officials, and others as it lacked clarity on venues, funding, and logistics. Very crucial, while Boston had several facilities that could be used for certain sports—Fenway Park, the Boston Garden, and arenas at several universities—it lacked the necessary infrastructure for the two most expensive events: an Olympic Stadium and an aquatic center. The IOC requires that the stadium had to be inside the host's city limits, ruling out Gillette Stadium where the Patriots played or the option of a stadium in lower-cost suburbs. Therefore, the Boston promoters proposed constructing a temporary stadium at South Bay. But not only did this blindside the property owners and businesses in that area, a major center for food processing and distribution employing over a thousand people, it surprised city officials who had not had time to consult neighbors in the densely-populated districts around that site. It was unlikely that the South Bay location would have worked in any case; the bid proposed that this be a temporary stadium, ignoring that it would be built on land that had been underwater until the 1960s and would have required a huge investment in foundation and site preparation to keep it from sinking into muck. Many of the other proposed venues had problems as well. The bid preparers had not consulted with the colleges and universities that owned the facilities they were proposing to use, for example, and had not prepared realistic cost estimates for adapting facilities for the games. Even a cursory analysis suggested that it would take billions of dollars to build the infrastructure in the plan.

This highlighted problems with funding. The IOC requires the host city to guarantee to pay for any deficits and cost overruns, meaning that the city and state had to commit to give billions to the games. But the City of Boston and Commonwealth of Massachusetts, having never been convinced they should support the bid, never were willing to pay for the games. Worse, because they had never been part of the bid preparation, they had not even begun the process of identifying funds to pay for this commitment. As 2015 began, the Boston Committee needed Mayor Walsh to sign a letter to the IOC promising to make up any deficit. Supporters suggested the letter was a mere formality, but Mayor Walsh balked, and Governor Charlie Baker, also angered that he had not been consulted about the bid, was not going to step to agree to fund the games either. The bid's finances were a mess.

As details and problems emerged, the Olympic organizers stumbled and sputtered. Stung by charges he had proposed hosting the games in order to profit from them, Fish pledged that his construction company would not bid on any projects associated with the games and offered to step down from organizing the games. Facing an outcry about the initial committee's lack of women and minorities (conjuring up images of the old Vault that many blamed for the problems of redevelopment and gentrification), it hastily sought to add new members to the committee and made its reputation worse when it clumsily contracted with former Governor Duval Patrick as a high-paid consultant. But the new expanded committee was still an embarrassment as it lacked any neighborhood representation. Then as residents in the city grew increasingly alarmed about the prospect of the games, the public debate became a nasty give and take between two wealthy white businessmen, one leading the bid process, the other opposed. But neither of them lived in Boston, and residents became angered that they were on the sidelines of a proposal that could have potentially reshaped the city.

The opposition to the games would have most likely remained disorganized and haphazard if not for two factors: just as the bid details were made public, Boston and eastern Massachusetts suffered from its snow catastrophe that shut down transportation and much of the city's life. A traumatized public astutely asked, could a public transit system that was in the middle of a collapse handle the pressures of the Olympics? Promoters proposed, without specifying how they would be paid for, important upgrades on the Red Line and other transit serving the proposed venues. But no one believed these would happen. Certainly the Governor was saying he would not fund any expansion or capital relief for the MBTA.

The other factor that shot down the bid was the involvement of Evan Falchuk, a failed third party candidate for governor in 2014 who belatedly learned how to use the media to move public opinion. Falchuk, using press releases, publicity stunts, social media outlets, and other methods, successfully rallied the disorganized opposition and forced bid proponents to back track, reframe their proposals, and eventually see their bid rescinded. Some of the arguments were emotionally urgent yet spurious: suggesting that money for the Olympics could instead be spent on providing support services to Boston public school students, for example, and complaining about traffic. Yet even car-using Atlanta and traffic-bound London found that the Olympics reduced traffic because people avoided the roads during the games. But other arguments, especially highlighting the problems with infrastructure and funding, were very powerful and ultimately helped convince the United States Olympic Committee to shift the bid from Boston to Los Angeles.

There was recrimination and finger pointing after the bid collapsed. Some suggested that Boston was incapable of thinking large and that it was hampered by a small-town mentality. Others grumbled that the wonderful alternatives for using Olympic funds advanced by opponents evaporated as soon as the bid was cancelled. But perhaps the real message was that the Boston's business community could not continue to ignore the great diversity of the city and that a proposal developed without strong local input was wrong for Boston.

- - -

Gay Pride Parade 2016. Some of the largest floats are produced by banks, hospitals, and insurance companies.

Veterans of the first Boston pride march in 1971 might be forgiven for a strong sense of disbelief if they watched the 2015 parade. John Mitzel had passed away in 2013, but he left the legacy a lifetime of activism and had served as an intellectual pillar of Boston's LGBT community for decades. He would have remarked on how the parade had changed. The first parade had focused on problems with bars, the police, state laws, and religion. In an important turn in the place of night clubs in Boston gay life, in the 1980s and 1990s some of the most popular floats in the parade were created by Boston gay bars that featured loud thumping music and scantily clad dancers who were greeted by cheers and salutes. By 2015, most of the bars were gone, victims of changing demographics and tastes, and so were their floats. Now a plurality of marchers and floats were by banks, insurance companies, pharmaceutical companies, and other large companies, each featuring dozens of their LGBT employees and allies. Not only were these employees not at risk of being fired, their presence was being promoted by their employers.

In 2015, some of the loudest cheers were for the New England Gay Officers Action League, police men and women from across the region who were openly gay. They were part of the way LGBT people had moved from being victims of law enforcement to incorporation into the mainstream. The 2015 parade also invited former mayor Thomas Menino to be honorary grand marshal, though his battle with cancer kept him away. He was honored for his decades of support for the LGBT community. In 1971, marchers had paused in front of the statehouse to protest discriminatory laws; in 2014, Governor Duval Patrick marched in the parade and was joined by many other politicians. The fourth stop in 1971 had been a protest against religious bigotry. Though in 2015 there were still denominations that were strongly anti-gay, the second largest number of groups in the parade were members of LGBT-friendly congregations. Mitzel prided himself on his radicalism and pursuit of justice, but he was kind to those to his political right and deeply loved irony. He would have flashed his enigmatic smile at the incongruity of what pride had become.

Prosperity did not solve all the city's issues. After decades of efforts, problems in the Boston Public Schools continued. The demographics of Boston's 54,000 students in 2015 were very different from what they had been in the 1970s. Now, 41 percent were Latino, 34 percent were black, 9 percent were Asian, and just 9 percent were white. Reflecting the high numbers of immigrants in Boston, 47 percent of students spoke a first language that was not English and 30 percent needed help learning English. Most of the students were poor enough to qualify for free lunch and breakfast, and there was a large gap between Boston and statewide performance on standardized tests. In the previous 10 years, the number of students declined by 5 percent while 13 percent of students dropped out of Boston high schools compared to 6 percent statewide. Though 72 percent of Boston students went on to higher education, this is 5 percentage points less than statewide numbers. The schools were now diverse and Boston students had a choice of traditional high schools, special School Department high schools known as pilot schools, a number of alternative schools, and charter schools not run by the School Department.[11]

Many students fare poorly on standardized tests and large gaps in performance between Asian and white students and black and Latino students persist. These differential outcomes reflect ongoing social and economic inequities in the city. Though there has been much attention paid to addressing the needs of disadvantaged students, the quality of their education continues to suffer.

The city's demographics have continued to evolve. Between 2001 and 2013, Boston's Latino population increased by 66.6 percent, Asians increased by 31.5 percent, whites by 1.5 percent, while blacks fell by 11.6 percent. The city's immigrant population increased to levels not seen in decades. People from the Dominican Republic, China, and Haiti made up the three largest sources of Boston's foreign born.[12] Whites were again a majority, though by just a very small amount, and the drop in Boston's black population is a concern as it reflects a continued inability to access the many benefits of the Boston boom.

One of the most important demographic shifts in the city occurred in East Boston as this longstanding Italian neighborhood shifted to being the largest Latino neighborhood in the city. The BHA's Maverick Development had long been an ethnic mix, but the first noticeable change in the neighborhood was the arrival of large numbers of Brazilian immigrants in the 1990s. Latinos moved in after 2000, mostly settling in the triple deckers in the central and southern parts of the neighborhood. In 1980 there had been fewer than 1,000 Latinos in East Boston; by 2010 there were more than 21,000. During the same thirty-year period, the number of Italians in East Boston dropped from 16,000 to 6,000. Though stalwarts such as Santarpio's Pizza have survived, East Boston now boasts bodegas, taquerias, and storefront churches serving Latinos. For the most part, this transition had been peaceful with new immigrants replacing elderly residents passing on, but there have been some tensions. Yet the arrival of new immigrants was easier to accept than a newer wave of residents. The era of Latino East Boston may not last long as there was a strong movement of young white college graduates moving into the neighborhood in search of affordable apartments with easy access to the city. East Boston was experiencing severe gentrification.

After twenty years in office, Boston's longest serving mayor, Thomas Menino, was in ill health and ready to step down. He could list many important successes from a strong economy to a city that had made peace with itself over its racial and economic divides. In contrast to when Kevin White had declined another term, there was no sense of unrest in the city or that there was a need for significant change. If anything, there was some anxiety regarding whether the next mayor could keep the good times going and not recreate the discord that was so common only a few decades earlier.

Relishing a chance for an open office, dozens of people considered running for Mayor, and there was hope that the city might finally elect a minority candidate. But despite gains on the City Council, the 2013 mayoral election showed the continued mixed strengths and weaknesses of minority politicians. Three strong minority candidates emerged in the crowded field of candidates. During the primary, there were calls for the minority community to unite around one candidate and rivals to drop out, but nothing came of them. John Barros had been a School Committee member and the respected head of the Dudley Street Neighborhood Initiative and Felix Arroyo was a citywide councilor and the son of another well-known politician, but it was Charlotte Golar-Ritchie who had the best chance of becoming mayor. She had been a state representative before taking high-level positions with the city and state in housing and community development. She was closely connected to Governor Duval Patrick and was a strong campaigner who had the potential to raise large sums of money. Yet she ran a lackluster campaign and finished third, failing to move on to the final. In the preliminary election, the total number of votes received by minority candidates was about equal to the combined votes for the top two finishers, both of whom were Irish men. The final would be another battle between inner-ward versus outer-ward Irish politicians.

The first-place finisher and inner-ward candidate was Marty Walsh, a state representative and labor union leader who was the son of Irish immigrants and a childhood cancer survivor. He was public about his past alcohol and drug abuse and a proud member of the recovering community. In second place was the outer-ward candidate was John Connelly, son of a long-term Massachusetts Secretary of State and a graduate of Boston College Law School. He had been an at-large member of the city council for several terms.

Connelly ran a particularly poor campaign, perhaps because he couldn't find a way to expand his constituency beyond the middle-class Irish wards. He repeatedly attacked Walsh over his connections to organized labor, implying that Walsh would not be able to negotiate contracts with them without bankrupting the city. He was helped in this effort by the *Boston Globe*, which suddenly tacked to the right to back the more conservative Connelly. In addition, Connelly made repeated attacks against the Boston Public Schools as he promoted charter schools and seemed to blame teachers for their failings.

These moves might have worked against James Michael Curley, Louise Day Hicks, or other past inner-ward Irish candidates, but in 2013 they helped drive blacks, Latinos, and Asians to support Walsh. After decades of integration, many municipal employees were now minorities, and most minority voters were close enough to the public schools to understand that their problems were too complex to be solved by threats against teachers. Broadening his coalition, Walsh reached out to Golar Richie, Barros, and Arroyo and together they campaigned on themes of unity and moving forward into the new century. In the end, Walsh beat Connelly by just under 5,000 votes. This represents an important change in Boston politics. Though they may not have enough numbers to elect one of their own as mayor, Boston's minority population is now the balance of power between the two factions of Irish in the city. Boston was a very different place than it had been in 1945.

1. Carr H. *The Brothers Bulger: How they Terrorized and Corrupted Boston for a Quarter Century.* New York: Grand Central Publishing, 2006.
2. MacDonald P. *All souls: A family history from Southie.* Boston: Beacon Press, 1999.

3. Gu Z, Mohammad S, Kladeftiras M and Xuto P. *Improving transportation access to the South Boston Seaport District.* Masters Thesis, Department of Civil and Environmental Engineering. MIT, 2014.

4. Campbell R. An urban eruption. *Boston Globe.* November 16, 2014, p. A1.

5. Quimby OS. *The Development of Boston's Seaport District: Employment Opportunities and Community Strategies.* Gaston Institute - University of Massachusetts Boston, 2001.

6. Zebrowski AE. *The Rose Fitzgerald Kennedy Greenway: Making the vision a reality.* Masters Thesis, University of Massachusetts - Amherst, 2011.

7. Palazzo AL. The Boston Greenway: Form and process issues at stake. *Journal of Urban Design.* 2014; 19: 352-67.

8. Agarwal A. *Business leadership in city planning: The case of the Central Artery.* Masters Thesis, MIT, 2005.

9. Shworm P. A celebration turns to bloody chaos. *Boston Globe.* April 16, 2013; p. A7.

10. Miller T. *The greening of community development: An analysis of ecological restoration and neighborhood planning in the Fenway.* Masters Thesis, DUSP. MIT, 2001.

11. Berardino M. *Latinos in Massachusetts Public Schools: Boston.* Gaston Institute, University of Massachusetts - Boston, 2015.

12. Granberry P. *Latinos in Massachusetts Selected Areas: Boston.* Gaston Institute, University of Massachusetts - Boston, 2015.

New Boston's Winners and Losers

B OSTON HAS BEEN radicaly transformed over the past seventy years: tens of millions of square feet of office space built, several hundred thousand housing units renovated or newly constructed, and its economy remade. Yet the city mostly looks the same physically. Its triple deckers, row houses, and historic buildings would be recognizable to anyone alive in World War II. But demographically, the transformation has been several orders of magnitude greater. In 1945 there were four major visible groups in the city: Irish, Italians, Jews, and blacks, as well as smaller numbers of Yankees, Greeks, Syrians, Poles, Lithuanians, and others. Invisible to outsiders were Boston's LGBT population, known to each other but forced into secrecy by society's repression.

Altogether, Boston is no longer as tribal as it once was, but it still consists of a number of distinct groups. These groups are not evenly spread across neighborhoods and some areas look very different than others. The city remains segregated and divided socially and this distribution tells us a lot about how the city functions in 2015.

The people who live in the city are very different today. There are still Jews, but there is no longer a distinct Jewish community inside the city. However, the population is thriving and they continue to contribute to the political and social life of the city. As evidence of this vitality, a bridge constructed as part of the Big Dig was named after the late Lenny Zakim, a Jewish civil rights advocate. Also highly visible is the city's LGBT population. It too now lacks a neighborhood that centers it in the city, though the South End comes close. It also is strong and vibrant despite its dispersion across the metropolitan area. To a great extent, these two groups have merged into the broader community of the city.

Most visible today is upscale Boston. Predominating in the Back Bay, Beacon Hill, Charlestown, downtown, the waterfront, and parts of the South End, Jamaica Plain, and South Boston, this group includes the great winners of the effort to make Boston a prosperous and well-connected city. Mostly white with a relatively high median age, this group occupies the condos, high-end apartments, and single-family homes that are generally within walking distance or a short transit ride of downtown. Many, if not most, of upscale Boston was not born here, though many have lived here for decades. Often they came for college or graduate school, were transferred here by their companies, or came here for the opportunities that the new Boston had to offer. Highly educated, most tend to vote for liberal Democrats, though they are more likely to go to the polls for national rather than local elections. Many work in medicine or medical research while others occupy the highest positions in legal, business services, and other cutting-edge industries. Some may only live here part time and spend the coldest months of the year in warmer climates. A very small percentage of this group are extremely wealthy, and their Boston homes represent just one property among many in their portfolio. These last are often very disconnected from the city, and some may not even know their way around town. Most of this demographic, however, are extremely supportive of the institutions that Boston is most famous for and a great many of them are patrons of the symphony, the Red Sox, and the trendiest restaurants. Many profess the great love for the city, and say they would never live any place.

Another winner in the New Boston is the middle class, many of whom are Irish. Despite years of displacement and the great migration of much of 1950s Boston to the suburbs, this group continues to hold on in several important parts of the city including South Boston, the southern portion of Dorchester, Jamaica Plain, West Roxbury, Brighton, and other enclaves scattered across the city. Boston's Irish population dropped much less than other groups, falling from 92,107 in 1980 to 77,610 in 2010. Yet even among these neighborhoods there has been differential change. In Charlestown, South Boston, and West Roxbury there has been little change in their numbers while in North and South Dorchester and Hyde Park, numbers have dropped by nearly 50 percent.

Overall the group is much more prosperous than their parents' and grandparents' generation. As a group, they tend to be well-educated and hold important positions in government and other service-related industries. This group tends to be very influential in politics and continues to dominate elected positions across the city as well as middle management in the bureaucracies that help make the city work. They are the most likely to have been born here of any of the groups in the city.

As a result of the great increase in college enrollment over the years, another major group in the city is student Boston. Centered in the Fenway, Allston-Brighton, and Mission Hill, students and young adults just out of college are a major demographic force in the city. Because of their willingness to live in overcrowded conditions and their inability to find safe and affordable housing, they tend to live in small to large apartments with many people per bedroom or in dormitories. At times it seems the city is awash with students who can be found at events such as the fireworks on the Esplanade and the Head of the Charles regatta. The group increasingly includes foreign students who often live in either extreme wealth or extreme poverty. There is increasing concern that Boston is losing its ability to retain students once they graduate and that too many return to places where they grew up or move to other cities that are equally or more attractive to young people. This may well be a real problem. However, the change from past times reflected the earlier demographics of Boston higher education. Decades ago, a higher percentage of students elected to stay in the region after graduation because they were born here or had family ties nearby. Now with almost every university having a global draw of students, many now elect to go back to places far away, near where they have family. However, as long as Boston institutions continue to attract students, there'll always be a fresh supply of young people moving into the city and adding to its vibrancy. For the most part this group is unaware of their role in the new Boston and they rarely vote, but they contribute to the economic engines of education and medical research.

Still yet to fully benefit from the New Boston is minority Boston. It includes a very diverse group of African Americans, some who can trace their ancestry in the city back over a hundred years, as well as newcomers from the Caribbean and Africa. Many have roots in the South, others claim families that came from Cape Verde and Haiti. The heart of the black community is a comma-shaped set of neighborhoods in the middle of the city starting in Mission Hill and Lower Roxbury and then heading south down to Hyde Park and Mattapan. The black population has been stable since 1980 when the census counted 122,102 blacks up to 2010 when it found 138,073. The main change has been the growth of the black population of Hyde Park, growing in these years from 4,282 to 17,049, and a sharp drop in the number of blacks in the South End, declining from 7,909 to 4,865.

Asians, the fastest growing group in the city, also trace their roots from a wide range of countries. There are engineers from India and China, students from Korea, and families who have children, parents, and grandparents born in this country. Their first languages range from English to Khmer. Many Asians live in Dorchester and Brighton as well as Chinatown (which has spread into the adjacent South End) and in student neighborhoods across the city. Some are among the most affluent in the city, others have high rates of unemployment and live in poverty. Their total numbers went from 16,073 in 1980 to 55,028 in 2010.

There is also a diverse group of Hispanics who predominate in many places such as East Boston, Jamaica Plain, the Dudley area, and elsewhere. Some Hispanics are from Puerto Rico, the Dominican Republic, and Cuba, others from Central and South America. Many are U. S. citizens by birth. Some speak only Spanish, others only English. Overall, their numbers increased from 36,068 in 1980 to 107,917 in 2010. As with Asians, there are large differences inside this community that make it difficult to generalize about their economic status.

Despite decades of advocacy, minority Boston is the most disconnected from the new prosperous Boston. Very few of the higher-paying jobs have gone to minorities, and most institutions have failed to incorporate people of color into their audiences and their constituencies whether they have tried to or not. Many of the city's minority communities are terribly afraid of gentrification and the prospect of being pushed out of the city to distant suburbs such as Brockton, Lowell, and Lynn. While the evidence that gentrification is active in Roxbury is mixed at this time, given the past history of displacement in the South End, Dorchester, and Jamaica Plain, this is not an unreasonable fear.

One group that lost in the revival of the city is white working-class Boston. At one time they dominated the city, providing the large electoral margins for Curley and other Irish mayors, and they had a hold on the well-paying yet low-skilled jobs in government, utilities, and construction. Most of the working-class Irish are gone, and with them has gone their dominance of Boston city hall. Many have left the state.

Another change that reflects the loss of working-class Boston is its loss of Italian neighborhoods. These were once the strongest citadels of this group. Though the North End and East Boston still feel Italian, the numbers of Italians are only a fraction of what they once were. In 1980 there were 48,392 people of Italian ancestry in Boston, in 2010, 37,983. The great Italian neighborhoods in the city are nearly gone. In East Boston, the number of Italians declined from 16,643 in 1980 to 6,243 in 2010; in the North End, the decline was from 5,786 to 2,803. The future of working-class whites in Boston is very unclear as Boston becomes a city of low-income minorities and affluent whites.

Given the vast changes in the city, what would Mayor Curley think of Boston today? Speculatively, he might be disappointed by the less lively politics of 2015: no one threatens to flood bank vaults anymore and campaign rallies no longer degenerate into drunken brawls. His personal style might not work in an era of instant messaging and cell phones at the ready to record videos and it's not certain that he could still connect to the remnants of his working-class Irish constituency. But most likely, he would be pleased with the state of the harbor, now cleaned up to showcase his foresight to remake the South Boston beaches, and he'd have to be impressed by the improvements of the city's housing stock. No longer does a third of the city live in squalor. Overall, the changes in the city have been positive, though some have come at great cost to residents, many of them once solid Curley supporters. We can be sure he would be proud of Boston's transformation and would take credit for it. But then, so would Hynes, Collins, White, and all the other leaders of the city over the past seventy years. Today's Boston has prosperity that all can easily see and its quality of life is high. Many might say they created the New Boston, but the ones who truly built it are its people.

INDEX

Gay and Lesbian Advocates and Defenders (GLAD), 145, 171, 210, 212, 213
Gay Community News, 140-1, 143-4
General Electric, 6
Gentrification, 69, 70, 88, 98, 113, 138, 151, 208,
Geoghan, John, 200, 202
George, Annissa Easaibi, 217
Golar-Ritchie, Charlotte, 251, 252
Goodridge, Hillary and Julie, 213, 214
Government Center, 48-9, 67, 73-5, 89, 109, 222
Greeks, 55
Greig, Catherine, 229
Gropius, Walter, 73, 147
Grove Hall, 86-87, 99, 112, 198
Grove Hall riot, 86-87

Haar, Charles, 176
Haitians, 3, 128, 150-1, 161, 166, 203, 250, 257
Harbor Walk, 183, 208
Harrington, John, 217, 218
Harrington, Kevin, 226
Harvard University, ix, 6, 35, 59, 62, 73, 76-7, 107, 118, 129, 147, 172, 193, 195, 200, 207, 213, 241
Haynes, Michael, 113
Hennigan, James, 107
Hennigan, Maura, 216
Henry, John, 218, 219
Hernandez, Jorge, 104
Hicks, Louise Day, 61-3, 65, 66, 89-90, 104, 105-6, 109, 110, 112-3, 123, 135, 252
highways, 3, 10-11, 34-7, 49, 51, 60, 70, 84, 100-2, 137, 146, 179-87, 205, 230, 232, 233
HIV/AIDS, 145, 151, 171-2
Hoffman, Amy, 143-4, 145
Holy Cross College, 202
Housing, viii, 8, 9-10, 18, 19, 21, 38-9, 41, 42, 47, 55, 69-70, 71, 72-3, 76-7,

82-3, 84-6, 96-8, 121-2, 126, 128, 130-4, 136-8, 142-3, 157, 161-4, 166-8, 191, 195-6, 198, 208-9, 224-5,
Huxtable, Ada Louise, 74
Hyde Park, 2, 100, 110, 150, 151, 256, 257,
Hynes, John, 13, 28-9, 32-5, 38, 39-40, 43, 48-9, 50-51, 54-55, 59, 67, 87, 115, 152, 191, 230, 259

Ianella, Christopher, 47, 89
IBM, 158
Indians, 3, 204, 257,
inner belt, 79, 100-2, 233
Inquilinos Boricuas en Accion (IBA), 97, 104
Irish, 3, 7, 8, 11, 12, 13, 16-17, 20, 21, 22, 23, 26, 29, 33, 34, 44, 46, 52, 54, 70, 72, 76, 77, 88, 90, 93, 96, 100, 103, 105, 107, 111, 123, 154, 166, 169, 176, 191, 200, 217, 225, 252, 254, 255-6, 258
Islam, 20
Italians, 3, 8, 13, 17, 21, 44-7, 55, 57, 66, 89, 100, 142-3, 166, 170, 190, 225-6, 250-1, 255, 258

Jackson, Ellen, 64-5, 113
Jacobs, Jane, 142
Jamaica Plain, 14, 17, 39, 64, 70, 94, 96, 103, 117, 121, 131, 137-8, 144, 168, 170, 198, 200, 241, 242, 255, 256, 257, 258
Japan, 5, 205
Jean-Louis, Yvon, 151
Jews, 8, 10, 13, 21, 26-8, 41, 55, 76, 77, 83, 88, 121-2, 166, 214, 254-5
John Paul II, Pope, 139
Johnson, Lyndon, 60
Joyce, Francis X., 227

Kallmann, Gerhard, 74
Kelly, James, 170
Kennedy, Edward, 90, 104, 109, 113, 182
Kennedy, John, 109